Publisher

Published by

THE BIBLE FOR TODAY PRESS
900 Park Avenue
Collingswood, New Jersey 08108
U.S.A.

Phone: 856-854-4452
Orders: 1-800-John 10:9
e-mail: BFT@BibleForToday.org
website: www.BibleForToday.org
fax: 856-854-2464

August, 2002
BFT2973

Copyright, 2002
All Rights Reserved

ISBN #1-56848-031-8
978-1-56848-031-2

Acknowledgments

I wish to acknowledge the assistance of the following people:

- **The Congregation** of the **Bible For Today Baptist Church** (for whom these messages were prepared and to whom they were delivered) who listened attentively and encouraged their Pastor as he preached;
- **Yvonne Sanborn Waite**, my wife, who encouraged the publication of these sermons, read the manuscript, and gave helpful suggestions;
- **Dianne W. Cosby**, for typing these messages from the cassette tapes and putting them in computer format;
- **Pastor Richard N. Waite**, for editing the messages on the computer format, inserting the texts of various verses used and making them consistent;
- **Daniel S. Waite**, the Assistant to the Bible For Today Director, who guided the book through the printing process;
- **Barbara Egan**, our Bible For Today secretary who also read the manuscript and offered valuable comments.

Foreword

- **The Beginning.** This book is the **third** in a planned series of books based on expository preaching from various books of the Bible. It is an attempt to bring to the minds of the readers two things: (1) the **meaning** of the words in the verses and (2) the practical **application** of those words to the lives of both saved and lost people.
- **Preached Sermons.** These are messages that have been preached to our **Bible For Today Baptist Church** in Collingswood, New Jersey, broadcast over radio, and placed on our website **(http://www.BibleFor-Today.org/audio_sermons.htm)** for people all over the world to listen to, should they wish. As the messages were originally preached, I took half a chapter each Sunday service, spending about forty-five minutes on each message.
- **Other Verses.** In connection with both meaning and application there are many verses from other places in the Bible that have been quoted for further elaboration of Paul's discussion. One of the unique features of this study is that all of the various verses of Scripture that are used to illustrate further truth are written out in full for easy reference.
- **A Transcription.** It should be noted that this book is made up largely from the transcription of the tape recordings of the messages. These recordings are available in both audio and video formats. Though there has been some editing, the words are basically the same as the ones I used as I preached the sermons. Though different in emphasis, this was also the method Dr. H. A. Ironside used in his Bible exposition books.
- **The Audience.** The audience aimed at is the same as the audience that listened to the messages in the first place. These studies are not meant to be overly scholarly though there is some reference to various Greek words used by Paul. My aim is to help lay people to understand the Words of God. It is my hope that I can get as many as possible of my expositions in print so that my children, grandchildren, and children in the faith may be able to rejoice with me in the things the Lord has brought to my attention as I have preached from the verses in Ephesians.

Yours For God's Words,

D. A. Waite

DAW/w   Pastor D. A. Waite, Th.D., Ph.D.
Bible For Today Baptist Church

Table of Contents

Publisher's Data I

Acknowledgments ii

Foreword iii

Table of Contents iv

Ephesians Chapter One 1

Ephesians Chapter Two 39

Ephesians Chapter Three 69

Ephesians Chapter Four 101

Ephesians Chapter Five 135

Ephesians Chapter Six 167

Index of Words and Phrases 199

About the Author 215

Order Blank Pages 217

Ephesians Chapter One

Introductory Remarks

The book of Ephesians is what has been called a "prison epistle." It is one of four of Paul's books written from his first imprisonment in Rome, Italy. His other three prison epistles are Philippians, Colossians, and Philemon. Though there is not unanimous agreement among Bible teachers on this point, I believe there were three books written from Paul's second Roman imprisonment. They are 1 Timothy, 2 Timothy, and Titus. These are called the "pastoral epistles" because both Timothy and Titus were pastors.

While Paul was in prison, he concentrated on Christ rather than on the severe conditions under which he lived. That is what we who are saved should do, even though we are not prisoners as Paul was. Who knows what may happen in our country. We could lose our freedoms before too many years, if conditions continue to accelerate rapidly. But, for now, we still have the freedom to meet in our church and to preach the gospel of the Lord Jesus Christ without hindrance. For this we are most thankful to our God. The background information about Paul's founding of the church in Ephesus is found in the book of Acts 18-29. Ephesus is a seaport city on the Aegean Sea. The Jews wanted to kill him. But Paul would not agree to that until he had been tried in Caesar's courts in Rome. He appealed unto Caesar.

- **Acts 25:11**
  For if I be an offender, or have committed any thing worthy of death, I refuse not to die: but if there be none of these things whereof these accuse me, no man may deliver me unto them. **I appeal unto Caesar**.

Paul's reasons for appealing to Caesar involved the Jews who wanted him to stay in Jerusalem so they could assassinate him without any trial at all.

- Acts 28:19
But when the Jews spake against *it*, I was constrained to appeal unto Caesar; not that I had ought to accuse my nation of.

At this point, Paul was in the prison at Caesarea. The Jews wanted to take him They wanted to take him from Caesarea and bring him down to Jerusalem. There were more than forty Jews who had bound themselves together with an oath that they would not eat or drink until they killed Paul. (Acts 23:12-13). One of the questions on our test of the book of Acts by one of the visiting Bible lecturers at Dallas Theological Seminary, when I was a student there, was this: "When did these Jews have their next meal?" They did not kill Paul. He did not go to Jerusalem.

The Lord knew what was going to happen, so Paul went to Rome. He almost got killed going to Rome when his ship was wrecked in Acts 28. But the Lord spared his life and that of all those on board. Paul does not make too many references to his being in prison. There are only three such references in the entire book of six chapters.

Ephesians 1:1

"Paul, an apostle of Jesus Christ by the will of God, to the saints which are at Ephesus, and to the faithful in Christ Jesus"

"Paul, an apostle of Jesus Christ by the will of God"

Paul was an *"apostle."* He was "one sent forth with a mission." He was a missionary and an evangelist who went all over the then-known world. Notice, he was an apostle *"by the will of God"* and not of his own will. Many preachers these days become preachers because of the will of their mother, their father, their grandmother, their grandfather or some other person--even themselves. Woe be unto that preacher who is not called by the Lord Jesus Christ to do the work of an evangelist, to be a pastor, or to go into some other sort of work we might call "full-time ministry."

I believe that the Lord Jesus Christ called Paul rather than Matthias to replace Judas. Matthias was chosen by the eleven remaining apostles to take the place of Judas. They drew lots (Acts 1:23-28). Whomever the lot fell upon was named the next apostle. The Lord Jesus Christ was the One who chose His apostles, not the other eleven. Christ picked Paul to replace Judas. I believe that the twelfth name to be listed with the *"names of the twelve apostles of the Lamb"* on those twelve foundations of the wall of the New Jerusalem (Revelation 21:14) will be Paul and not Matthias. After his "election" by the other apostles, Matthias was never heard from again. Paul's ministry, however, dominated the entire book of Acts.

"to the saints which are at Ephesus, and to the faithful in Christ Jesus" This book was addressed to the "*saints*" at Ephesus. This is not a reference to the saints of the Roman Catholic Church. Everyone who is born-again and regenerated by the Holy Spirit of God is a "*saint*." The word, "saint," means one who is "*set apart*." The book was also written "*to the faithful in Christ Jesus*." May the Lord give us faithfulness, and keep us faithful. May the Lord keep us faithful to at least these eight things.

We Need Faithfulness:
1. to the Lord Jesus Christ
2. to the Scriptures
3. to our church fellowship
4. to our Bible reading
5. to our praying
6. to our mates
7. to our children, and
8. to our grandchildren.

Though there are many more things that require our faithfulness, these eight are very important. God wants us to be "*faithful*," not unfaithful.

Ephesians 1:2

"Grace *be* to you, and peace, from God our Father, and from the Lord Jesus Christ" Here is the greeting of "*grace*." Grace is getting something we do not deserve. It leads us to salvation if we avail ourselves of God's grace made possible through His Son, the Lord Jesus Christ.

- **Ephesians 2:8**
"For **by grace are ye saved through faith**; and that not of yourselves: *it is* the gift of God"

There is also a mention made in this greeting of "*peace*." This is the possession of all those who have repented of their sins and put their faith in the Lord Jesus Christ.

- **Romans 5:1**
Therefore being justified by faith, **we have peace with God** through our Lord Jesus Christ:

Notice that both *"grace"* and *"peace"* are *"from God our Father"* and *"the Lord Jesus Christ."* There is a unity in the Trinity. Many modernists and liberals do not believe that the Lord Jesus Christ is a member of the Trinity possessing all the attributes of Deity found in God the Father, and in God the Holy Spirit. These are Unitarians in doctrine. They believe that the Lord Jesus Christ was only a man, but not God the Son. The Scriptures clearly show that the Lord Jesus is, as the Father and the Holy Spirit are, all co-equal, co-powerful, and co-eternal.

Ephesians 1:3

"Blessed *be* the God and Father of our Lord Jesus Christ, who hath blessed us with all spiritual blessings in heavenly *places* in Christ" One of the distinctions between Israel and the Church is that to **Israel** God has promised predominantly, though not exclusively, **earthly blessings**. This is not to say that the church does not have any earthly blessings. But to the **Church**, God has promised predominately, though not exclusively, **spiritual blessings**. These blessings are *"all spiritual blessings in heavenly places."* Those who are saved have been redeemed by the Lord Jesus Christ. He has bought us with His blood. These blessings are the result of our redemption. He has given us *"all"* spiritual blessings, not just a few. The blessings that God has bestowed upon those who are saved are possessed by every sinner who is saved by God's grace. These blessings are not just for a certain number of people. The question is why do we not realize this? Why do not all believers get themselves in a spiritual state instead of a carnal state so they can enjoy fully these *"spiritual blessings"*? The Lord Jesus has gone to the *"heavenly places"* where the saved will one day go also.

- **Ephesians 1:20**
  Which he wrought in Christ, when he raised him from the dead, and **set *him* at his own right hand in the heavenly *places***,
- Ephesians 2:6
  And hath raised *us* up together, and **made *us* sit together in heavenly *places* in Christ Jesus**:

As far as the Lord is concerned, the redeemed are seated together with *"Christ Jesus"* in *"heavenly places."* We are with Christ even now. This phrase *"spiritual blessings in heavenly places in Christ"* is a phrase which explains things that take place in Heaven. This is the source of our blessings. They are based in Heaven itself.

The blessings of this earth are one thing. The blessings of Heaven are another. Some people do not care about blessings from Heaven. All they want is the "here and now." They do not care about the hereafter. If you ask people on the street if they are concerned about eternity, many will say that they do not care. Some will say they are doing well and prospering. I heard on the radio that the Thanksgiving buying spree this year is higher than any other year. We will spend over one hundred and sixty billion dollars this Thanksgiving season. Some people just live for the "bitter here-and-now," and don't care about the "sweet by-and-by." We have to remember that the Lord has blessed believers with heavenly blessings.

Ephesians 1:4

"According as he hath chosen us in him before the foundation of the world, that we should be holy and without blame before him in love"

"According as he hath chosen us in him" There should be no doubt about the fact that the Bible teaches that God *"chose"* certain groups. *"He hath chosen us in Him."* The problem is coming to a proper understanding of the meaning of *"chosen."* I like to explain this by a "corporate election." I believe, for example, that the Lord chose the nation of Israel as an elect people, as a "corporate" body. I believe He has chosen the Church also as a "corporate" body or group. I believe that He has chosen the church as an entity. This is called "corporate election." The Lord founded and established the church as a corporate body before the foundation of the world. As the believers trust Christ as Saviour and redeemer, they become members of that corporate body, the church, which was chosen before the foundation of the world. That is how I harmonize all of these things.

Those who are hyper-Calvinist believe in the "five points" of the acronym TULIP.

The T.U.L.I.P. of Calvinism

T stands for total depravity.
U stands for unconditional election.
L stands for limited atonement.
I stands for irresistible grace.
P stands for perseverance of the saints.

These hyper Calvinists do not believe that "whosoever will may come" to Christ and be saved. They believe that only the "elect" may come. Only those who are specially favored by God are able to come. This false system teaches that Christ died only for the sins of the "elect" but He did not die for the sins of the entire world. a hyper-Calvinist preacher cannot say to all the audience that "Christ died for your sins." You have to realize that if you are not of the elect, that preacher does not believe that Christ died for you. This is not Scriptural.

- **John 3:16**
  For **God so loved the world**, that he gave his only begotten Son, that **whosoever believeth in him should not perish, but have everlasting life**.

First of all, the verse declares that God loved the entire *"world,"* not just the "elect." It does not say that if the "elect" believe. It says *"whosoever believeth."* This includes the so-called "elect" and everyone else you could think of. It is clear that God loved the entire *"world"* and Christ died for the sins of the entire world. That is what the Scriptures teach.

"before the foundation of the world" This phrase *foundation of the world* is used ten times throughout the Bible. Here are the nine other uses.

- **Matthew 13:35**
  That it might be fulfilled which was spoken by the prophet, saying, I will open my mouth in parables; I will utter things which have been **kept secret from the foundation of the world**.

God is not in "time." He is in "eternity." He has things planned out *"from the foundation of the world."*

- **Matthew 25:34**
  Then shall the King say unto them on his right hand, Come, ye blessed of my Father, **inherit the kingdom prepared for you from the foundation of the world**:

- **Luke 11:50**
  That the blood of all the prophets, **which was shed from the foundation of the world**, may be required of this generation;

- **John 17:24**
  Father, I will that they also, whom thou hast given me, be with me where I am; that they may behold my glory, which thou hast given me: **for thou lovedst me before the foundation of the world**.

The Father and the Son loved one another in eternity past, before the world was ever created.

- **Hebrews 4:3**
  For we which have believed do enter into rest, as he said, As I have sworn in my wrath, if they shall enter into my rest: although **the works were finished from the foundation of the world**.

- **Hebrews 9:26**
  For then must he often have suffered since the foundation of the world: but now once in the end of the world hath he appeared to put away sin by the sacrifice of himself.
- **1 Peter 1:20**
  Who verily was foreordained before the foundation of the world, but was manifest in these last times for you,
- **Revelation 17:8**
  The beast that thou sawest was, and is not; and shall ascend out of the bottomless pit, and go into perdition: and they that dwell on the earth shall wonder, **whose names were not written in the book of life from the foundation of the world**, when they behold the beast that was, and is not, and yet is.
- **Revelation 13:8**
  And all that dwell upon the earth shall worship him, whose names are not written in the book of life of **the Lamb slain from the foundation of the world**.

We cannot fully understand that because we are creatures of time. How could the Lord Jesus Christ, the Lamb of God, be *"slain from the foundation of the world"* when He was not slain until He was placed upon Calvary's cross of shame? In God's timing and in God's plan, He was slain. It was done!

A few weeks ago someone asked me this question. "Was Old Testament salvation the same as New Testament salvation?" The answer is "Yes." They both are based on the death of Christ, the Lamb who was *"slain from the foundation of the world."* Old Testament salvation was by grace through faith looking forward to that Lamb. The Jews had the gospel preached to them.

"that we should be holy and without blame before him in love" The purpose for which God has *"chosen us in Him"* is that we who are saved *"should be holy."* Many people say "We do not want to be holy." We look down our noses at the holy rollers as they used to be called. We think that some of them are not Scripturally sound. Many of their doctrines are not, but holiness is not just for the holiness people. It is for all Christians. God wants us to be holy.

- **Leviticus 20:7**
  Sanctify yourselves therefore, and **be ye holy**: for I *am* the LORD your God.

We cannot be holy except by the Holy Spirit. The Holy Spirit dwells within all those whom He has saved and regenerated. He is the only One who can make us holy.

- 1 Peter 1:15-16
  But **as he which hath called you is holy, so be ye holy in all manner of conversation**; Because it is written, Be ye holy; for I am holy.

God wants us to be just like His Son. That word *"be ye holy"* is in the present tense in the Greek language which shows a continuous action. Therefore, it means that we should be holy all the time, continuously. That means do not just be holy when you come to church, or one day a week, or one hour, or one minute. If we belong to the Lord Jesus Christ, we are to be holy continuously. Being holy means being separated unto the Father and separated unto the Son. It also means being separated from sin, separated from self, and separated from the world. That is what holiness requires and demands. It is difficult to be holy in an unholy world, but that is what God expects of his redeemed people. He wants us to be holy and *"without blame."* He chose us *"that we should be holy and without blame before Him."* Here in this world we may have blame, but before Him we are *"without blame"* because of our standing in Christ. We are to be holy before Him in love. This is God's standard for us if we're saved. That is what He wants for us.

Ephesians 1:5

"Having predestinated us unto the adoption of children by Jesus Christ to himself, according to the good pleasure of his will"

"Having predestinated us" That word, *"predestinate,"* is found also in Romans 8:29. To predestinate, PROORIZO, means *"to predetermine, decide before hand."* It comes from two words. PRO means *"before"* and HORIZO means *"to mark out the boundaries or limits of any place or thing."* So the word predestinate means *"to mark out the boundaries or limits before hand."* We get the word "horizon" from the Greek word HORIZO. The horizon separates Heaven and earth. God has separated us beforehand.

- Romans 8:29
  For whom he did foreknow, **he also did predestinate *to be conformed to the image of his Son***, that he might be the firstborn among many brethren.
- Romans 8:30
  Moreover whom **he did predestinate**, them he also called: and whom he **called**, them he also justified: and whom he **justified**, them he also **glorified**.

I believe in predestination according to Scripture. I believe that predestination refers to what is taught in Romans 8:29. Every saved person will one day be absolutely *"conformed to the image of His Son."*

- **1 John 3:2**
  Beloved, now are we the sons of God, and it doth not yet appear what we shall be: but we know that, when he shall appear, **we shall be like him**; for we shall see him as he is.

We shall be *"like Him"* in Glory, not on this earth. But that is our goal. Since we are going to be *"conformed to the image of His Son,"* let us start now. That is where holiness comes in. That is Bible predestination.

- **Ephesians 1:11**
  In whom also we have obtained an inheritance, **being predestinated according to the purpose of him who worketh all things after the counsel of his own will**:

God did this all according to His own *"purpose."* I realize that there are some of our friends who believe in predestination a different way, but the Romans 8:29 way is the best and most Biblical way to explain it.

"unto the adoption of children by Jesus Christ to himself, according to the good pleasure of his will" God foreordained that we should be adopted as His children.

- **Romans 8:15**
  For ye have not received the spirit of bondage again to fear; but **ye have received the Spirit of adoption, whereby we cry, Abba, Father**.

That *"adoption"* is a *"full fledged placing as a son."* We are no longer children. We are no longer under the age of twenty-one. The minute we are saved, God places us as full mature children.

- **Galatians 4:5**
  To redeem them that were under the law, **that we might receive the adoption of sons**.

Even though we are just newly saved Christians, we are still completely adopted.

He does not want every believer who is saved to be a little baby. He does not want us to be a little skinny dwarf. Have you seen the little ponies as you drive along? They are beautiful little ponies frisking around in the field. When we are saved, God does not make us little ponies but big full grown horses. He wants us full grown, and He made us full-grown. Let us act that way. People sometimes say "Act your age, not your shoe size." That is a good saying. If we act our shoe size, we are in trouble. God has made us fully mature, grown children. We are able to have our inheritance right away. We do not have to wait until we are twenty-one years in Christ. We can have it right away.

Ephesians 1:6

"To the praise of the glory of his grace, wherein he hath made us accepted in the beloved"

"To the praise of the glory of his grace" All of this saving grace and all of this making us approved children is to the "*praise*" or the commendation of His "*grace.*" He did this because it pleased Him.

"wherein he hath made us accepted in the beloved" What a wonderful phrase. He made us accepted. The "*Beloved*" One is the Lord Jesus Christ. We cannot make ourselves accepted by Him. We can only be "*accepted in the beloved*" by grace through faith. There is no other way for any man, woman, or child to be "*accepted*" but by personal, saving faith in the "*Beloved*" One, the Lord Jesus Christ.

Ephesians 1:7

"In whom we have redemption through his blood, the forgiveness of sins, according to the riches of his grace"

"In whom we have redemption through his blood" John MacArthur does not believe that "*blood*" means "*blood.*" He believes that blood is a metonym for death. There are many others who are following John MacArthur's teaching on this. It is a heresy. There are many verses which speak of the literal blood of Christ. It is not death. It is blood. Christ did die for our sins, but He shed His blood. In the Bible God specifically mentions the literal blood of Christ and says that His blood does certain things.

I believe the following "Rule" makes sense when it comes to the interpretation of our Bible.

The Golden Rule of Interpretation

"When the plain sense of Scripture makes common sense, seek no other sense. Therefore, take every word at its primary, ordinary, usual, literal meaning unless the facts of the immediate context studied in the light of related passages and axiomatic and fundamental truths indicate clearly otherwise. God in revealing His Word neither intends nor permits the reader to be confused. He wants His children to understand."

When God uses the word, "*blood,*" He means "*blood.*" When He uses the word, "*death,*" He means "*death.*" These two nouns are separate and distinct in Hebrew, in Greek, in English, and in every other language of the world. Let us keep them separate.

There are at least fourteen effects of the literal blood of Christ.

> First, there is **REDEMPTION** (atonement, substitution, remission, salvation, or purchase) through the literal blood of Christ.

- Leviticus 17:11
  For the life of the flesh *is* in the blood: and I have given it to you upon the altar to make an atonement for your souls: **for it *is* the blood *that* maketh an atonement for the soul.**
- Matthew 26:28
  For **this is my blood of the new testament, which is shed for many for the remission of sins.**
- Mark 14:24
  And he said unto them, **This is my blood of the new testament, which is shed for many.**
- Luke 22:20
  Likewise also the cup after supper, saying, **This cup *is* the new testament in my blood, which is shed for you.**
- Acts 20:28
  Take heed therefore unto yourselves, and to all the flock, over the which the Holy Ghost hath made you overseers, to feed the church of God, **which he hath purchased with his own blood.**
- Romans 5:9
  Much more then, being now justified by his blood, we shall be saved from wrath through him.
- Ephesians 1:7
  In whom we have redemption through his blood, the forgiveness of sins, according to the riches of his grace;
- Colossians 1:14
  In whom we have redemption through his blood, *even* the forgiveness of sins:
- 1 Peter 1:18-19
  Forasmuch as ye know that **ye were not redeemed with corruptible things,** *as* silver and gold, from your vain conversation *received* by tradition from your fathers; **But with the precious blood of Christ,** as of a lamb without blemish and without spot:

- **Revelation 5:9**
  And they sung a new song, saying, Thou art worthy to take the book, and to open the seals thereof: for thou wast slain, and **hast redeemed us to God by thy blood** out of every kindred, and tongue, and people, and nation;

The "blood" of Christ and the "death" of Christ are not the same thing. They are two different concepts. Notice the distinction with the example of the passover lamb (Exodus 12:1-7). Moses was told to take a lamb, make sure he was pure and clean, slay it, and then catch its blood in a basin. After slaying the lamb, the people were to put some of its blood on the "*two side posts*" and "*upper door post*" of their houses. The death of the lamb was one thing. The application of its blood was another thing. The death and the blood were two separate concepts.

Second, there is PROPITIATION through the literal blood of Christ.

- **Romans 3:25**
  Whom God hath set forth *to be* **a propitiation through faith in his blood**, to declare his righteousness for the remission of sins that are past, through the forbearance of God;

Third, there is JUSTIFICATION through the literal blood of a Christ.

- **Romans 5:9**
  Much more then, **being now justified by his blood**, we shall be saved from wrath through him.

Fourth, there is FELLOWSHIP through the literal blood of Christ.

- **Ephesians 2:13**
  But now in Christ Jesus **ye who sometimes were far off are made nigh by the blood of Christ.**

Fifth, there is PEACE through the literal blood of Christ.

- Colossians 1:20
  And, **having made peace through the blood of his cross**, by him to reconcile all things unto himself; by him, *I say*, whether *they be* things in earth, or things in Heaven.

> Sixth, there is **FORGIVENESS** through the literal blood of Christ.

- Ephesians 1:7
  In whom we have redemption **through his blood, the forgiveness of sins**, according to the riches of his grace;
- Colossians 1:14
  In whom we have redemption **through his blood,** *even* **the forgiveness of sins**:

> Seventh, there is **SANCTIFICATION** through the literal blood of Christ.

- Hebrews 13:12
  Wherefore Jesus also, **that he might sanctify the people with his own blood**, suffered without the gate.

> Eighth, there is **RECONCILIATION** through the literal blood of Christ.

- Colossians 1:20
  And, having made peace **through the blood of his cross, by him to reconcile all things unto himself**; by him, *I say*, whether *they be* things in earth, or things in Heaven.

> Ninth, there is **CLEANSING** (purging, washing, purifying) through the literal blood of Christ.

- Hebrews 9:14
  How much more shall the blood of Christ, who through the eternal Spirit offered himself without spot to God, **purge your conscience** from dead works to serve the living God?

- **Hebrews 9:22-23**
  And almost all things are by the law **purged with blood**; and without shedding of blood is no remission. *It was* **therefore necessary that the patterns of things in the heavens should be purified with these**; but the heavenly things themselves with better sacrifices than these.
- **1 John 1:7**
  But if we walk in the light, as he is in the light, we have fellowship one with another, and **the blood of Jesus Christ his Son cleanseth us** from all sin.
- **Revelation 1:5**
  And from Jesus Christ, *who is* the faithful witness, *and* the first begotten of the dead, and the prince of the kings of the earth. Unto him that loved us, and **washed us from our sins in his own blood.**
- **Revelation 7:14**
  And I said unto him, Sir, thou knowest. And he said to me, These are they which came out of great tribulation, and **have washed their robes, and made them white in the blood of the Lamb.**

> Tenth, there is **REMEMBRANCE** through the literal blood of Christ.

- **1 Corinthians 11:25**
  After the same manner also *he took* the cup, when he had supped, saying, **This cup is the new testament in my blood: this do ye, as oft as ye drink** *it*, **in remembrance of me.**

> Eleventh, there is **BOLDNESS** and **ACCESS** to God's throne through the literal blood of Christ.

- **Hebrews 10:19**
  Having therefore, brethren, **boldness to enter into the holiest by the blood of Jesus,**

> Twelfth, there is **MATURITY** in doing God's will through the literal blood of Christ.

- **Hebrews 13:20-21**
  Now the God of peace, that brought again from the dead our Lord Jesus, that great shepherd of the sheep, **through the blood of the everlasting covenant, Make you perfect** in every good work **to do his will**, working in you that which is wellpleasing in his sight, through Jesus Christ; to whom *be* glory for ever and ever. Amen.

Thirteenth, if we mistreat it, there is PUNISHMENT (weakness, sickness, or death) through the literal blood of Christ.

- **Hebrews 10:29**
  Of how much sorer punishment, suppose ye, shall he be thought worthy, who hath trodden under foot the Son of God, and **hath counted the blood of the covenant, wherewith he was sanctified, an unholy thing**, and hath done despite unto the Spirit of grace?
- **1 Corinthians 11:27-30**
  Wherefore **whosoever shall eat this bread, and drink** *this* **cup of the Lord, unworthily, shall be guilty of the body and blood of the Lord.** For he that eateth and drinketh unworthily, eateth and **drinketh damnation to himself**, not discerning the Lord's body. For this cause many *are* **weak** and **sickly** among you, and **many sleep**.

Fourteenth, there is VICTORY over Satan through the literal blood of Christ.

- **Revelation 12:9, 11**
  And the great dragon was cast out, **that old serpent, called the Devil, and Satan**, which deceiveth the whole world: he was cast out into the earth, and his angels were cast out with him. . . . And **they overcame him by the blood of the Lamb**, and by the word of their testimony; and they loved not their lives unto the death.

I think that these verses clearly teach us that "blood" means "blood." When God says we have all these results by the literal blood of Christ, let us take God at His Word. He means it. Do not let John MacArthur or any of his followers twist our minds when he says that "blood" means "death." He makes a joke of the blood of Christ. I consider this to be both blasphemy and heresy!

"the forgiveness of sins" The Greek word for *"forgiveness,"* APHIEMI, is made up of APO which means *"from or away"* and HIEMI which means *"to send."* Forgiveness is *"to send away."* As far as God is concerned, the sins of the saved people are *"sent away"* from them and placed on Christ. This is a wonderful position to be in. There are at least seven important passages that talk about forgiveness.

- Acts 5:31
  Him hath God exalted with his right hand *to be* a Prince and a Saviour, **for to give repentance to Israel, and forgiveness of sins.**
- Acts 13:38
  Be it known unto you therefore, men *and* brethren, that **through this man is preached unto you the forgiveness of sins**:
- Acts 26:18
  To open their eyes, *and* to turn *them* from darkness to light, and *from* the power of Satan unto God, **that they may receive forgiveness of sins**, and inheritance among them which are sanctified by faith that is in me.
- Romans 4:7
  Saying, **Blessed** *are* **they whose iniquities are forgiven**, and whose sins are covered.
- Ephesians 4:32
  And be ye kind one to another, tenderhearted, **forgiving one another, even as God for Christ's sake hath forgiven you**.

We must forgive our fellow believers for any harm we might have caused them.

- Colossians 1:14
  In whom we have redemption through his blood, *even* **the forgiveness of sins**:
- 1 John 1:9
  If we confess our sins, **he is faithful and just to forgive us** *our* **sins**, and to cleanse us from all unrighteousness.

That is forgiveness.

"according to the riches of his grace" Dr. Lewis Sperry Chafer, my teacher at Dallas Theological Seminary from 1948 through 1952, lists thirty-three things that we have by the "Riches of Divine Grace." This is listed in the third volume of his systematic theology. If any of us become discouraged, we need to consider the riches of God's grace. We may be poor and may not have many material possessions; but just read over the list of what God has given those who have been saved by His grace through personal and genuine faith in Christ.

The Riches Of Divine Grace

1. We are redeemed.
2. We are reconciled.
3. We are related to God through propitiation.
4. We are forgiven all trespasses.
5. We are vitally conjoined to Christ for the judgment of the old man to a new walk.
6. We are free from the law.
7. We are children of God.
8. We are adopted.
9. We are acceptable to God by Jesus Christ.
10. We are justified.
11. We are made nigh.
12. We are delivered from the power of darkness.
13. We are translated into the kingdom of His dear Son.
14. We are on the Rock Christ Jesus.
15. We are a gift from God the Father to Christ.
16. We are circumcised in Christ.
17. We are made partakers of the holy and royal priesthood.
18. We are a chosen generation.
19. We are a holy nation.
20. We are a peculiar people.
21. We are heavenly citizens.
22. We are of the family and household of God.
23. We are in the fellowship of the saints.
24. We have a heavenly association.
25. We have access to God.
26. We are within the much more care of God.
27. We are His inheritance and are the inheritance of the saints.
28. We are light in the Lord.
29. We are vitally united to the Father Son and Holy Spirit.
30. We are blessed with the earnest of the Holy Spirit.
31. We are blessed with the first fruits of the Spirit.
32. We are glorified and completed in Him.
33. We possess every spiritual blessing.

These are thirty-three tremendous things that we have if we are born-again Christians. These are found in volume three, pages 234-265, of Dr. Chafer's original eight-volume *Systematic Theology*. At present, the Seminary has condensed these eight volumes into two volumes, using the flawed New International Version instead of the King James Bible. I don't know whether or not they have retained these thirty-three "Riches of Divine Grace."

Ephesians 1:8

"Wherein he hath abounded toward us in all wisdom and prudence"

"Wherein he hath abounded toward us" Do you know what "*abounded*" means? It means "*something that is filled up to the top and running over.*" A cup that is half full is not abounding. A cup that is three-fourths full is not abounding. A cup that is ninety-nine per cent full is not abounding. A cup is abounding when it is full and running over. God has super abounded to us because he has given us His grace and the "Riches of Divine Grace."

"in all wisdom and prudence" "*Wisdom*" is found in the Word of God. He has given it to us. We have it. Why do we not use it? Why do we not believe it? Why do we not memorize from it? Why do we not put it into practice and action? He has abounded to us all "*wisdom*" which is found in the Word of God. That is why we try to preach the Word. "*Wisdom*" is knowing a lot of things, but "*prudence*" is understanding these things. After we have it and know it, prudence says, "I understand it." God has given us that prudence. When there are many different positions on various issues, the Scriptures give us prudence to see the differences. Remember there is a serenity prayer often used by Alcoholics Anonymous which says:

The Serenity Prayer

"God grant me the serenity to accept the things that I cannot change, the courage to change the things that I can, and the wisdom to know the difference."

We have this prayer in our kitchen. While I differ with that organization and the one who wrote this prayer, it makes sense. The wisdom which God has given to us is found in the pages of His Word. What a wonderful thing that God has given to us His wisdom within the pages of His Book. That's why we must use the proper Hebrew Old Testament Masoretic Text and the proper Greek New

Testament Textus Receptus which underlie our King James Bible as well as the King James Bible itself rather than the many spurious Hebrew, Greek, and English versions.

Ephesians 1:9

"Having made known unto us the mystery of his will, according to his good pleasure which he hath purposed in himself"

"Having made known unto us the mystery of his will" The word, "*mystery*," is MUSTERION. It is merely a transliteration of the Greek word. A mystery has been defined as a "sacred secret." God has made know to us the mystery of His will. Where is His will? It is found in His Word. My wife's mother, Gertrude G. Sanborn, always used to tell me this. She was my teacher when I was a new Christian. She would give me theology and doctrine books. She would write me about different Bible subjects and doctrinal statements when I was a student at the University of Michigan. She lived in Berea, Ohio, near Cleveland. One statement that she always quoted was: "*Full knowledge of God's will is found in the full knowledge of God's Word.*" Those two terms, "*God's will*" and "*God's Word*" are inextricably bound up together. God has made known to us the mystery of His will. It is in His Word. It is in the Bible. Make sure you are using the right Bible, the King James Bible in English.

"according to his good pleasure which he hath purposed in himself" This mystery which was kept hidden in the Old Testament is the Lord Jesus Christ, "*the Lamb slain from the foundation of the world*" (Revelation 13:8). The Lord Jesus Christ would one day come into the world and believers in Him would be transformed by His grace. They would be forgiven by faith and made whole "*according to His good pleasure which He purposed in Himself.*"

You might ask what is going to happen between now and eternity? If you want to find some answers, just read the Bible. It tells you what is going to happen. There is going to be a rapture or a "snatching away" of all the regenerated people one of these days. It could be today, or it could be tomorrow. It could occur at any time. It is imminent. The Lord Jesus Christ is going to take out the regenerated ones. He will catch them up into the air (1 Thessalonians 4:16-18). The "rapture" as it is called, is the next event on God's prophetic calendar. Then there will be a seven-year period of tribulation called Daniel's seventieth week (Daniel 9:24). There will be judgment upon this earth the like of which we have never seen. This will make the year two thousand computer scare or any other doomsday prediction insignificant by comparison. It will be a terrific judgment. The Antichrist will appear. People are going to worship him and think that he is a great fellow. They will think he is a wonderful leader, but he will be the Devil himself incarnate.

Then, at the end of that tribulation, the Lord Jesus Himself is going to come back with the saved multitudes. He will set His feet on the Mount of Olives causing it to split from north to south, making an opening east to west (Zechariah 14:4). He will open up a fresh and pure river that will flow from the temple of Jerusalem eastward (Zechariah 14:8) to make that whole desert "*blossom as the rose*" (Isaiah 35:1). He will reign out of Jerusalem with the saved ones for a thousand years (Revelation 20:6). Then the Devil will be loosed, and he will gather the nations to attack the saints in Jerusalem (Revelation 20:7-9). The Lord will put that down with fire from Heaven (Revelation 20:9). This will usher in the eternal state.

We know what will happen. God has made known the mystery of His will. The future is right in the Scriptures. We do not know when, but we know what. The one thing we know is that in Heaven, as the gospel song says, "*God's own Son will be the leading one in the meeting in the air.*" There will be no big shots. There will be no denominational hierarchies. There will be no popes. There will be no preachers. There will be no presidents or any other kind of leaders. Christ will be the leading one in that meeting in the air.

Ephesians 1:10

"That in the dispensation of the fulness of times he might gather together in one all things in Christ, both which are in heaven, and which are on earth; *even* **in him"**

"That in the dispensation of the fulness of times he might gather together in one all things in Christ" One day God is going to "*gather together in one*" every saved person. It is in the dispensation of the fullness of times. That is going to take place when the believers are raptured. Jesus will come to meet the saved ones in the air, snatching the true believers from every nation of the world.

- 1 Thessalonians 4:16-17
  For the Lord himself shall descend from heaven with a shout, with the voice of the archangel, and with the trump of God: and the dead in Christ shall rise first: **Then we which are alive** *and* **remain shall be caught up together with them in the clouds**, to meet the Lord in the air: and so shall we ever be with the Lord.

The ones who are not saved will not be brought "*together in one.*" Only the ones who are redeemed will be brought together with those who have gone before us.

"both which are in heaven, and which are on earth; even in him" All things that are in Heaven (the spirits and souls who have gone before) and in earth will be brought *"together in one."* There is a great day coming. We do not know when it will be. If you are unsaved, you need to trust the Lord Jesus Christ. You need to be saved so on that day it will not take you unawares. Only the ones who are redeemed by the precious blood of Christ will be taken up on that day.

Ephesians 1:11

"In whom also we have obtained an inheritance, being predestinated according to the purpose of him who worketh all things after the counsel of his own will" The *"we"* refers to genuine believers. Paul the prisoner is writing to the church at Ephesus. God has predestinated or *"known beforehand"* that we have this *"inheritance."* We have a predestinated inheritance. There are at least eight important verses on this *"inheritance."*

- Acts 20:32
  And now, brethren, I commend you to God, and to the word of his grace, which is able to build you up, and **to give you an inheritance** among all them which are sanctified.
- Acts 26:18
  To open their eyes, *and* to turn *them* from darkness to light, and *from* the power of Satan unto God, **that they may receive forgiveness of sins, and inheritance** among them which are sanctified by faith that is in me.

That was the testimony that Paul gave before King Agrippa.

- Ephesians 1:14
  Which is the earnest of our inheritance until the redemption of the purchased possession, unto the praise of his glory.
- Ephesians 1:18
  The eyes of your understanding being enlightened; that ye may know what is the hope of his calling, and **what the riches of the glory of his inheritance** in the saints,
- Colossians 1:12
  Giving thanks unto the Father, which hath made us meet to be **partakers of the inheritance** of the saints in light:
- Colossians 3:24
  Knowing that of the Lord **ye shall receive the reward of the inheritance**: for ye serve the Lord Christ.

- **Hebrews 9:15**
  And for this cause he is the mediator of the new testament, that by means of death, for the redemption of the transgressions *that were* under the first testament, they which are called **might receive the promise of eternal inheritance**.
- **1 Peter 1:4**
  To an inheritance incorruptible, and undefiled, and that fadeth not away, reserved in heaven for you,

All of these verses are on the subject of the saved person's inheritance.

What are you going to get from your inheritance? Or have you already received it? If you have a father, a mother, a grandfather, or a grandmother who has died, perhaps they have left you a physical inheritance. My wife has an inheritance from her father. Most of it is taking care of his youngest daughter, Beverly, who is not able to speak. My dad died and left me an inheritance. I shared it with my two sisters, so the three of us split it. Maybe some of you have had an inheritance whether small or great. This verse is speaking of an eternal inheritance that will not fade away. This incorruptible inheritance is reserved in Heaven for believers. There is nothing on this earth that can compare with the inheritance that is awaiting the born-again believers in Heaven.

You might know some millionaires who have three-million-dollar houses, yachts, and many servants. That is fine if they can afford it. Some of them have all of that and ill health to go with it. On the other hand, some of them are very strong, healthy, and robust until the day that they die. I know some of these things because my dad and mom were yachting people. My dad had many yachts in his day. He was a member for many years of the Vermilion Yacht Club in Vermilion, Ohio. They were around many millionaires who had these boats. Sam works at a hotel where millionaires live. I asked Sam what they were like. Sam said they are miserable. He said they are grumpy.

The inheritance of Heaven cannot compare to that which is on earth. Paul said *"having food and raiment let us be therewith content."* (1 Timothy 6:8) In our country we have more than food and raiment. This country is filled with much more food, clothes, possessions, and other items than Liberia. These people hardly have clothes to put on their back. They hardly have a roof over their heads. They hardly have rice enough to feed their empty stomachs. Disease is rampant, and there is hardly enough clean water. We have plenty in this country. But whatever we have here on earth cannot compare with the inheritance we who are saved have in Heaven. That inheritance is *"incorruptible and undefiled, and that fadeth not away"* (1 Peter 1:4). It is reserved in Heaven for us. What a great inheritance!

Ephesians 1:12

"That we should be to the praise of his glory, who first trusted in Christ"

"That we should be to the praise of his glory" That word for "praise," EPAINOS, means *"approbation, [official approval] commendation."* God wants us with our inheritance to be approved unto *"the praise of His glory."* He wants us holy. He wants us without blame.

"who first trusted in Christ" Trusting in Christ is the beginning of it all. Once we have sincere trust in the Lord Jesus Christ, we have everything that God has given to us. We are heirs of God and joint heirs with Jesus Christ. There is not a single thing that the Father has that the Son does not also have. If we are saved, we are in Christ and have everything that the Son of God has. We are *"joint-heirs with Christ"* (Romans 8:17). That is our inheritance in Heaven which we received when we first trusted Christ. I am glad that Paul did not dwell on his circumstances. He dwelt on Christ. I do not think Paul has mentioned his bonds once so far in this book. He does not even say he is a prisoner. He does not ask for money, food, or Bibles. He does not want them to cry for him because he is in torment. He does not moan and groan about his surroundings, but he exalts his Saviour. That is what we should do also.

Ephesians 1:13

"In whom ye also *trusted*, after that ye heard the word of truth, the gospel of your salvation: in whom also after that ye believed, ye were sealed with that holy Spirit of promise"

"In whom ye also *trusted*, after that ye heard the word of truth, the gospel of your salvation" Remember, Ephesus was a major seaport on the Aegean Sea in what used to be called Asia Minor which is now called Turkey. Paul was writing them from prison in Rome. He had founded the church of Ephesus on one of his earlier missionary journeys. They had trusted the Lord Jesus Christ. They trusted in the Lord Jesus Christ after they heard the gospel of salvation. The thing that brings a person to Christ is their repentance for their sins and their turning in genuine faith to the One Who died for their sins. The Scriptures taught in truth will lead people to open their hearts and receive the Lord Jesus Christ as their Saviour.

The Holy Spirit works with His Word of Truth. That is why we stand, in our church, for the King James Bible. We believe it to be the only accurate English translation from its Hebrew and Greek manuscripts. We believe it to be the best. There are versions and perversions all over, but we believe the King James Bible is founded on the proper Hebrew and Greek texts. Along with the proper text, it had the proper translators and the proper translation technique. It also has the proper theology.

When they heard the Word of Truth, these Ephesian Christians opened their hearts and received Christ. The Holy Spirit must work, but He works through the Word. Notice what the good news of the gospel is. The first part is bad news. The bad news is that all men, women, boys, and girls are lost and bound for Hell. That is bad news for us, but it does not stop there. God loved sinners even when we were dead in our sins. He sent His Son, the Lord Jesus Christ, to be our Saviour. God the Son, the second Person of the Trinity, left Heaven and took upon Himself a body. Then he was nailed to the cross and died in our stead for our sins, our guilt, and our shame. That is the gospel of our salvation. We must realize we're sinners, repent of our sins, and have a genuine trust in Christ Who died for our sins. That brings us to Christ and makes us saved.

"In whom also after that ye believed, ye were sealed with that holy Spirit of promise" These Ephesian Christians had heard the Word and had trusted Christ. At the time of salvation, they were sealed with the Holy Spirit. We are neither Arminians nor hyper-Calvinists, but we believe the Bible. The Bible says that once we are saved we are sealed with the Holy Spirit of God. That seal can never be broken. We have eternal life, and that will never leave us. Once we have been born, we cannot be unborn by the Spirit of God. The Holy Spirit of God has sealed us.

- John 6:27
  Labour not for the meat which perisheth, but for that meat which endureth unto everlasting life, which the Son of man shall give unto you: **for him hath God the Father sealed.**

God the Father has sealed His Son. He has also sealed the believers who have been saved.

- 2 Corinthians 1:22
  Who hath also sealed us, and given the earnest of the Spirit in our hearts.
- Ephesians 4:30
  And grieve not the holy Spirit of God, **whereby ye are sealed unto the day of redemption.**

That is the length and duration of the seal. There is no end to it until we are caught up to be like Him and have bodies like Christ's body. This seal is something that God has put on us by the Holy Spirit of God.

A seal is something for security. Have you been sealed by the Holy Spirit of God? When you are saved by repentant faith in Christ, then the Holy Spirit

enters your body. That is what it says in Scripture. That Holy Spirit seals us. Once we are saved, we are always saved. This is what the Lord Jesus said.
- **John 10:27**
  My sheep hear my voice, and **I know them, and they follow me**:

The sealing is permanent. It is by the Holy Spirit of God. We do not believe that we can lose our salvation. We may lose the joy of our salvation if we choose to walk after the flesh instead of after the Spirit. This is just like when we rebel against our mom and dad and so on. We may lose the fellowship of mom and dad, but we will not lose the sonship or daughtership of mom and dad. So it is with our relationship with our heavenly Father.

Ephesians 1:14

"Which is the earnest of our inheritance until the redemption of the purchased possession, unto the praise of his glory" The *"which"* goes back to the Holy Spirit mentioned in the previous verse. People do not very often understand what *"earnest"* means. Earnest money is money that you put up front before you pay the full price of a house. You put a down payment on that house. The Holy Spirit is that down payment.

- **2 Corinthians 1:22**
  Who hath also sealed us, **and given the earnest of the Spirit** in our hearts.

That is the first down payment. The fact is that one day God is going to redeem fully the saved ones and take their bodies and make them like the body of the Lord Jesus Christ. First of all, He gives us a down payment. God says if you are regenerated, then the Holy Spirit is placed in our bodies. That is the first step. God has promised that He will do a work in these bodies one day and make them just like Christ's body. We will be redeemed from all sin and iniquity, and we will be made just like God's Son, the Lord Jesus Christ.

- **2 Corinthians 5:5**
  Now he that hath wrought us for the selfsame thing *is* God, who also **hath given unto us the earnest of the Spirit**.

God is going to see us through.

- **Romans 8:23**
  And not only *they*, but ourselves also, which have the firstfruits of the Spirit, even we ourselves groan within ourselves, **waiting for the adoption,** *to wit*, **the redemption of our body.**

One day, if we are saved, our body is going to be redeemed. Our spirit and soul are redeemed as soon as we trust Christ as Saviour, but our bodies are not redeemed. That is why we have the old nature which is the flesh and the new nature which is the Spirit of God dwelling within us. Until the final redemption, we have to walk by faith and do what is right. But one day we are going to be redeemed totally even to the receiving of a glorified body which will have no sin nature in it at all.

- **Ephesians 4:30**
  And grieve not the holy Spirit of God, **whereby ye are sealed unto the day of redemption.**

The money that is given as a pledge or down payment guarantees that the full amount will subsequently be paid. That is what earnest money is. God has pledged that He is going to carry this thing through. I just simply believe this. When God saved me, He gave me the Holy Spirit into my heart and mind. I just believe He will carry the rest through. One day I am going to go to Heaven and have a body just like the Lord Jesus' body. That is a precious promise indeed.

Ephesians 1:15

"Wherefore I also, after I heard of your faith in the Lord Jesus, and love unto all the saints" Paul was in prison a thousand miles or so away, yet he heard about their faith and their church which was growing. He heard also of their *"love unto all the saints."* Some of the saints are just plain unlovely. Did you know that? Are any of you here unlovely saints? *"Saints"* is a good word for believers. It means *"separated ones."* We are separated unto the Lord Jesus Christ. We do not have to be in the Roman Catholic Church to be called saints. We do not have to wait until we die and the pope pronounces us saints. Believers who are saved by genuine faith in Christ are called saints. This is one of the words that is left out in some of the new versions. They do not call New Testament believers *"saints."* They are called God's children or other things. I do not want to placate Rome by leaving out the word *"saint"* for all saved people.

There are two things to keep in mind when it comes to saints. There are some who call themselves saints who are not, and there are those who are saints but at times do not walk too saintly. Mark this down. Some who profess to be saints are not saints. The Lord Jesus spoke of this.

- **Matthew 7:22-23**

Many will say to me in that day, Lord, Lord, have we not prophesied in thy name? and in thy name have cast out devils? and in thy name done many wonderful works? And **then will I profess unto them, I never knew you: depart from me, ye that work iniquity.**

We want those who walk after the flesh to get straightened out and have them walk by faith and not by sight. They need to walk by the Spirit and not by the flesh. We have to be saintly. God calls us to be saints, and so we must act like the saints that we are.

Christians should have love for all the saints even though we shy away from some of the saints who are most unlovely. In this verse, we see that these Ephesian Christians loved all the saints. Christ loved me when I was lost. He loved you when you were lost. We were wretched, lost, and bound for Hell, but God sent a Saviour. I like this saying in our bulletin,

Our Greatest Need

"If our greatest need had been information, God would have sent us an educator. If our greatest need had been technology, God would have sent us a scientist. If our greatest need had been money, God would have sent us an economist. If our greatest need had been pleasure, God would have sent us an entertainer. But our greatest need was forgiveness, so God sent a Saviour." [Copied]

God knew our greatest need, and that is important to us. God loved all the saints. He loved the sinners too.

- **Romans 5:8**
  But **God commendeth his love toward us, in that, while we were yet sinners**, Christ died for us.

We should have a love for all the saints. Sometimes our love for the unlovely saints who know Jesus Christ as personal Saviour, even to those who do not act too saintly, will make them be drawn closer to the Lord as they see our love toward them. They may even hate us. They may even not want to be around us. Those Christians who are walking after the flesh are not comfortable with those who are walking after the Spirit and do not want to be around them. This is true of the unbelievers, too.

I remember one of the ladies who used to come to our home Bible study class. She said that this was all right for us in the class to try to follow the Bible's teachings, but she could not. She did not feel like she could walk according to the things of the Word. I am sorry she is not still with us. She could begin to grow in Christ, and then she could see that with God all things are possible. We cannot do this in our flesh, but the Lord is able to cause us to love all the saints and to walk in His Word.

In summary, Paul not only heard about the Ephesian Christians' faith, but he also heard about their love for all the saints. We may not always agree with all of the believers. There are many saints whom we do not believe are walking Scripturally when we see that they have compromise in their lives. We do not have to agree with all their ways, but we can still love them. You can love somebody even though you may disagree with them. If we are born again, we can do that. We do not have to follow their practices. We believe there are certain doctrines that they have that are not Scriptural. We do not walk with them, but we can love them.

Ephesians 1:16

"Cease not to give thanks for you, making mention of you in my prayers" Paul in prison ceased not *"to give thanks"* for these Ephesians because of their faith and love. He thanked the Lord for them. Can you imagine a man in prison with not much to eat, without much warmth on cold nights, and without much comfort sleeping on a hard bed praying and giving thanks for the people that he led to Christ on one of his former missionary journeys there in Ephesus?

I hope that you can *"give thanks"* for me, and that I can *"give thanks"* for you. We should give thanks for one another. Thanks that God has caused us to come unto Christ and be saved by his grace through faith. We need to be thankful Christians. I am glad that we have been singing, "Thank You Jesus for All You've Done." It's a beautiful gospel song. Paul made mention of these Christians in his prayers.

- Philippians 4:6-7

  Be careful for nothing; but in every thing by prayer and supplication with thanksgiving let your requests be made known unto God. And the peace of God, which passeth all understanding, shall keep your hearts and minds through Christ Jesus.

The way some people read this verse in their lives is *"be careful and anxious for everything."* The Bible says to be careful for nothing or do not be anxious about anything.

- Colossians 2:7

  Rooted and built up in him, and stablished in the faith, as ye have been taught, **abounding therein with thanksgiving.**

- Colossians 4:2

  Continue in prayer, and **watch in the same with thanksgiving**;

- Revelation 7:12

  Saying, Amen: Blessing, and glory, and wisdom, **and thanksgiving**, and honour, and power, and might, *be* unto our God for ever and ever. Amen.

We ought to thank our Lord Jesus Christ for what He has done for us. We ought to be thankful for our fellow believers who are in Christ. This word for

"prayers," PROSEUCHE, is *"a place set apart or suited for the offering of prayer."* Sometimes it is used for the word synagogue. It is
> *"a place in the open air where the Jews were wont to pray, outside the cities, where they had no synagogue. Such places were situated upon the bank of a stream or the shore of a sea, where there was a supply of water for washing the hands before prayer."*

The river bank was historically the place where people picked a place to pray. That is why Lydia was *"by a river side, where prayer was wont to be made."* (Acts 16:13) Paul visited her in the city of Philippi. This is the word for prayer.

Ephesians 1:17

"That the God of our Lord Jesus Christ, the Father of glory, may give unto you the spirit of wisdom and revelation in the knowledge of him" Paul is praying that God would give unto these believers *"the spirit of wisdom."* We have some wisdom in high schools and in colleges, but that is not the wisdom that he is talking about here. There is nothing wrong with good wisdom that is founded upon truth, but it is important that wisdom be founded upon God and His Words. Harvard College was founded on this basis. Now look at it. It is apostate. Princeton was founded on this. Temple University was founded on this. Many of these great schools were founded so that they might have wisdom and knowledge of the Lord Jesus Christ. They have gone astray from that. We have to know Him.

- Philippians 3:8
  Yea doubtless, and I count all things *but* loss for the excellency of the knowledge of Christ Jesus my Lord: for whom I have suffered the loss of all things, and do count them *but* dung, that I may win Christ,
- Philippians 3:10
  That I may know him, and the power of his resurrection, and the fellowship of his sufferings, being made conformable unto his death;

Knowing Him was important to Paul. Where are you going to find that knowledge? The only place is in the Word of God!

- Luke 24:27
  And beginning at Moses and all the prophets, **he expounded unto them in all the scriptures the things concerning himself**.

These disciples on the road to Emmaus did not know it was the Lord Jesus Christ. I would have loved to have been in that audience to know the things in all the Scriptures concerning Himself that He expounded unto them that day (Luke 24:27). We can read from Genesis to Revelation and wonder what He means. Jesus knew the Scriptures because He was the Author of the Scriptures. I believe the Lord Jesus Christ, the Revelator, the Logos of God, gave the Words of all the Old Testament Scriptures and He gave the revelation of the Words of the New Testament. This is what Jesus said about the giving of the New Testament.

- **John 16:13**
  Howbeit when he, the Spirit of truth, is come, he will guide you into all truth: for he shall not speak of himself; [or from Himself as the source] but **whatsoever he shall hear, *that* shall he speak: and he will shew you things to come.**
- **Luke 24:30-31**
  And it came to pass, as he sat at meat with them, **he took bread, and blessed *it*,** and brake, and gave to them. **And their eyes were opened, and they knew him**; and he vanished out of their sight.

Probably when Christ broke the bread, they saw the scars of Calvary. Yes, He had a new body. It will be the only body in Glory that will be scarred. I believe all of our bodies, no matter what scars we have now, will be perfect but not His. I realize that Harold Camping, President of Family Radio, does not believe this. He thinks that Christ's body is without scars. I would like to draw his attention to Thomas's question.

- **John 20:25**
  The other disciples therefore said unto him, We have seen the Lord. But he said unto them, **Except I shall see in his hands the print of the nails, and put my finger into the print of the nails, and thrust my hand into his side, I will not believe.**

When Jesus met Thomas in the upper room, he showed Thomas the scars on his body.

- **John 20:27-28**
  Then saith he to Thomas, **Reach hither thy finger, and behold my hands; and reach hither thy hand, and thrust *it* into my side**: and be not faithless, but believing. And Thomas answered and said unto him, **My Lord and my God**.

Thomas did not even touch Him. He knew He was Lord by the scars on His body. I believe that as He broke the bread before those two men on the road to Emmaus just outside of Jerusalem, they recognized Him by the scars on His hands.

- Luke 24:32
  And they said one to another, **Did not our heart burn within us**, while he talked with us by the way, and **while he opened to us the scriptures**?

That is not heartburn like we talk about today. This is a good type of burning, the burning of our hearts. When the Scriptures are opened up to us, this makes our hearts warm to the things of the Lord. Paul wanted to know Christ, and he wanted the Christians at Ephesus and the Christians today also to know Christ. Before the Lord Jesus Christ ascended into Heaven, the two angels said: "... *this same Jesus, which is taken up from you into heaven, shall so come in like manner as ye have seen Him go into heaven*" (Acts 1:11b)

Ephesians 1:18

"The eyes of your understanding being enlightened; that ye may know what is the hope of his calling, and what the riches of the glory of his inheritance in the saints"

"The eyes of your understanding being enlightened"
Paul also prayed that the eyes of their "*understanding*" would be "*enlightened.*" Before we are saved, our eyes and our understanding are darkened. We are blind.

- 2 Corinthians 4:3-4
  But if our gospel be hid, **it is hid to them that are lost**: In whom the god of this world hath **blinded the minds of them which believe not**, lest the light of the glorious gospel of Christ, who is the image of God, should shine unto them.

He prays that their understanding would be opened up and that they would be able to see.

"that ye may know what is the hope of his calling, and what the riches of the glory of his inheritance in the saints" The "*hope of His calling*" is that one day the saved ones will see Him and be with Him in Glory. That is the hope of His calling. When He called us, He said, "*Come unto me, all ye that labour and are heavy laden, and I will give you rest*" (Matthew 11:28). He called everyone of us who are saved. If we are regenerated, there was a time when the gospel was preached and the Holy Spirit of God touched our hearts. We said, "Yes, I repent of my sins, accept, and believe on Christ." Then we are saved and redeemed. That is the hope-- to be saved and to be in Heaven with Him for all eternity.

We have not seen His glory on this earth. The Lord Jesus saw God the Father's glory and then left that glory. He came down and veiled His glory in His perfect human body. He veiled perfect deity so that we would not be blinded with the glory of God. That is why Moses could not see the Lord in all of His perfection and glory. The Lord had to hide Moses in *"a clift of the rock"* to shelter him (Exodus 33:22). That is where we get that hymn, "Hiding in Thee." After Moses was in the Lord's presence, he had to wear a veil over his face because the people said that Moses' face was too bright (Exodus 34:35). This brightness came after only seeing the "back parts" of the Lord and not even His face (Exodus 33:23). One day the redeemed will see His glory because we will have perfect bodies like Christ's body that can behold the glory of God. We could not last seeing God's glory in these bodies. Remember the dazzling atomic brightness and the beams that wounded and killed people at Hiroshima? The Lord has some sort of "atomic radiation" which will not be deadly to us in our glorified bodies. The Bible tells us that flesh and blood shall not inherit the kingdom of Heaven (1 Corinthians 15:50). We cannot go there in our flesh and blood bodies. We just cannot do it. Our new bodies will be like unto Christ's body, and we shall behold His glory. Peter, James, and John beheld, in a small measure, the Lord's glory on the mount of transfiguration. While they were on the mount, Moses and Elijah appeared. The Lord's garment was as white as snow and as bright as the sunshine (Matthew 17:1-3). He was glorified a little bit in front of them. John said that *"we beheld His glory"* (John 1:14). One day we will see his full glory, and we will be able to exist in its presence. As the gospel song says, there will be "Only Glory By and By."

Ephesians 1:19

"And what *is* the exceeding greatness of his power to us-ward who believe, according to the working of his mighty power" Paul prayed that they would understand the greatness of God's power. I would like you to look with me at just thirteen verses about power because this is what he was praying about.

- **Matthew 9:6**
  But that ye may know that **the Son of man hath power on earth to forgive sins**, (then saith he to the sick of the palsy,) Arise, take up thy bed, and go unto thine house.
- **Matthew 28:18**
  And Jesus came and spake unto them, saying, **All power is given unto me in heaven and in earth**.
- **Luke 24:49**
  And, behold, I send the promise of my Father upon you: but tarry ye in the city of Jerusalem, **until ye be endued with power from on high**.

- Acts 1:8
  But ye shall receive power, after that the Holy Ghost is come upon you: and ye shall be witnesses unto me both in Jerusalem, and in all Judea, and in Samaria, and unto the uttermost part of the earth.
- Romans 1:20
  For the invisible things of him from the creation of the world are clearly seen, being understood by the things that are made, *even* **his eternal power and Godhead**; so that they are without excuse:
- Romans 15:13
  Now the God of hope fill you with all joy and peace in believing, that ye may abound in hope, **through the power of the Holy Ghost**.
- 1 Corinthians 1:18
  For the preaching of the cross is to them that perish foolishness; **but unto us which are saved it is the power of God**.
- 1 Corinthians 1:24
  But unto them which are called, both Jews and Greeks, **Christ the power of God**, and the wisdom of God.
- 1 Corinthians 2:4-5
  And my speech and my preaching *was* not with enticing words of man's wisdom, **but in demonstration of the Spirit and of power**: That your faith should not stand in the wisdom of men, but in the power of God.

There are a lot of wise men, but if it is just the wisdom of men and not the power of God, nothing will be accomplished for the Lord.

- 2 Corinthians 12:9
  And he said unto me, My grace is sufficient for thee: for my strength is made perfect in weakness. Most gladly therefore will I rather glory in my infirmities, **that the power of Christ may rest upon me**.

When we are weak, we can see God's power. When we are strong, we do not need God's power because we are strong within ourselves. The people in the world who are lost in their sins think they do not need God because they are strong. *"They that are whole need not a physician, but they that are sick."* (Matthew 9:12) Praise God that we who are saved have the power of Christ resting upon us.

- **Ephesians 3:20**
  Now unto him that is able to do exceeding abundantly above all that we ask or think, **according to the power that worketh in us,**
- **Ephesians 6:10**
  Finally, my brethren, **be strong in the Lord, and in the power of his might.**

The power is in the Lord's might, and not our might. Why do you think David slew Goliath? It was the power of God. Goliath was much bigger than David and much more skilled in battle. David had only a sling and five smooth stones. The Lord had given him victory over a lion and a bear, and David said that the Lord would give him victory over this Philistine. God directed the stone because David trusted in Him and His power (1 Samuel 17:37).

Ephesians 1:20

"Which he wrought in Christ, when he raised him from the dead, and set *him* at his own right hand in the heavenly *places*" This power which God the Father *"wrought in Christ"* is a greater power than any power on this earth. Notice God showed His power in His Son in two things. He *"raised Him from the dead,"* and He *"set Him at His own right hand."* There are many manifestations of God's power.

Nine Manifestations of God's Power

1. God showed His power in the creation of the world.
2. God showed His power in the creation of man.
3. God showed His power and miracles in delivering Israel from Egypt.
4. God showed His power in the miracles of Elijah, Elisha, and other Old Testament characters.
5. God showed His power in the various miracles of our Lord Jesus Christ.
6. God showed His power in the various miracles by the apostles.
7. God shows His power in the miracle of the new birth when He saves sinners.
8. God showed His power in the resurrection power of the Lord Jesus Christ.
9. God showed His power in setting His Son at His own right hand in the heavenly places.

- **John 10:17**
  Therefore doth my Father love me, because **I lay down my life, that I might take it again.**
The Lord Jesus Christ had the power to take His life back again in resurrection glory.
- **1 Corinthians 6:14**
  And **God hath both raised up the Lord**, and will also raise up us by his own power.
The resurrection is the greatest power on this earth.
- **1 Corinthians 15:43**
  It is sown in dishonour; it is raised in glory: it is sown in weakness; **it is raised in power:**
Our bodies are going to be powerful when we go to be with Christ.
- **Philippians 3:10**
  That I may know him, and **the power of his resurrection**, and the fellowship of his sufferings, being made conformable unto his death;
There is great power. To sum up, God the Father showed His power in two things that he did to the Lord Jesus Christ.

<u>First of all</u>: God showed His power when He raised Jesus from the dead. Man cannot do that even though he may try. There is the science of cryonics. Cryonics is
"the practice of freezing the body of a person who has just died in order to preserve it for possible resuscitation in the future, as when a cure for the disease that caused death has been found."
I do not believe that man will ever do that. God has the power of life. Man can make a lot of things, but the raising from the dead is the power of God.

<u>Second of all</u>: God showed His power when He set the Lord Jesus in the heavenly places. Jesus is seated on the Father's right hand. His ascension shows another power that no man can do. We had a failure in the power of the Mar's probe. Everybody was expecting to see the pictures from Mars, but they are lost. It cost one-hundred and sixty million dollars to get to that point, and it failed. Our astronauts have had a lot of practice, and they still failed. Our Lord Jesus did not have any practice; yet God, in His power, took the resurrected glorified body of our Lord Jesus Christ up through the atmosphere with the coldness, the pressure, no oxygen, no gravity. He instantaneously took Him into the heavens and *"set Him at His own right hand in heavenly places."*

We have never seen that power. Men can try and try, but they can never go into the Heaven of Heavens. Man can only go into the starry heaven. The Devil can go into the earthly sphere around us, but he can never again go take his former exalted place in the third Heaven, as Paul speaks of it. He has been banned from that former exalted position since his fall into sin and pride. I do not know how many planets man is going to try to go to, but God's power was manifested as He raised Christ from the dead and set Him on His right hand in glory. He is there for believers. The Lord Jesus Christ is there at the Father's right hand as our great High Priest. We are not Roman Catholics, but we believe in a High Priest, the Lord Jesus Christ. He makes intercession for every believer.

- 1 John 2:1-3
  My little children, these things write I unto you, that ye sin not. And if any man sin, **we have an advocate with the Father**, Jesus Christ the righteous:

He is our Advocate. He does not want us to sin. But if we do sin, we can pray to Him, and He can forgive our sins and make us right.

- 1 John 1:9
  If we confess our sins, **he is faithful and just to forgive us our sins**, and to cleanse us from all unrighteousness.

Ephesians 1:21

"Far above all principality, and power, and might, and dominion, and every name that is named, not only in this world, but also in that which is to come" Jesus is above all of these powers. He is above mayors, governors, presidents, kings, emperors, and all other powers. At the Father's right hand, Jesus is above all of them. He is above every name that is named.

- Isaiah 45:23
  I have sworn by myself, the word is gone out of my mouth *in* righteousness, and shall not return, That unto me **every knee shall bow, every tongue shall swear**.
- Acts 4:12
  Neither is there salvation in any other: for **there is none other name under heaven given among men, whereby we must be saved**.

That Name of the Lord Jesus Christ is the only Name *"under heaven" "whereby we must be saved."* None other Name will do. Mohammed won't do. The leaders of Shinto won't do. The leaders of the Taoism won't do. The leaders of the New Age won't do. Confucius won't do. None but the Name of the Lord Jesus Christ of the Bible is able to bring salvation to the soul.

- Philippians 2:9-11
  Wherefore God also hath highly exalted him, and **given him a name which is above every name: That at the name of Jesus every knee should bow**, of *things* in heaven, and

Ephesians 1:21-22

things in earth, and *things* under the earth; And *that* every tongue should confess that Jesus Christ *is* Lord, to the glory of God the Father.

One day that is going to happen. All who are lost and bound for Hell who refuse to bow before Him on this earth will one day have to bow their knee before Him.

There are many hymns about the name of the Lord Jesus Christ. Here are a few of them:

Hymns About Christ's Name

"The Name of Jesus is So Sweet"
"There's Something About That Name"
"Jesus Sweetest Name I Know"
" Oh How I Love Jesus"
"His Name Is Wonderful"
"O Hail the Name of Jesus"
"Glory To His Name"
"There Is a Name I Highly Treasure"
"Jesus Name I Love"
"That Beautiful Name"
"Take the Name of Jesus With You"

Ephesians 1:22

"And hath put all *things* under his feet, and gave him *to be* the head over all *things* to the church"

"And hath put all *things* under his feet" One day when Jesus reigns in His millennial glory, He will have everything *"under His feet."* Most people never used the word millennium much until the turn of the century in the year 2000. Christians have always talked about the millennium which is the one-thousand-year reign of the Lord Jesus Christ upon this earth. At that time everything will be put under His feet.

"and gave him *to be* the head over all *things* to the church" The Lord Jesus is the head of the church. He is the Good Shepherd. Pastors are undershepherds but the Lord Jesus is the Chief Shepherd.

> ## Christ Our Threefold Shepherd
> **Psalm 22 speaks of His past ministry.**
> Jesus is the Good Shepherd who gave His life for the sheep.
> **Psalm 23 speaks of His present ministry.**
> Jesus is the Great Shepherd who intercedes for His sheep.
> **Psalm 24 speaks of His future ministry.**
> Jesus is the Chief Shepherd who shall one day reign with His sheep.

The ones who are born again make up the body of Christ. Jesus is the Head of the body. These days the body is pretty weak and anemic, and it is getting weaker. Oh, there are believers who profess salvation, but they do not hold on to the Head, the Lord Jesus, to be strong. The body of Christ is made up of those who are born again, saved, and regenerated by the Spirit of God. Even those of us who are regenerated and saved by the Spirit of God are in pretty sad shape. We have to keep strong and be strengthened as we hold up the Head who is our Saviour.

Ephesians 1:23

"Which is his body, the fulness of him that filleth all in all"

"Which is his body" The body of Christ is composed of the believers found in our local church. We help one another. We care for one another. We are glad to be in fellowship one with another. The Lord Jesus is the Head of this body.

"the fulness of him that filleth all in all" The world knows no other message but the message that we have in our bodies as we represent Him. We who are saved are an epistle *"known and read of all men."* (2 Corinthians 3:2) If we have a blank page in our "epistle," that is what they will read. If our letter is blank, they read it blank. If the believers are the *"fullness"* of the Lord on this earth, let us be a little fuller. Sometimes we are half empty. The Lord Jesus considers the believers here to be His fullness.

Ephesians Chapter Two

Ephesians 2:1

"And you *hath he quickened,* **who were dead in trespasses and sins"** Here is a description of our lost condition before we were saved. The Lord is very specific. He is talking to these Ephesian believers who were saved, but, remember, they were first lost. The words "*hath he quickened*" are in italic type because they are supplied from the Greek words used in verse five later on. It is important that we see that before we were saved, we were not just sick; we were dead. Apostate preachers and theologians teach that men, women, boys and girls are alive and not dead. They teach that everyone will go to Heaven. That is not what the Bible teaches. The Bible teaches that all of us are lost and need a Saviour in Christ. Some people teach that we are not all dead. They say that we are just a little bit sick. They say there is a spark within us and that we just have to fan the flame by good works. That is not what the Bible teaches. The Bible pronounces that we are "*dead in trespasses and sins*." We are dead from the standpoint of sins and trespasses, not that we are physically dead.

There is a heresy in this world of preachers and teachers that believe that we are so dead that we are not capable of believing on the Lord Jesus Christ. They say that not a single person can believe on the Lord Jesus Christ. Only those who are of the elect can believe. So they are saying the gospel is not to "whosoever will" but to only the elect. That is a heresy, I believe.

In what sense are we dead? We are dead in the sense that we cannot do anything to save ourselves. That is our deadness. We cannot be saved except for the grace of Christ. I have heard Mr. Harold Camping on Family Radio say that faith is a work, and so you cannot be saved by faith because faith is a work. I believe in the total depravity of man, but I do not believe in the total inability of man. That is what the hyper-Calvinists or the strict five-point Calvinists believe. Total depravity means we are lost, and we cannot be saved by our own works of any kind. This salvation comes only by faith in the Lord Jesus Christ Who alone can save us. This faith is not a work, deed, or something we have to accomplish. If our hands are tied and we cannot call upon the Lord Jesus Christ to be saved, why did Paul tell the Philippian jailer to believe on the Lord Jesus in order to be saved? He said, *"Believe on the Lord Jesus Christ, and thou shalt be saved and thy house."* (Acts 16:31) He believed and his house believed, and they were saved. That is the Scripture, and we cannot go beyond the Scripture. He did not know whether he was elect or not. Paul did not know that Philippian jailor and his family. Paul just simply said to believe on the Lord Jesus Christ. Pastor Carl Elgena, when he was the Pastor of the Bethel Baptist Church in Cherry Hill, New Jersey, used to say years ago, *"Those who go out and knock on doors and preach the gospel to those who are there in the houses just happen to find more of the elect than those who don't."* That is a very interesting and important point.

Ephesians 2:2

"Wherein in time past ye walked according to the course of this world, according to the prince of the power of the air, the spirit that now worketh in the children of disobedience"

"Wherein in time past ye walked according to the course of this world" This is the past of these believers in Ephesus. Some of you, perhaps, were saved as a young person. I was saved when I was sixteen (almost seventeen). These verses one to three have to do with a past condition. They walked in the wickedness of this world. Before we were saved, we walked according to this world's course also.

"according to the prince of the power of the air, the spirit that now worketh in the children of disobedience" The *"prince of the power of the air"* is Satan. We were Satan's children before we were saved.

- **John 8:44**
  Ye are of *your* father the devil, and the lusts of your father ye will do. He was a murderer from the beginning, and abode not in the truth, because there is no truth in him. When he speaketh a lie, he speaketh of his own: for he is a liar, and the father of it.

There is an evil spirit that works inside of every unsaved person. Every unsaved person *"walks"* in accord with this evil spirit. Here are some other verses having to do with walking in the wrong way.

- **Ephesians 4:17**
 This I say therefore, and testify in the Lord, that ye henceforth **walk not as other Gentiles walk, in the vanity of their mind,**

They used to walk in the old sinful nature, but now they should not do so.
- **Philippians 3:18**
 (For **many walk,** of whom I have told you often, and now tell you even weeping, *that they* **are the enemies of the cross** of Christ:

The people who do not walk according to the things of the Lord are *"enemies of the cross of Christ."*
- **1 Peter 4:3**
 For the time past of *our* life may suffice us to have wrought the will of the Gentiles, **when we walked in lasciviousness, lusts, excess of wine, revellings, banquetings, and abominable idolatries**:
- **2 Peter 2:10**
 But chiefly them that **walk after the flesh in the lust of uncleanness**, and despise government. Presumptuous *are they*, selfwilled, they are not afraid to speak evil of dignities.
- **2 Peter 3:3**
 Knowing this first, that there shall come in the last days scoffers, **walking after their own lusts,**
- **Jude 16**
 These are murmurers, complainers, **walking after their own lusts**; and their mouth speaketh great swelling *words*, having men's persons in admiration because of advantage.
- **Jude 18**
 How that they told you there should be mockers in the last time, who should **walk after their own ungodly lusts**.

Everyone who is unsaved and is walking according to their own desires and lusts is empowered by Satan. You might wonder about this nice little old lady who helps people. How can she be walking according to the flesh. If she is unsaved, she is walking according to the flesh. Satan is that *"prince of the power of the air."* Unsaved people are walking according to a different power. It is not the power of God, but it is the power of the flesh, the power of the Devil, and the power of this world.

Satan is called the *"prince of the power of the air."* It is interesting to note that word for *"air,"* AER, refers to the *"lower and denser air as distinguished from the higher and rarer air."* It refers to the air just surrounding this earth. This is the Devil's domain right now. He is not up in the first heaven which is the atmospheric heaven, or the second heaven which is the starry heaven, or the third Heaven which is God's Heaven. Satan is empowered to go into those areas, but his domain and the domain of his evil spirits is right in the air immediately surrounding this earth.

Ephesians 2:3

"Among whom also we all had our conversation in times past in the lusts of our flesh, fulfilling the desires of the flesh and of the mind; and were by nature the children of wrath, even as others"

"Among whom also we all had our conversation in times past in the lusts of our flesh" This is referring to times past. These Ephesian Christians who were now saved did these things in the past. Sometimes it is good to go back and think about what we were in the past. We are not to dwell on it, but if we are saved, we must realize what God has brought us out of. It is good to remember where we came from so that we don't go back into that terrible pit.

"fulfilling the desires of the flesh and of the mind; and were by nature the children of wrath, even as others" Sin does not only come to the *"flesh"* but also to the *"mind."* We can sin with our mind as well as the flesh. We have to keep our minds clean and straight and in tune with the Word of God. We are by nature the children of wrath, that is, children who are destined to the wrath of God. You say, "Well, isn't the Lord a God of love." Yes, He is a God of love, but He is also a God of wrath in the judgment of sin. That is why God punished His only begotten Son Who was sent from Heaven to be our Substitute and to bear our wrath in His own body.

There are two ways of paying for your sins. First, you can either bear them yourself and pay for your own sins for all eternity in Hell, the lake of fire. If that is what you want, that is what you can do. The second way is to trust and believe that the Lord Jesus Christ paid for your sins as He did on the cross of Calvary. Jesus paid for the sins of everyone and gives eternal life to those who trust in Him, accept Him, and receive Him as their Saviour. That is what the gospel is. That is what the Lord wants everyone to do. But without Christ we are the children of wrath. Liberals, modernists, and unbelievers do not like to have people called *"children of wrath."* They do not like that because it is negative. If it is in the Bible, it ought to be preached whether it is negative or positive.

Here are a few verses about the lusts and *"desires of the flesh."*

- **John 8:44**
  Ye are of *your* father the devil, and **the lusts of your father ye will do**. He was a murderer from the beginning, and abode not in the truth, because there is no truth in him. When he speaketh a lie, he speaketh of his own: for he is a liar, and the father of it.

The Lord Jesus is speaking here to the Pharisees. He is describing the lusts of their father. The Devil is their father and also the father of a lie.

- **Romans 1:24**
  Wherefore God also gave them up to uncleanness **through the lusts of their own hearts**, to dishonour their own bodies between themselves:
- **Romans 6:12**
  Let not sin therefore reign in your mortal body, **that ye should obey it in the lusts thereof.**

This is speaking to the believer.

- **Romans 13:14**
  But put ye on the Lord Jesus Christ, and **make not provision for the flesh, to** *fulfil* **the lusts** *thereof*.
- **2 Timothy 2:22**
  Flee also youthful lusts: but follow righteousness, faith, charity, peace, with them that call on the Lord out of a pure heart.
- **Titus 2:12**
  Teaching us that, **denying ungodliness and worldly lusts,** we should live soberly, righteously, and godly, in this present world;
- **Titus 3:3**
  For we ourselves also were sometimes foolish, disobedient, deceived, **serving divers lusts and pleasures,** living in malice and envy, hateful, *and* hating one another.

There are the up-and-outers, and there are the down-and-outers. You do not have to be on skid row and drunk to be lost. Even the high and mighty are lost if they have not received Christ as their personal Lord and Saviour.

- **1 Peter 2:11**
  Dearly beloved, I beseech *you* as strangers and pilgrims, **abstain from fleshly lusts,** which war against the soul;
- **1 Peter 1:14**
  As obedient children, **not fashioning yourselves according to the former lusts** in your ignorance:

That Greek word for "*lust,*" is EPITHUMIA. It means "*desire, craving, longing, desire for what is forbidden.*" The flesh is "*the sensuous nature of man, that depraved animal nature.*" We have a body, but inside that body we have an evil nature. You say, "Well, once we are saved doesn't that nature go away? " No, it does not. We still have it. If you do not believe it, just ask your spouse or your children. They'll tell you about your old nature very quickly.

Whenever he got righteously indignant, Dr. David Otis Fuller used to ask if it were his new nature or his old nature. If we are saved, we have two natures. The unbeliever just has one nature. The Holy Spirit of God, who is indwelling every believer, has the power to knock out the power and dominion of the flesh and is able to give us victory.

This is in the past of the believer. We were dead in trespasses and sins. We were walking according to the world. We were walking with the prince of the power of the air. It was a horrible condition!

Ephesians 2:4

"But God, who is rich in mercy, for his great love wherewith he loved us"

"But God" That first word, "*but,*" makes all the difference in the world. That is the contrast-- "*but God.*" The only way that any of us can get out of the "Slough of Despond" as it says in John Bunyan's *Pilgrim's Progress* is by faith in the Lord Jesus Christ. God must do it. He is the only one Who can save us. We cannot save ourselves.

"who is rich in mercy, for his great love wherewith he loved us" Here in verse four we see the combination of mercy and love. There are many good verses about God's rich "*mercy.*"

- **Matthew 20:30.**
  And, behold, two blind men sitting by the way side, when they heard that Jesus passed by, cried out, saying, **Have mercy on us, O Lord**, *thou* Son of David.

They needed God's mercy as well as His grace.

- **Luke 16:24**
  And he cried and said, **Father Abraham, have mercy on me**, and send Lazarus, that he may dip the tip of his finger in water, and cool my tongue; for I am tormented in this flame.

- **1 Timothy 1:12-13**
  Who was before a blasphemer, and a persecutor, and injurious: **but I obtained mercy**, because I did *it* ignorantly in unbelief.

If we are saved, God has given us His mercy. We have done many things ignorantly in unbelief, but we have obtained mercy from God.

- **1 Peter 1:3**
  Blessed *be* the God and Father of our Lord Jesus Christ, which **according to his abundant mercy** hath begotten us again unto a lively hope by the resurrection of Jesus Christ from the dead,

Mercy has been defined as *"kindness or good will towards the miserable and the afflicted, joined with a desire to help them."* That is what that word *"mercy,"* ELEOS, means. We were miserable and sometimes are still miserable. I think most of us are sometimes on the miserable side. That is why we need God's mercy.

Grace and Mercy Contrasted

Grace is positive--getting something we don't deserve--**Heaven.**

Mercy is negative--not getting something we do deserve--**Hell.**

We need God's mercy. He could take us out to His woodshed very easily. As mentioned before, mercy is kindness toward the miserable and the afflicted. It is having the desire to help them. I am glad that God has the desire to help us. The mercies of God are great and innumerable. God shows his mercy towards men in general providence. He shows his mercy and clemency towards us by providing an offering for our sins in the Person of His beloved Son. He provides salvation through faith in the Lord Jesus Christ. That is His mercy that endureth forever (Psalm 106:1).

Ephesians 2:5

"Even when we were dead in sins, hath quickened us together with Christ, (by grace ye are saved;)"

"Even when we were dead in sins, hath quickened us together with Christ" The word, *"quickened,"* means *"to be made alive."* That is what dead people need. They need to be alive. You cannot be made alive by man. Man is making all kinds of provisions for bringing people back to life, such as by cryogenics. But only God is able to *"quicken"* a person. He created life, and He is the only One who can make life.

Last Thursday we had a question in our Bible study service on cremation. My conviction is that it is unscriptural. There are many Christians who do not see anything wrong with cremation. They say that it is easier, and it is cheaper. We were talking to a Christian gentleman who had recently lost his wife. She was a godly woman. Sadly, he told us that his wife was cremated. That is bad enough, but she also had her ashes scattered so her remains were not even in one place. The Lord is able to pick up all those ashes and bring her back. There is no problem there just like there is no problem with the ones who die at sea and the sharks might eat them. God is able in the resurrection to *"quicken"* those bodies and give them incorruptible resurrection bodies. He is the only One who is able to do that. Then this man told us that he was going to be cremated also. He said that he was too poor to be buried. He did tell us that he knew that it was unscriptural. We did not say a word to this man. We did not pick on him. He is a friend from way back, so we just let it ride.

The Lord is able to quicken us even when we were *"dead in sins."* Notice this word, *"together."* There are three *"togethers"* in this section of the Word of God. There is one here in verse five, *"quickened us together with Christ."* The next two *"togethers"* are in verse six, *"raised us up together"* and *"made us sit together in heavenly places."* He has quickened us together with Christ. When we are saved, we are made alive by the Lord Jesus Christ. God the Father quickens us with Christ. We are in Christ.

- **John 5:21**
  For as the Father raiseth up the dead, and quickeneth *them*; even so **the Son quickeneth whom he will.**
- **Romans 4:17**
  (As it is written, I have made thee a father of many nations,) before him whom he believed, *even* God, **who quickeneth the dead**, and calleth those things which be not as though they were.
- **Romans 8:11**
  But if the Spirit of him that raised up Jesus from the dead dwell in you, he that raised up Christ from the dead **shall also quicken your mortal bodies by his Spirit that dwelleth in you.**
- **Colossians 2:13**
  And you, being dead in your sins and the uncircumcision of your flesh, hath **he quickened together with him**, having forgiven you all trespasses;

"(by grace ye are saved)" As I've said before, grace is *"getting something we don't deserve."* Salvation is something we don't deserve, and it is certainly not earned by works. This word grace, CHARIS, speaks of

"the merciful kindness by which God, exerting His holy influence upon souls; turns them to Christ, keeps, strengthens, increases them in Christian faith, knowledge, affection, and kindles them to the exercise of Christian virtues."

It is the Lord that gives us His grace.

Notice that *"by grace ye are saved."* We are going to look at that in another verse a little later, but that word, "*saved*" is in the Greek perfect tense. The perfect tense speaks of something that has happened in the past, continues to the present, and then continues right on into the future. Everything that God does in salvation is permanent. That word saved, SOZO, means "*to keep safe and sound, to rescue from danger or destruction.*" Once God saves us, that is permanent.

Many people think that once they are saved, they can be lost. This is not true. The Lord Jesus gives unto His sheep "*eternal life, and they shall never perish*" (John 10:28).

- Matthew 7:21-23
Not every one that saith unto me, Lord, Lord, shall enter into the kingdom of heaven; but he that doeth the will of my Father which is in heaven. **Many will say to me in that day, Lord, Lord, have we not prophesied in thy name**? and in thy name have cast out devils? and in thy name done many wonderful works? And then will I profess unto them, **I never knew you: depart from me, ye that work iniquity.**

There are some who think they are saved, but they are not. If we know we are saved and the Lord Jesus Christ is our Saviour and our Redeemer, we are safe in the arms of Jesus.

Ephesians 2:6

"And hath raised *us* up together, and made *us* sit together in heavenly *places* in Christ Jesus:" God has not only "*raised us up together*" with Christ, but He also has "*made us sit together in heavenly places in Christ Jesus.*" As far as the Lord is concerned, those who are saved and regenerated by the Holy Spirit of God are seated with Christ at the right hand of the Father. Now, we are seated physically right here in this auditorium. I am standing, and you are seated. But according to God's plan and according to His way of looking at things, we are also seated with Christ at the Father's right hand. This is our positional seating. We have to understand that. Also, He has seated us in heavenly places where the Lord Jesus Christ is with God the Father in Glory. One day we who are saved are going to be in the heavenly places physically with our new resurrected and glorified bodies.

Ephesians 2:7

"That in the ages to come he might shew the exceeding riches of his grace in *his* kindness toward us through Christ Jesus." God has a plan "*in the ages to come*" for saved people. The Lord is going put us on display as those whom He has redeemed from the dirt and dust of sin. God is rich in "*His grace.*" Nor is He

impoverished in *"kindness."* As believers, we should have a little kindness ourselves.
- **Colossians 3:12**
  Put on therefore, as the elect of God, holy and beloved, **bowels of mercies, kindness**, humbleness of mind, meekness, longsuffering;

This is what God tells us to have. Not only does God show kindness to us, but we have to show kindness to other people.

Do not go to Arizona if you want to find polite drivers. We can say that about any state. While we were in Arizona, we counted three different times where people either cut us off, honked their horn, or did some other strange thing. We almost got into several serious situations because of these drivers. Where is the kindness? If they are lost or unsaved, they do not have to be kind. They are just after "me first." They are just thinking about number one. We as believers should be kind because God tells us to be kind.
- **Titus 3:4-5**
  But after that **the kindness and love of God our Saviour toward man appeared**, Not by works of righteousness which we have done, but **according to his mercy he saved us**, by the washing of regeneration, and renewing of the Holy Ghost;

We are to show mercy and kindness one to another just like God showed mercy and kindness to us. God has a plan. He wants to openly display us for all eternity as trophies of his matchless grace and kindness. We are God's masterpiece of grace through and because of the Lord Jesus Christ.

Ephesians 2:8

"For by grace are ye saved through faith; and that not of yourselves: *it is* the gift of God:" Here is God's plan for salvation. First of all, it is *"by grace."* I repeat once again, grace is *"getting something we don't deserve."* We cannot work for salvation. It is by God's grace. Secondly, it is *"through faith."* Faith is not a work. It is very wrong to say that faith is a work. This is strange to me, but you have many, such as Mr. Harold Camping (who is heard over the Family Radio network all over the world) and other hyper-Calvinists, who say that faith is a work.

We are saved by grace through faith. Years ago I wrote a dissertation on Ephesians 2:1-10 in the Greek text for my Master of Theology thesis at Dallas Theological Seminary. I faced the controversy concerning the reference to the word, *"that,"* in this verse. What does the word *"that"* refer to in the phrase *"and **that** not of yourselves"*? The hyper-Calvinists say that it refers to faith. They are saying that you cannot have faith by yourself. They even say you have to be saved before you can have faith. Paul said to the Philippian jailer, "*believe on the Lord Jesus Christ and thou shalt be saved.*" (Acts 16:31) That is the order. It is faith and then salvation. They reverse it. They say first you have to be of the elect and be saved, and then God will give you the faith. One of the verses that they use to prove their point is this verse right here.

There are a few problems with this interpretation. First of all, both "*grace*" and "*faith*" are in the feminine gender in the Greek language. All the nouns in the Greek language have genders. They are either masculine, feminine, or neuter. In the Greek grammatical construction, the gender endings must match up with the gender endings of the words that they modify. Generally there has to be feminines with feminines and masculines with masculines. The word, "*that,*" is a demonstrative pronoun. As such, it must refer back to a noun of the same gender. It is neuter in gender. Therefore, it cannot refer either to "*faith*" or "*grace*" which are both feminine in gender. What does it refer to? It refers to the whole concept of "*salvation.*" "*For by grace are ye saved through faith; and **that***" [meaning the whole idea of being saved] is "*not of yourselves.*" The word for "saved," SESOSMENOI, is a perfect passive participle. That makes sense. Salvation is "*not of yourselves, it is a gift of God.*"

Salvation is "*not of works lest any man should boast.*" It comes beautifully together that salvation is not of yourselves. "*Faith*" is the way we get salvation. "*Faith cometh by hearing, and hearing by the word of God*" (Romans 10:17). You cannot work for a gift, can you? You may work for many things. But when you work, you get wages. If it is wages, the IRS will tax you on it. You will be paying taxes on your wages.

- **Romans 6:23**
  For **the wages of sin *is* death**; but the gift of God *is* eternal life through Jesus Christ our Lord.

If you are looking for wages, God will give you a payday some day. It is going to be eternal death if you do not trust Christ as your Saviour. "*The wages of sin is death.*" This gift is salvation, not grace or faith. "*But the gift of God is eternal life.*"

Ephesians 2:9

"**Not of works, lest any man should boast.**" If we were saved by works or the deeds we do, we would be saving ourselves. It is not possible to save ourselves. Only God can save us. Only the Lord Jesus Christ through His shed blood on Calvary and His death on the cross can save us when we trust wholly in Him. Salvation is not of works or by works. Why? It says "*lest any man should boast.*" There will be no braggers or boasters in Heaven. Nobody will say they have arrived in Heaven by themselves. If you have done it by yourself, you will not be in Heaven. You will be in Hell. That is where you will be.

There are two kinds of religions in this world. One is in the present tense, and one is in the past tense. One kind says "*do*," and the other kind says "*done*." Satan's religions all say "*do*." You have to do this and this and this. Christ's salvation says "*done*." As the gospel song goes:

"Jesus paid it all.
All to Him I owe.
Sin had left a crimson stain.
He washed it white as snow."

Salvation is "*not of works*." I am glad that it is not of works because I know that none of us could earn it if it were by our works.

Why do you think the God of Heaven had to send His Son, the Lord Jesus Christ, to save the miserable sinners that we are? Jesus came because we could not save ourselves. That is why Jesus came to earth. God realized that none of us could save ourselves. Look at Adam and Eve in the garden of Eden. They were innocent and had not yet sinned by disobeying the will of God. Even then they could not do it. God could not foresee anybody who could save himself by works. That is why He sent us His Son to save us by His grace and to give us the gift of God which is eternal life through genuine faith in Jesus Christ our Lord.

I will tell you in Whom we can boast. We can boast in the Lord Jesus Christ. Paul says that he boasted in Christ. He was glad in Christ. He said that in Christ he would glory. The hymn writer says, "In the Cross of Christ I Glory." We can glory and boast in Him. He is a great Saviour. He is a loving Saviour. We can always boast in what He has done for us.

Ephesians 2:10

"For we are his workmanship, created in Christ Jesus unto good works, which God hath before ordained that we should walk in them." Notice, it says that this all happens after we have been saved by grace through genuine faith. These two verses lay the foundation of salvation. It is "*not of works, lest any man should boast*," but in verse ten it also says that those who have been saved are God's "*workmanship*." God has worked upon those who have been saved by His grace through faith. We are His workmanship now. We have been created anew at our salvation. You might think that creation stopped after the six days. Well, it did, but only so far as the physical world is concerned.

Some people might think that since they have been saved by grace, it doesn't matter how they live afterwards. No, that is not salvation through grace by faith. Biblically, if you have been saved by grace, you have repented of your sinful life and are going to have a different desire and motivation.

- **2 Corinthians 5:17**
  Therefore if any man *be* in Christ, *he is* a new creature: **old things are passed away; behold, all things are become new**.

You do not live for the world, the flesh, or the Devil once you are saved. God has created you in Christ Jesus *"unto good works."* Those are works after you are saved. Although works cannot save you, God expects good works once you are saved. He expects fruit. If we do not see any fruit, we wonder if there has been any seed planted. If there is no fruit, we wonder about the source. There is the root, and there is the fruit. If there is no fruit, you wonder if there is no root.

Sometimes a person claims to have been saved as a little child. But you look at them now, and they are living for the world, the flesh, and the Devil. The Lord knows their heart. But as far as we are concerned, we cannot rest in the fact that this person is saved. All we can see is a regular worldly person.

Some people have the attitude that Heaven is just a fire escape from Hell. That is not God's plan. God's plan is that you are not saved by works. But once you are saved, you are created unto good works *"which God hath foreordained that we should walk in them."* God expects us to walk in good works and to do that which pleases Him.

We cannot put the cart before the horse. Recently, there has been talk in Philadelphia about getting rid of the horse-drawn carriages. Many of us in this room do not even know about horses and carts. The horse does not go behind the cart and push it. The horse goes in front of the cart to pull it. If you have works and salvation mixed up, you have the cart of good works before the horse of salvation. Salvation comes first and then the good works should follow. If the works do not follow, we wonder if there is any salvation there at all. God wants us to walk in the Lord Jesus Christ and remember what He has done for us by grace through faith.

Ephesians 2:11

"Wherefore remember, that ye *being* in time past Gentiles in the flesh, who are called Uncircumcision by that which is called the Circumcision in the flesh made by hands" These Ephesians were "Gentiles in the flesh," not Jews. As Gentiles they were not a part of the promises of God. Those of us who are Gentiles have been changed by Christ into Christians. We are no longer Gentiles. Saved Jews today are no longer considered to be Jews, but now God considers them to be Christians. We, too, can say that in times past we were lost sinners in the flesh. We were lost and undone and without Christ.

This subject of salvation by grace is important, indeed, for anyone who is in this world. Are you certain that you are saved? If you sometimes have doubts, you can get certain. God is able to give you certainty. There is a tract which was written by one of the Plymouth Brethren years ago called, "Safety, Certainty, and Enjoyment." You can have all three of these things if you will have genuine faith in Christ.

- **1 John 5:13**
  These things have I written unto you that believe on the name of the Son of God; **that ye may know that ye have eternal life**, and that ye may believe on the name of the Son of God.

There is nothing so miserable as someone who thinks he is saved but is not sure. They are hanging in the balance. But you can make sure. You can repent of your sins and have genuine trust in the Lord Jesus Christ as your Saviour. You can realize that it is by His grace that you are saved through faith and not of yourselves. We are grateful for this gift of God.

Ephesians 2:12

"That at that time ye were without Christ, being aliens from the commonwealth of Israel, and strangers from the covenants of promise, having no hope, and without God in the world"

"That at that time ye were without Christ, being aliens from the commonwealth of Israel, and strangers from the covenants of promise" Paul says that before they were saved, these Gentiles were barbarians. They were "*without Christ*." We know many people who are without Christ. Oh, they may say that they are Christians as opposed to being Jews. But they are without Christ. They need a Saviour in their heart and in their life. These Ephesians were "*aliens*." We hear a lot about aliens now. I do not know if there are aliens or not. People have pictures of them on space ships and so on. Who knows? I am not going to speculate. An alien is "*someone from another planet*." If you are an alien without Christ, you are from another planet. You are from the planet of Satan and from the town of Satanville.

I hope nobody in this room is a "*stranger*" from one another. If you do not know each other say "Hello." In the realm of eternity, those outside of Christ are "*strangers from the covenants of promise*." They had nothing to do with the covenant promises made to Abraham, Isaac, and Jacob.

"having no hope, and without God in the world" They were hopeless also. That is the worse thing of all. People talk about the Christmas season of joy, but it is also a great season of grief as well. People without their families are very sad. The suicide rates at Christmas time are very high. There are billions of dollars spent on Christmas alone. When the bills come due, depression, despair, and hopelessness also come. God says that without Christ we are without hope. Here are a few verses on hope.

- **Romans 15:4**
  For whatsoever things were written aforetime were written for our learning, **that we through patience and comfort of the scriptures might have hope.**

There is hope in the Word of God.

- **Romans 15:13**
  Now the God of hope fill you with all joy and peace in believing, that ye may abound in hope, through the power of the Holy Ghost.

He is the God of hope.

- **Colossians 1:5**
  For the hope which is laid up for you in heaven, whereof ye heard before in the word of the truth of the gospel;

That is the hope of all hope. If we're saved we have the hope of a future in Heaven.

- **Colossians 1:27**
  To whom God would make known what *is* the riches of the glory of this mystery among the Gentiles; which is **Christ in you, the hope of glory**:

This was the theme when I went to Liberia, West Africa at one of their Bible conferences in the 1990's, "Christ in You, the Hope of Glory. Those Liberians have nothing compared with what we have here. Still if Christ is in them, they have "*the hope of glory.*" If they do not have Christ, they have no hope either physically or spiritually. Pastor Joah is still going strong, giving the Liberian people hope in Christ. That is the thing that all of us need more than anything in the world.

- **1 Thessalonians 4:13**
  But I would not have you to be ignorant, brethren, concerning them which are asleep, that ye **sorrow not, even as others which have no hope.**

Those words are spoken at the grave side of many Christians who are buried. Paul tells us not to sorrow as others who "*have no hope.*" We sorrow, but it is not the same as others who are hopeless.

- **1 Thessalonians 5:8**
  But let us, who are of the day, be sober, putting on the breastplate of faith and love; and for an helmet, **the hope of salvation.**

- **Titus 2:13**
  Looking for that blessed hope, and the glorious appearing of the great God and our Saviour Jesus Christ;

Here is *"blessed hope."* Jesus is coming again one day to take away and snatch the saved ones out of this wicked world. That hope is imminent. It may occur at any moment.

- **Titus 3:7**
  That being justified by his grace, **we should be made heirs according to the hope of eternal life.**

These Ephesian believers had no hope before Christ. Now, with Christ, there is hope. An alien is someone who is shut out from one's fellowship and intimacy. That is what is true of every lost person in this world. There is no hope, and they are strangers and aliens from the commonwealth of Israel. Hope is a *"joyful confident expectation of eternal salvation."* We are not a hopeless people if we have Christ as our Saviour.

Ephesians 2:13

"But now in Christ Jesus ye who sometimes were far off are made nigh by the blood of Christ" Those in Christ Jesus are *"made nigh by the blood of Christ."* I have talked before about John MacArthur's teaching on the blood of Christ. There are many people who are following John MacArthur. He has a radio program, a college, and has written many books. He is teaching that the blood of Christ does not mean the blood of Christ, but it only means the death of Christ. He says that *"blood"* is a metonym or figure of speech for *"death."*

God put two separate and distinct words in the Greek language to make this clear. One word is used for *"blood,"* HAIMA, and one word is used for *"death,"* THANATOS. They are two distinct things. When the Passover lamb was slain in Exodus chapter twelve, they took the blood and put it over the top and side posts of their doors. God did not say, "When I see the animal dead, I will pass over you." God said *"when I see the blood I will pass over you"* (Exodus 12:13). John MacArthur believes that the literal blood of Christ does not make us *"nigh."*

There are fourteen effects that the Lord has specified in the New Testament by the literal blood of Christ. Though I have listed these before (under **Ephesians 1:7**) here are the fourteen effects again for emphasis.

First, there is **REDEMPTION** (atonement, substitution, remission, salvation, or purchase) through the literal blood of Christ.

Ephesians 2:13

- **Leviticus 17:11**
  For the life of the flesh *is* in the blood: and I have given it to you upon the altar to make an atonement for your souls: **for it *is* the blood *that* maketh an atonement for the soul.**
- **Matthew 26:28**
  For **this is my blood of the new testament, which is shed for many for the remission of sins.**
- **Mark 14:24**
  And he said unto them, **This is my blood of the new testament, which is shed for many.**
- **Luke 22:20**
  Likewise also the cup after supper, saying, **This cup *is* the new testament in my blood, which is shed for you.**
- **Acts 20:28**
  Take heed therefore unto yourselves, and to all the flock, over the which the Holy Ghost hath made you overseers, to feed the church of God, **which he hath purchased with his own blood.**
- **Romans 5:9**
  Much more then, being now justified by his blood, we shall be saved from wrath through him.
- **Ephesians 1:7**
  In whom we have redemption through his blood, the forgiveness of sins, according to the riches of his grace;
- **Colossians 1:14**
  In whom we have redemption through his blood, *even* the forgiveness of sins:
- **1 Peter 1:18-19**
  Forasmuch as ye know that **ye were not redeemed with corruptible things**, *as* silver and gold, from your vain conversation *received* by tradition from your fathers; **But with the precious blood of Christ**, as of a lamb without blemish and without spot:
- **Revelation 5:9**
  And they sung a new song, saying, Thou art worthy to take the book, and to open the seals thereof: for thou wast slain, and **hast redeemed us to God by thy blood** out of every kindred, and tongue, and people, and nation;

The blood of Christ and the death of Christ are not identical. They are entirely different. Notice the distinction with the example of the passover lamb (Exodus 12:1-7). Moses was told to take a lamb, make sure he was pure and clean, slay it, and then catch its blood in a basin. After slaying the lamb, then the people were to put some of its blood on the "*two side posts*" and "*upper door post*" of their house. The death of the lamb was one event. The application of its blood was another and separate event. The death and the blood were two separate entities that cannot be made to be the same, no matter how loud and long John MacArthur (and his followers) might argue that they are.

> Second, there is **PROPITIATION** through the literal blood of Christ.

- Romans 3:25
  Whom God hath set forth *to be* **a propitiation through faith in his blood,** to declare his righteousness for the remission of sins that are past, through the forbearance of God;

> Third, there is **JUSTIFICATION** through the literal blood of Christ.

- Romans 5:9
  Much more then, **being now justified by his blood**, we shall be saved from wrath through him.

> Fourth, there is **FELLOWSHIP** through the literal blood of Christ.

- Ephesians 2:13
  But now in Christ Jesus **ye who sometimes were far off are made nigh by the blood of Christ.**

> Fifth, there is **PEACE** through the literal blood of Christ.

- Colossians 1:20
  And, **having made peace through the blood of his cross**, by him to reconcile all things unto himself; by him, *I say*, whether *they be* things in earth, or things in Heaven.

> Sixth, there is **FORGIVENESS** through the literal blood of Christ.

- **Ephesians 1:7**
  In whom we have redemption **through his blood, the forgiveness of sins**, according to the riches of his grace;
- **Colossians 1:14**
  In whom we have redemption **through his blood,** *even* **the forgiveness of sins**:

> Seventh, there is **SANCTIFICATION** through the literal blood of Christ.

- **Hebrews 13:12**
  Wherefore Jesus also, **that he might sanctify the people with his own blood**, suffered without the gate.

> Eighth, there is **RECONCILIATION** through the literal blood of Christ.

- **Colossians 1:20**
  And, having made peace **through the blood of his cross, by him to reconcile all things unto himself**; by him, *I say*, whether *they be* things in earth, or things in heaven.

> Ninth, there is **CLEANSING** (purging, washing, purifying) through the literal blood of Christ.

- **Hebrews 9:14**
  How much more shall the blood of Christ, who through the eternal Spirit offered himself without spot to God, **purge your conscience** from dead works to serve the living God?
- **Hebrews 9:22-23**
  And almost all things are by the law **purged with blood**; and without shedding of blood is no remission. *It was* **therefore necessary that the patterns of things in the heavens should be purified with these**; but the heavenly things themselves with better sacrifices than these.
- **1 John 1:7**
  But if we walk in the light, as he is in the light, we have fellowship one with another, and **the blood of Jesus Christ his Son cleanseth us** from all sin.

- Revelation 1:5
  And from Jesus Christ, *who is* the faithful witness, *and* the first begotten of the dead, and the prince of the kings of the earth. Unto him that loved us, and **washed us from our sins in his own blood.**
- Revelation 7:14
  And I said unto him, Sir, thou knowest. And he said to me, These are they which came out of great tribulation, and **have washed their robes, and made them white in the blood of the Lamb.**

> Tenth, there is **REMEMBRANCE** through the literal blood of Christ.

- 1 Corinthians 11:25
  After the same manner also *he took* the cup, when he had supped, saying, **This cup is the new testament in my blood: this do ye, as oft as ye drink** *it*, **in remembrance of me**.

> Eleventh, there is **BOLDNESS** and **ACCESS** to God's throne through the literal blood of Christ.

- Hebrews 10:19
  Having therefore, brethren, **boldness to enter into the holiest by the blood of Jesus,**

> Twelfth, there is **MATURITY** in doing God's will through the literal blood of Christ.

- Hebrews 13:20-21
  Now the God of peace, that brought again from the dead our Lord Jesus, that great shepherd of the sheep, **through the blood of the everlasting covenant, Make you perfect** in every good work **to do his will**, working in you that which is wellpleasing in his sight, through Jesus Christ; to whom *be* glory for ever and ever. Amen.

> Thirteenth, if we mistreat it, there is **PUNISHMENT** (weakness, sickness, or death) through the literal blood of Christ.

- Hebrews 10:29
  Of how much sorer punishment, suppose ye, shall he be thought worthy, who hath trodden under foot the Son of God, and **hath counted the blood of the covenant, wherewith he was sanctified, an unholy thing**, and hath done despite unto the Spirit of grace?
- 1 Corinthians 11:27-30
  Wherefore **whosoever shall eat this bread, and drink *this* cup of the Lord, unworthily, shall be guilty of the body and blood of the Lord.** For he that eateth and drinketh unworthily, eateth and **drinketh damnation to himself**, not discerning the Lord's body. For this cause many *are* **weak** and **sickly** among you, and **many sleep**.

> Fourteenth, there is **VICTORY** over Satan through the literal blood of Christ.

- Revelation 12:9, 11
  And the great dragon was cast out, **that old serpent, called the Devil, and Satan**, which deceiveth the whole world: he was cast out into the earth, and his angels were cast out with him. . . . And **they overcame him by the blood of the Lamb**, and by the word of their testimony; and they loved not their lives unto the death.

I think that these verses clearly teach us that "*blood*" means blood. When God says we have all these things by the literal blood of Christ, let us take what God says. He means it. Do not let John MacArthur or any of his followers twist our minds when he says that "*blood*" means "*death*." He makes a joke of the blood of Christ. I consider this to be both blasphemy and heresy.

Ephesians 2:14

"For he is our peace, who hath made both one, and hath broken down the middle wall of partition *between us*"
Jesus is our "*peace*." There are three verses in this chapter that have to do with peace. They are verses fourteen, fifteen, and seventeen. The "*middle wall of partition*" has been broken down through the Lord Jesus Christ.

There used to be a partition wall that would keep the Jews from the Gentiles. Jesus is our peace. The Greek word for "peace," is EIRENE.

> ## God's Peace
> "Peace is the tranquil state of a soul, assured of its salvation through Christ, and so fearing nothing from God, and content with its earthly lot, of whatever sort that it is."

It is also *"an exemption from the rage and havoc of war."* The Lord Jesus Christ has broken the wall down for the saved ones. The Jew and the Gentile could not have any peace between them. There was a wall separating them. That wall separates or prevents the two from coming together. That wall was like the veil in the temple that prevented people from coming into the very presence of God.

If that wall was broken down, why are not Jews and Gentiles happy together? Why is there all the fighting and war between the two? They are at war because they have not trusted in the Christ who came to break down the wall. They have not trusted in the Redeemer. I do not believe that any fundamental, Bible-believing, born-again, regenerated Christian has any problem with the Jews. We want to win them to Christ. We do not hate them. Many unsaved Gentiles hate Jews. Many unsaved Jews hate Gentiles. When you mention the name of Christ to an orthodox Jew, they hate that Name. The Lord Jesus Christ came to break down that enmity and to bring peace to both groups.

Here are some verses on *"peace."*

- **Matthew 10:34**
  Think not that I am come to send peace on earth: **I came not to send peace, but a sword**.

The Lord Jesus did not come for *"peace"* the first time. At the cross He made *"peace."*

- **Mark 4:39**
  And he arose, and rebuked the wind, and said unto the sea, **Peace, be still. And the wind ceased**, and there was a great calm.

Jesus Christ has the power to bring *"peace"* to the troubled sea. If He can bring *"peace"* to the troubled sea, He certainly can bring peace to troubled hearts. He has brought *"peace"* to our troubled hearts if we are saved.

- **Luke 1:79**
  To give light to them that sit in darkness and *in* the shadow of death, **to guide our feet into the way of peace**.

We talk about *"peace"* at the time of the incarnation.

- **Luke 2:14**
 Glory to God in the highest, and **on earth peace**, good will toward men.

To bring "*peace*" is why the Lord Jesus came. He made "*peace*," not at His birth, but at His death. He made "*peace*" by the shedding of His blood for the sins of the world on the cross of Calvary. That is where "*peace*" really comes.

- **John 14:27**
 Peace I leave with you, my peace I give unto you: not as the world giveth, give I unto you. Let not your heart be troubled, neither let it be afraid.

The "*you*" in this verse does not refer to the world of the unsaved. It refers to the believers, the saved people. That is Christ's "*peace*."

- **John 16:33**
 These things I have spoken unto you, that **in me ye might have peace**. In the world ye shall have tribulation: but be of good cheer; I have overcome the world.

In the world you will have all kinds of trouble.

- **Acts 10:36**
 The word which *God* sent unto the children of Israel, **preaching peace by Jesus Christ**: (he is Lord of all:)

The Lord Jesus can bring peace to troubled hearts. We are to preach "*peace*" by Him and through Him.

- **Romans 5:1**
 Therefore being justified by faith, **we have peace with God** through our Lord Jesus Christ:

He is the One who can give us "*peace*."

- **Romans 10:15**
 And how shall they preach, except they be sent? as it is written, **How beautiful are the feet of them that preach the gospel of peace**, and bring glad tidings of good things!

Did you ever think your feet were "*beautiful*"? God says if you preach the gospel of "*peace*," your feet are beautiful.

- **Philippians 4:7**
 And the peace of God, which passeth all understanding, shall keep your hearts and minds through Christ Jesus.

Here is the "*peace*" of God.

- **Colossians 1:20**
 And, **having made peace through the blood of his cross**, by him to reconcile all things unto himself; by him, *I say*, whether *they be* things in earth, or things in heaven.

The Lord Jesus is a peacemaker. The Jews and the Arabs can talk all they want, but I do not think that there will ever be perfect "*peace*" between them until they come to Calvary. There will be no "*peace*" in Israel until they look on the Messiah whom they have pierced and say blessed is he that cometh in the name of the Lord. Until then there will be wars and not peace.

Ephesians 2:15

"Having abolished in his flesh the enmity, *even* the law of commandments *contained* in ordinances; for to make in himself of twain one new man, *so* making peace" Jesus "*abolished*" the hatred between Jew and Gentile on the cross of Calvary. It is only possible to make one fresh "*new man*" through the cross of Christ.

There are two Greek words for "*new.*" One word, NEOS, means chronologically new. The other means new in the sense of a fresh, new look at a thing or a change that is different. This word, KAINOS, means a "*fresh new look.*" That is why I believe the Jews and Gentiles should worship at the same church. I do not see that there is any reason to have "Jews for Jesus" or the other groups that separate some Christians from other Christians. If you are a saved Christian, though in the flesh you are either a Jew or a Gentile, God does not consider you as such in the spiritual relationship with Christ. You are neither Jew nor Gentile, but a Christian.

- **1 Corinthians 10:32**
  Give none offence, **neither to the Jews, nor to the Gentiles, nor to the church of God**:

There are only three categories here, either "*Jews*" or "*Gentiles*" or "*the church of God*" which is a reference to saved Christians.

- **Galatians 3:28**
  There is neither Jew nor Greek, there is neither bond nor free, there is neither male nor female: for **ye are all one in Christ Jesus**.

This is a very clear verse on the unity of believers in Christ. Though there are some people who differ with me on this point, I believe the Scriptures are clear. Paul never advocated that Jewish Christians should worship separately from Gentile Christians. This is the very opposite of what salvation means.

Ephesians 2:16

"And that he might reconcile both unto God in one body by the cross, having slain the enmity thereby" The purpose of the cross of Calvary was to "*reconcile*" both Jews and Gentiles unto God. The Lord Jesus Christ has slain the enmity, the hatred, and the bitter antagonism. Paul was a Jew, and he was saved by Christ through faith. He was redeemed. Now, he was preaching to these Ephesian Gentiles. Paul does not hate Gentiles. He loves them and wants to win them to Christ. Paul is exhibit number one as to how that enmity between Jew and Gentile has been slain. Before he was saved, he hated Christians. He hated everybody who was not a Jew. God through His Son and the cross of Calvary made the difference. Paul's heart was melted and broken.

Before I was saved, I did not respect my father, for example. It was a sad thing that I hated my dad. I disliked him because he disciplined me. He did not let me run around on the highways and byways as a young person. He was right in these actions. When I was saved at the age of seventeen, the enmity was gone. The love was there because I knew Christ. When my dad was in his eighties, while he was in our town having an eye operation, he came to know the Lord Jesus Christ as his Saviour after many years of prayer. The Lord makes a difference. He slays the *"enmity"* or the hatred that you may have.

You may hate your next door neighbor or someone you work with, but in the Lord you can show the love of Christ. I had some problems with one here in Collingswood, New Jersey. His name was Dr. Carl McIntire. I was his associate for three years. I taught at Shelton College in Cape May, New Jersey. When I submitted to him my letter of resignation, he told me that if I resigned from him, he would fire me. Figure that one out! He further said that within twenty-four hours I had to remove all my personal files and possessions from the Reformation Building. He also said that he would publish in his *Christian Beacon* world-wide newspaper that I was no good. He carried out all three of those threats. On March 19, 2002, as this book is being written, Dr. McIntire died at the age of 95. Now, if I wanted to waste my life hating Dr. McIntire, that would be foolish. We lived in the same town. We even used to go to the same barber. Our human flesh is capable of hating and despising anyone. But life is too short to have it consumed by hatred. When we hate, our whole being is taken up with hatred. Our whole outlook is changed.

Here are some verses on the doctrine of *"reconciliation."* The word means *"to change, to exchange one thing for another, to transform."*

- **Romans 5:10**
  For if, when we were enemies, **we were reconciled to God by the death of his Son**, much more, being reconciled, we shall be saved by his life.
- **2 Corinthians 5:19**
  To wit, that **God was in Christ, reconciling the world unto himself**, not imputing their trespasses unto them; and hath committed unto us the word of reconciliation.

The Lord can reconcile not only Jew and Gentile but all people who are saved.

Ephesians 2:17

"And came and preached peace to you which were afar off, and to them that were nigh." Both groups needed *"peace"* preached to them. The Jews needed *"peace"* in Christ and the Gentiles needed *"peace"* in Christ. So Paul came and preached peace to both of them.

Ephesians 2:18

"For through him we both have access by one Spirit unto the Father." This *"access"* is a wonderful thing to have. Do you have *"access"* to God the Father? Think of all the things to which we do not have access.

There is not supposed to be access to the pilot's cabin in a commercial airliner. They lock the door because of people who might take over that cabin. They still have high jackings even with that precaution. Look what happened when four commercial planes were taken over and crashed into the World Trade Towers, the Pentagon, and the Pennsylvania field on September 11, 2001. Over 2,000 people were killed because these terrorists had *"access"* by force to the airplanes' cockpits. The doors have now been strengthened since that unfortunate day. No one except authorized people should have access to the pilot's cabin. Let them do their work.

There is no access to the governor's or the president's office unless you get permission. You cannot just barge into these offices. There is no access to the vaults at the bank. You cannot go in there and open up all the drawers and see all the money and the gold.

There was no access to anyone entering into the king of Persia's inner court, unless the king held out his golden sceptre. If that were not done, the person would be put to death (Esther 4:11).

But there is *"access"* to God the Father in Heaven for every redeemed believer. It is only through the Lord Jesus Christ that we can have that access. It is an "open door" policy. First of all, we are to come unto Him and be saved. Then we can open our hearts and pray to Him and have access by the Holy Spirit of God unto the Father. He bids us to come.

They could not have this *"access"* to the Lord in the Old Testament. The tabernacle is an illustration of this. There were two different compartments in the tabernacle proper. The holy place and the Holy of Holies were separated by a thick curtain. Only once a year the high priest had *"access"* to the Holy of Holies. And on that day he needed to enter with the blood of a bullock and a goat to atone for the sins of himself and the people. When the Lord Jesus Christ came, His flesh was like the veil (Hebrews 10:20) that was rent in two after the crucifixion (Matthew 27:51). At His death the veil of the temple was rent from top to bottom. Man did not do that. Man did not cut the veil from the bottom up. God tore the veil from top to bottom. This showed that access to God the Father was now open.

- **Romans 5:1-2**
  Therefore being justified by faith, we have peace with God through our Lord Jesus Christ: **By whom also we have access by faith** into this grace wherein we stand, and rejoice in hope of the glory of God.
- Ephesians 3:11-12
  According to the eternal purpose which he purposed in Christ Jesus our Lord: **In whom we have boldness and access with confidence** by the faith of him.

That access is an approach to God the Father. It is a relationship with God whereby the saved ones are acceptable to Him. Through Christ, we have assurance that God the Father is favorably disposed toward us.

Ephesians 2:19

"Now therefore ye are no more strangers and foreigners, but fellowcitizens with the saints, and of the household of God" If we are saved, we considered to be "*in Christ.*" There is no more alienation. We are part of the family. Everyone of us who is saved are saints. It is not just special Roman Catholics who are saints. There is a song in our hymnal (page 304) entitled "*I'm Adopted.*" It is by Ron Hamilton. Here's the first verse:

"*I am adopted. I'm a child of the King. God is my Father, and He owns everything. He walks beside me. He's my very best friend. Praise God, I'll never be lonely again.*"

That is access. That is fellowship. That is being "*fellow citizens with the saints*" of God. Here's the second verse:

"*My Father chose me, and He loves me, I know. He will be with me wherever I go. I'll never worry; I have joined royalty. I am a member of the King's family.*"

Here's the chorus:

"*I'm adopted, hallelujah! I've got a new song. I'm adopted, hallelujah! I finally belong. I've got a brand new family overflowing with love. I'm a child of my Father above.*"

That is a nice little song. This is what God has done for us if we are saved. He has adopted us into His family by the death of His Son so that we are no longer "*strangers and foreigners.*" We are now "*fellowcitizens with the saints.*" We are members of the "*household of God.*"

Ephesians 2:20

"And are built upon the foundation of the apostles and prophets, Jesus Christ himself being the chief corner stone" The Lord gives us many pictures of the church. We are a body. He is the Vine, and we are the branches (John 15:5). This illustration is that we are a building, and He is the Corner Stone.
- 1 Corinthians 3:11
  For other **foundation** can no man lay than that is laid, **which is Jesus Christ.**

As believers we have to be careful of our building materials. If we use hay, wood, or stubble, it will be burned up. Gold, silver, and precious stone will abide in the fire and be purified. Christ is the Foundation which started with the apostles and prophets.

Later on in chapter four of Ephesians, we are going to see that there are various gifts that God has given to the church. Some are prophets. Some are apostles. Some are evangelists. Some are pastors and teachers. Evangelists, pastors, and teachers are still here, but apostles and prophets are no more. We have the Foundation, and Christ has given us Himself as that Foundation and commands the believers to build upon it.

We have the Scriptures in completed form, Old and New Testaments. The canon of Scriptures (the list of approved books) has been closed for centuries. We have no need for apostles or prophets. Prophets foretold and told forth the Words of God. We now have the Words of God preserved in Hebrew/Aramaic and Greek. In English, these Words have been properly translated in the King James Bible. The Mormon church is wrong in most things. One of them is that they still have apostles. I listened to an interview with one of their elders the other night. They have a different Christ, a different gospel, and a different Bible.

Some people interpret that word, *"prophet"* as one who tells forth God's Word. They believe that a pastor is a *"prophet."* I like to use the real meaning of prophet. The charismatic movement claims to have the gift of *"prophecy."* Many years ago, my wife and I attended a charismatic rally at Arrowhead Stadium as reporters. Every night on that platform they had a whole group of about twenty people giving prophecies. They would say what would happen. They added to the Words of God, but God says that the Word of God is closed and the Scripture has been completed. When the book of Revelation was finished, that was the end of the canon of Scripture. Christ is our Master and our Shepherd. Pastors are undershepherds. The Lord Jesus Christ should get all the glory as the Chief Cornerstone. He is the One Who is the most important.

Ephesians 2:21
"In whom all the building fitly framed together groweth unto an holy temple in the Lord"

"In whom all the building fitly framed together" The believers are not only the bride and the body, but they are also a building. That word, *"fitly,"* SUNARMOLOGEO, means *"to join closely together, to frame together parts of the building."* Because I am not a builder, I would lay a brick wall that would be crooked. The Lord Jesus Christ is not crooked. His walls are built tightly together. That is where fellowship comes with the fellow-believers in our local church. We must be knitted closely together as part of a building. In Christ, the building is framed together closely.

"Groweth unto an holy temple in the Lord" The church grows unto a holy temple unto the Lord. We are glad for the growth of our little church here. Our church is probably the most non-conforming Baptist church in the world. We meet in a home. We do not as yet have official elected deacons, though we do have those who serve (which is what *"deacon"* means). We do not have membership. As far as I am concerned, we vote with our feet. When we walk in, we are part of the congregation. Most of us are saved, but unsaved are welcome to attend if they wish. If we walk out and do not return, then we are no longer part of the congregation. We do not try to keep anybody either in or out.

I know exactly what a Baptist church is supposed to be. I have been in Baptist churches since 1944, and I know how they are supposed to be from "A" to "Z." This time, in our Bible For Today Baptist Church, I just wanted to be a kind of a maverick, nonconformist Baptist church. I just wanted to be a Bible-believing, Bible-preaching preacher. I just wanted to open my home even if only two or three people would be in attendance. The first Sunday there were twenty-four people here.

For the rest of my life, I want to preach the Word, verse by verse as I have been trained and prepared to do at the old Dallas Theological Seminary (1948 through 1953). I want to put these messages on some radio stations, in audio, and video tapes and in books as the Lord provides. If any of my children, grandchildren, or great grandchildren (or others) want to listen to these messages, or read them in books when I am gone home to be with the Lord, and grow stronger for the Lord Jesus Christ, then I would rejoice. In the seminary where I went, the old Dallas Theological Seminary (not the new Dallas), they trained us to *"preach the Word"* (2 Timothy 4:2). That was the motto of the school. Those words appear in Greek on the school's shield.

God wants us to grow into a *"holy temple."* I do not want unholiness do you? I want my own body as well as this church to be a *"holy temple"* for the

Lord's use. So many Christians are tied up with unholiness. God wants our lives pure, clean, clear, and transparent. I appreciate all of you who have that same desire.

Ephesians 2:22

"In whom ye also are builded together for an habitation of God through the Spirit" The Holy Spirit of God indwells those who are saved and redeemed. Let us look at a few verses about the indwelling Holy Spirit.

- **Matthew 28:20**
  Teaching them to observe all things whatsoever I have commanded you: and, **lo, I am with you alway**, *even* unto the end of the world. Amen.

The Lord Jesus Christ is with us *"alway"* in the power of the Holy Spirit of God.

- **John 7:33**
  Then said Jesus unto them, **Yet a little while am I with you, and *then* I go** unto him that sent me.

The Lord Jesus Christ went away, back to Heaven whence He came, but He sent God the Holy Spirit back down to this earth to indwell the saved ones.

- **John 14:16**
  And I will pray the Father, and **he shall give you another Comforter, that he may abide with you for ever**;

Jesus is talking to His disciples about the indwelling power of the Holy Spirit. We cannot build a church without Holy Spirit-regenerated people. You cannot have it. That would not be a church. It would just be a gathering of people.

- **1 Corinthians 6:19**
  What? know ye not that **your body is the temple of the Holy Ghost *which is* in you**, which ye have of God, and ye are not your own?

The Holy Spirit of God dwells within the bodies of all redeemed people. The Lord Jesus Christ is at the right hand of the throne of God the Father in Heaven. Both He and the Father have sent God the Holy Spirit as *"another comforter,"* advocate, or helper to help those of us who are saved by faith in Christ.

Ephesians Chapter Three

Ephesians 3:1

"For this cause I Paul, the prisoner of Jesus Christ for you Gentiles" Paul is the writer of Ephesians. Many apostates do not believe that Paul wrote anything, even though it says he wrote it. When the Bible says that Paul wrote something, he wrote it. That settles it. Paul was a Jew who was preaching to the Gentiles. He was converted to Christianity for the express purpose to preach to these heathen people.

Here Paul mentions that he is a *"prisoner."* Up until this time in chapter one and chapter two, Paul does not say anything about being in chains. There are at least five different references to Paul's being a *"prisoner."*

- Acts 23:18
  So he took him, and brought *him* to the chief captain, and said, **Paul the prisoner** called me unto *him*, and prayed me to bring this young man unto thee, who hath something to say unto thee.
- Ephesians 4:1
  I therefore, the prisoner of the Lord, beseech you that ye walk worthy of the vocation wherewith ye are called,
- 2 Timothy 1:8
  Be not thou therefore ashamed of the testimony of our Lord, **nor of me his prisoner**: but be thou partaker of the afflictions of the gospel according to the power of God;
- Philemon 1
  Paul, a prisoner of Jesus Christ, and Timothy *our* brother, unto Philemon our dearly beloved, and fellowlabourer,
- Philemon 9
  Yet for love's sake I rather beseech *thee*, being such an one as Paul the aged, and **now also a prisoner of Jesus Christ**.

Notice, he is the *"prisoner of Jesus Christ."* He is not a prisoner because of his own sin or corruption. He did not steal anything. He did not rob anybody. He was a prisoner because of his faith in Christ. He would not relent. He would not change. He just kept on preaching and preaching no matter what they did to him or no matter how many jails they put him in.

What were the prison conditions in Paul's day? I looked up something in that regard.

"Most prisoners wore chains. Their feet might be shackled. Their hands were manacled or even attached to their neck by another chain. Their movements were further restricted by their chain fastened to a post. Some prisoners were also kept in wooden stocks. These were devices to restrain the feet, hands, or even the neck of an individual. The jails did not have any windows so that the prisoners were in the dark. The inner area of the prison is mentioned in Acts 16:24. Unscrupulous guards might at times withhold food or even torture the prisoners in order to extort money from prisoners or their relatives."

Paul refers to himself many times as one who is in prison. In fact, the *"prisoner of Jesus Christ"* is almost a definition of Paul. He was in so many jails as a prisoner of Christ because he would not relent. Paul praised the Lord Jesus Christ even in His status as a *"prisoner."* He found God's grace to be sufficient for him even in those bad conditions. When Paul was converted, (Acts 9) the Lord Jesus told him that He was going to send him far away unto the Gentiles. He was told that he would give testimony of Christ to kings and other rulers. That is exactly what Paul's ministry was.

Ephesians 3:2

"If ye have heard of the dispensation of the grace of God which is given me to you-ward"

"If ye have heard of the dispensation of the grace of God" In Ephesians 1:10 Paul made reference to the *"dispensation of the fullness of times."* That word, *"dispensation,"* OIKONOMIA is made up of the words, OIKOS, "house" and NOMOS, "law." It means *"the law of the house."* It is *"the management of a household or of household affairs."*

Our church believes in dispensationalism. We believe there are certain times of testing that are different in this current age than in the age of the law. There are four dispensations which are smaller in length. They are the dispensation of innocence, the dispensation of conscience, the dispensation of human government, and the dispensation of promise. There is one dispensation that is of longer duration, the dispensation of the law. The dispensation of grace is the present dispensation. The last dispensation will be the dispensation of the kingdom . It will be the 1,000-year reign of the Lord Jesus Christ on this earth.

We hear much talk these days about the new millennium of 2000 or 2001 to be exact. In the future, there is going to be a real thousand year reign of the Lord Jesus Christ in the millennium spoken of in the Bible. Some of the newspapers and the commentators do not even know how to spell that word. That is one of the words that some professors say we should never use again. Every once in a while a professor comes up and says that these various words and terms need to be thrown away from our vocabulary. We are not going to throw away *"millennium"* because we believe in that word. It means *"thousand years."* The Greek term for it is used six times in the New Testament (Revelation 20:2-7).

"which is given me to you-ward" The word, *"given,"* DIDOMI, means *"to give over to one's care, intrust, commit."* Paul was the great administrator of the age of grace. Paul wrote more about the grace of God than any other human writer in Scripture. He wrote more books of the Bible than any other human writer.

Ephesians 3:3

"How that by revelation he made known unto me the mystery; (as I wrote afore in few words" That word, "mystery," MUSTERION, means *"a hidden thing, secret, mystery."* That is all it is. It was a "sacred secret." It was something that was not known. It was hidden until the time that it was to be revealed. After it was revealed, it was a revealed secret. Notice it says, *"how that by revelation he made known unto me."*

The *"revelation"* itself is different from the interpretation of that revelation. We have the Bible now. That is God's revelation. He gave us His Hebrew Words. He gave us His Greek Words. He gave us a few Aramaic Words. That is His *"revelation."* God promised to preserve these revealed Hebrew/Aramaic and Greek Words for all time. I believe He has done so in the Masoretic Hebrew Words and the Received Greek Words underlying our King James Bible. The Words of that *"revelation"* will never be changed or added to. His *"revelation"* is finished. It is completed.

That is where some churches disagree. The Mormon Church has the *Book of Mormon* which adds to the revelation of God. I believe that this is unscriptural. The Christian Science Church has the *Science and Health With the Keys to the Scripture.* That is adding to the Words of God and is unscriptural. The charismatics have revelation groups, and they add to the Words of God. I believe that is unscriptural. I believe that the *"revelation"* has been completed. There is nothing more that needs to be added or should be added. Adding to the Scripures are strickly prohibited (Revealtion 22:18).

Those who teach or imply (as Dr. Peter Ruckman and others) that the King James Bible itself is a *"revelation"* are in serious error. The King James Bible is **not** a *"revelation"* which was *"given by inspiration of God"* (2 Timothy 3:16) completed in 1611. It is a translation. If that were true, then it would mean that the English of the King James Bible would supersede the Hebrew and Greek of the autographs. That is absolute foolishness, in my judgment. I believe that the King James Bible is the only accurate translation of the preserved *"revelation"* in its Hebrew/Aramaic and Greek Words that underlie it. I believe God's *"revelation"* has been given to us originally and preserved for us Word for Word.

The King James Bible is an accurate translation. It should never be considered as a *"revelation."* If we consider it to be a further *"revelation"* completed in 1611, over and above and in addition to the Hebrew/Aramaic and Greek *"revelation,"* then there might possibly be more *"revelation"* for us today. How would we know that the New International Version is not a *"revelation"*? How would we know that the New American Standard Version or any other version is not a *"revelation"*? This teaching is an absurd picture of what the King James Bible is. I believe God has preserved the Words of the Hebrew Old Testament and the Words of the Greek New Testament in the texts that underlie the King James Bible.

The new look from the Fundamentalist world is to deny the preservation of God's Hebrew and Greek words. Bob Jones University is leading the whole fundamentalist world into the dangerous error of saying that God has preserved only His "message" but not His Hebrew and Greek Words. Their President has backed a book entitled *From the Mind of God to the Mind of Man.* That title is a misleading title. God did not just give us His mind. He gave us His Words. Bob Jones University has been joined in this by at least three other leading Fundamentalist schools: (1) Detroit Baptist Theological Seminary in Detroit, Michigan, (2) Central Baptist Theological Seminary in Minneapolis, Minnesota, and (3) Calvary Baptist Theological Seminary in Lansdale, Pennsylvania. There are several other institutions as well.

This is how these Fundamentalist institutions desire to take us away from the preservation of God's Words. They say, in essence (at least on paper),

> *"Let us respect everyone's views of the Bible. Those who hold the Critical Greek Text are all right. Those who hold the Majority Greek Text (which departs from the Textus Receptus in at least 1,800 places) are all right. Those who hold the Textus Receptus are all right. Let us respect the views of everybody."*

They also say that various English translations are all right--the King James Bible, the New King James Version, the New American Standard Version, or even the New International Version. Use anyone you want to. The cold hard facts, statistical facts, are that there are some 5,604 places of difference between the Greek text underlying the King James Bible and Greek texts of the NASV, the NIV, and most other modern English translations. They can't all be right.

In fact, Dr. Jack Moorman, a Baptist missionary to London, England, is presently making a study of the differences in the King James Bible's Textus Receptus Greek and the Critical Greek Text. He has found and cataloged in his computer data base **over 8,000 differences**.

These Fundamentalist leaders are talking about unity. But we must never have unity at the expense of truth. It is better to be "divided by truth" than to be "united by error." We need truth at whatever costs that might entail. God gave us His *"revelation"* in the first place. He has kept and preserved that "revelation" through the Biblical preservation of His Hebrew and Greek Words. If God had not given us His *"revelation"* plenarily (fully and completely from Genesis to Revelation) and verbally (Word by Word) in the first place, then it would be impossible for us to have it today preserved plenarily and verbally. If, however, God gave us *"revelation"* Word for Word (and He did), and if He has promised to preserve the Words of His *"revelation"* Word for Word (and he did), why also has He not kept His promise by means of His omnipotence to actually preserve those Words for us Word for Word? This is where the battle lines are drawn today. It is not enough to say God has "preserved" His "Word" (meaning only "message," "ideas," "thoughts," or "concepts"). This is what the quartet of institutions mentioned above believes. We must believe that God has preserved His Hebrew/Aramaic and Greek "Words."

Ephesians 3:4

"Whereby, when ye read, ye may understand my knowledge in the mystery of Christ)" Paul was given a revelation. When he reveals to these Ephesian Christians what this mystery is, they could not understand his knowledge. Paul was not making this up. Many times preachers seem to make up things. It is good to use illustrations, but sometimes in the pursuit of doctrine they make up things that are not in the Bible. That is a strange thing.

Paul did not want to be accused of making up this special revelation. This revelation was given to him by the Lord Jesus Christ. Do you remember how Paul was taught of God for three years in the desert of Arabia. For three years he did not go up to Jerusalem (Galatians 1:17-18). He had special training by the Lord Jesus Christ. The other apostles had three years of ministry with the Lord Jesus Christ. Paul was not neglected either. He had three years as well. He was specially trained. Some of this special revelation from the Lord Jesus Christ we find in the books of Ephesians, Philippians, and Colossians.

Paul did not make these things up. They were not just his ideas. Some people say we have to hate Paul because he taught that women should not be preachers. People get up in arms and say that Paul did not like women. Friends, that is a revelation of God and His Word. The words "Pastor," "bishop," and "elder" are always masculine, never feminine. There are no women preachers who are the *"husband of one wife"* (1 Timothy 3:2; Titus 1:6). That is a qualification of a preacher. People say that now we have a new look. No, we do not have a new look. It is still in the Book clear as crystal. Paul did not make up these things. He got them by revelation. His knowledge is the *"mystery of Christ."*

Ephesians 3:5

"Which in other ages was not made known unto the sons of men, as it is now revealed unto his holy apostles and prophets by the Spirit"

"Which in other ages was not made known unto the sons of men" This phrase, *"in other ages,"* is probably referring to the other dispensations. As I said before, the three large dispensations are the dispensation of law, the dispensation of grace, and the dispensation of the millennial kingdom. The other four shorter dispensations are the dispensation of innocence, the dispensation of conscience, the dispensation of human government, and the dispensation of promise. Here is a listing of the seven dispensations in order.

The Seven "Ages" or Dispensations

1. The Dispensation of Innocence
2. The Dispensation of Conscience
3. The Dispensation of Human Government
4. The Dispensation of Promise
5. The Dispensation of Law
6. The Dispensation of Grace (or Church)
7. The Dispensation of the Kingdom (or Millennium)

"as it is now revealed" In the ages past, God never revealed this special "secret." They never could know what Paul is now revealing. This is what he is going to be talking about in the next few verses. Sometimes God does not make everything plain in the Bible until the time comes. The Lord Jesus Christ was *"the Lamb slain from the foundation of the world"* (Revelation 13:8). He was the One who was always to be the Saviour and the Redeemer of us who are lost. God did not reveal the details until the New Testament era. Abraham had the gospel preached unto him as it says in the book of Galatians (Galatians 3:8).

Ephesians 3:5

Although we are not certain of the details, God *"preached before the gospel unto Abraham"* as He talked about his son Isaac and probably also about His own Son Who would one day come to take away the sins of the world.

But some of the things were not revealed to the people in the Old Testament. Therefore, they were in darkness. The Holy Spirit of God saw to it that the Old Testament writers wrote accurately. The Holy Spirit guided their words even though they could not always understand their words. In 1 Peter it says that the prophets did not understand what manner of things they were writing when they wrote *"about the sufferings of Christ and the glory that should follow"* (1 Peter 1:11). Just because the human writers could not understand the words they were writing as they spoke of future things does not mean that the Holy Spirit of God did not give them the very words so that they would be true and straight.

Revelation is a special thing that is no longer possible. There was a discussion on this point at one of the founding meetings of the Independent Baptist Fellowship of North America (IBFNA). I was one of the men they had asked to write the doctrinal statement on the Bible and various other truths. One of the men, who was a teacher at a Fundamental Baptist Seminary, asked how do we know that the revelation is complete and that the Bible is finished? He said that maybe there is something else that God is going to reveal in the tribulation period. He was trying to make the point that God had some special future revelation that is not in the Scripture. I could not understand how a fundamentalist Baptist who is a teacher in one of the seminaries could come up with such a false idea. I and others fought this view, so that it did not become part of this group's doctrinal statement. The case is closed. The canon of Scripture is closed. The Bible is closed. We do not look for anything else. God has completed His special revelation in Scripture in the Hebrew and Greek documents underlying the King James Bible! He has given us the Bible. That is all that He wants us to know.

This is not to say that there are not other things for those of us who are saved to know about Him when we get to Glory. He will reveal them to us. All that there is for us to know now, He has given to us in the Scriptures. There are thirty-nine books in the Old Testament and twenty-seven books in the New Testament, and that is it. We want to know what that revelation is.

"unto his holy apostles and prophets by the Spirit"
Notice the two groups of people to whom God revealed His Word. They are the holy apostles and prophets. I said previously that those two groups are the foundation of the church. When the New Testament was completed, those two offices disappeared. We believe there are no more apostles, no more prophets, and no more special revelations. This includes the false revelation of Christian Science, or Mormonism, and even some of the views of some of the followers of Dr. Peter Ruckman to the effect that the King James Bible is a special and

"advanced" revelation which even contradicts the Hebrew and Greek on which it was based. We do not need anything more foretold. The other offices that we will come to in chapter four of Ephesians (evangelists, pastors, and teachers) are still with us today. These are the ones who take the revelation of Christ to the world. They are to be preaching and winning souls to Christ all over the world. They are to be building up the saints. It is by the Spirit that the apostles were given these revelations.

Ephesians 3:6

"That the Gentiles should be fellowheirs, and of the same body, and partakers of his promise in Christ by the gospel:" That is the "secret." That is the "*mystery.*" That is what was not revealed in the ages past. The mystery is that the Jews and the Gentiles will be fellow-partakers or "*fellowheirs*" one with the other. In the past, the Jews were unique. They were the chosen earthly people of Israel. They still are the chosen earthly people, but believers in this dispensation are the chosen heavenly people. They have been chosen in Christ (John 15:16). If you wanted to be blessed of God, you had to be a convert or a proselyte to Judaism. But that is no more.

If you are not saved, you are either a Jew or a Gentile. If you are saved, you are a member of the "*church of God*" and are neither a Jew or a Gentile but a Christian.

- **1 Corinthians 10:32**
  Give none offence, **neither to the Jews, nor to the Gentiles, nor to the church of God**:

God promised Abraham that in him all the world would be blessed.

- **Genesis 12:3**
  And I will bless them that bless thee, and curse him that curseth thee: and **in thee shall all families of the earth be blessed**.

That promise was not limited to Israel. "*All families of the earth,*" including the Gentiles (heathen people), can be saved and blessed by the gospel if they trust Christ and receive Him as their Saviour. The gospel is what makes us "*fellowheirs.*" A "*fellowheir,*" SUGKLERONOMOS, is "*one who obtains something assigned to himself with others, a joint participant.*" In the book of Revelation, you see that the Heavenly City has twelve gates and twelve foundations. The twelve gates have the names of the twelve tribes of Israel on them (Revelation 21:12). The twelve foundations have the names of the twelve apostles on them (Revelation 21:14). Here you have a combination of the Old Testament saints and the New Testament saints in the "*same body*" and "*partakers of His promise in Christ by the gospel.*" This is the "secret" mystery that was kept hidden.

Ephesians 3:7

"Whereof I was made a minister, according to the gift of the grace of God given unto me by the effectual working of his power" It was a great miracle of God that Paul was *"made a minister."* Before his conversion Paul was a Jew who hated Christians. The book of Acts tells us that Paul was on his way to Damascus to imprison, torture, and kill Christians (Acts 26:10). He was a dedicated persecutor of the body of Christ. God stopped Paul on the way to Damascus. When he was blinded with a light far brighter than the sun, Paul asked, *"Lord, what wilt thou have me to do?"* (Acts 9:6) Jesus told Paul that he was persecuting Him. *"Why persecutest thou me?"* (Acts 9:4) The Lord turned him around, saving him, blinding him, and then having him taken into the city of Damascus. Ananias helped him to receive his sight and told him what he should do.

God made him a minister of this wonderful gospel. Notice, he was *"made a minister."* Paul did not call himself into the ministry. He was a Jew who hated Christians. He was not suddenly going to change into somebody who loved Christ. It took a miracle of God's grace to transform a Jew who hated Christians into a fervent apostle of Christ. That is exactly what the Lord did to Paul. Every minister of the gospel today must be *"made a minister"* by Christ. If you are a self-made minister, you are going to fall flat on your face. There are altogether too many self-proclaimed, self-made ministers all over the world. Some of them are modernist liberals. Some of them are apostates. I am sure that God never called anyone to be a minister who denies the Word of God. I am sad to say there are even some who are Bible-believing ministers who are self appointed. Maybe their fathers were ministers so they just took it up as a vocation. If you are not called into the ministry by the Lord Jesus Christ, forget it, do not enter into this work.

I was called by the Lord to be His servant. I was not sure what that service was going to be. I did not know whether it would be as a Navy chaplain, which I was for five years on active duty, or whether it would be as a pastor of a local church, which I was for five years there in Massachusetts, or whether it would be with the work in the Bible For Today ministry. I was called to give my life to serve the Lord Jesus Christ. I am glad that He called me back into this preaching ministry in our Bible For Today Baptist Church. God's calling for me to preach and teach His Word has not left me either.

That is why I want you to pray for Dr. Jung who visits our church frequently. He has a Ph.D. and is a teacher of mechanical engineering. He is a well-versed young man at age forty. He and his wife want to start a Baptist church in South Korea in an area where there is no church. The closest church is several hours away. They have had Bible studies in their home for many years. He wants to start a church. I encouraged him to go ahead and do this. If the Lord's calling, you go forward, too.

In South Korea a minister needs to go to seminary. Dr Jung is taking some courses at Pensacola Christian College. If you do not have a seminary degree in Korea, you get no respect. In Korea you do not start a church in a house. They do not do things in Korea that way. I told Dr. Jung that Paul did not go to seminary. Paul was trained in the Jewish faith, but Christ called him and gave him a personal three-year course of theological education on the backside of the desert of Arabia (Galatians 1:17-18). But Paul never saw the inside of a traditional theological seminary. Titus and Timothy also did not go to seminary. In South Korea if you are not trained by some seminary, you are nothing. Well, let him be nothing, but let him start.

Pray for that couple and their three young daughters. They are not sure when to start. I shared how we started our little church here. We had a meeting with another couple. From there we decided to start a local church. I believed the Lord was leading me so I decided to go ahead and start this local church. Dr. Jung and his team have accurately translated the entire Bible into the South Korean language. He has worked very hard. God has given him a gift to do that. Very few people would have the patience to do this, but he is burdened that the Word of God be in his language accurately. They plan to publish this Bible which will be faithful to the Textus Receptus Greek and the Masoretic Hebrew Text just like our King James Bible. He also wants to establish a Bible institute to train others in his country. [Since preaching this message, Dr. Jung has begun the Victory Baptist Church of Inchon, South Korea. He has also published his Korean Bible as well as a parallel Korean and King James Bible.]

Paul was "*made a minister.*" That is what God is in the business of doing. Ministers who are working under their own steam are not going to get too far. But if they are in the effectual working of the power of the Lord Jesus Christ, they will go forward in God's will. Paul was a whirlwind. I cannot imagine how he would be going to so many places on his three missionary journeys. When he was offered freedom from jail if he would be quiet about the things of Christ, he rejected the offer. He appealed to Caesar. He kept preaching even when he was in prison. Here he is writing this prison letter. He did not quit. He did not stop. He did not say it was all over.

How much does it take to stop you? That is a good question. It is an important question. I hope that nothing will stop us in the things of the Lord. I hope that nothing will stop us from preaching the Word and witnessing to others.

Ephesians 3:8

"Unto me, who am less than the least of all saints, is this grace given, that I should preach among the Gentiles the unsearchable riches of Christ" Paul was not a proud, arrogant man. He was brought up *"at the feet of Gamaliel"* (Acts 22:3). Gamaliel was one of the most knowledgeable teachers of the law of Moses in his day. Paul did do a little boasting because people were saying he was not an apostle and he did not know anything, but he could not be considered a boastful man. We should not be boastful. Paul said that he was *"less than the least of all saints."* He also said: *"For I am **the least of the apostles**, that am not meet to be called an apostle, because I persecuted the church of God."* (1 Corinthians 15:9)

Paul preached *"the unsearchable riches of Christ."*

"Unsearchable" means something *"that cannot be searched out, that cannot be comprehended."* The word, *"unsearchable,"* appears in our Bible at least five times.

- **Job 5:9**
  Which doeth great things and **unsearchable; marvellous things** without number:
- **Psalm 145:3**
  Great *is* the LORD, and greatly to be praised; and **his greatness *is* unsearchable**.
- **Proverbs 25:3**
  The heaven for height, and the earth for depth, and **the heart of kings *is* unsearchable**.
- **Romans 11:33**
  O the depth of the riches both of the wisdom and knowledge of God! **how unsearchable *are* his judgments**, and his ways past finding out!
- **Ephesians 3:8**
  Unto me, who am less than the least of all saints, is this grace given, that I should preach among the Gentiles **the unsearchable riches of Christ**;

The names of the Lord are *"unsearchable."* There are at least 160 Names for the Lord Jesus Christ. If you want the entire list, they can be found in **B.F.T. #1529**. Let me list a few of them from A to Z.

Some Names For Christ

He has a Name written which no man knoweth.
He is Acquainted with grief.
He is the Afflicted One.
He is the Alpha and Omega.
He is the Altogether Lovely One.
He is the Amen.
He is the Angel of the Lord.
He is the Anointed One.
He is the Author of our faith.
He is the Beginning.
He is the Beloved One.
He is the Beloved Son.
He is the Bishop of our souls.
He is the Branch.
He is the Bridegroom.
He is the Brightness of God's glory.
He is the Bright Star.
He is the Bruised One.
He is the Chief Cornerstone.
He is the Chief Shepherd.
He is the Chiefest of ten thousand.
He is a Child, a Holy Child, and a Young Child.
He is Christ.
He is Christ Jesus.
He is the Counselor.
He is the Daystar.
He is the Despised One.
He is the Door.
He is the Elect Cornerstone.
He is the Emmanuel.
He is the End.
He is the Everlasting Father.
He is the Express Image of God's Person.

He is the Faithful One.
He is the Faithful Witness.
He is the Finisher of our Faith.
He is the First Begotten of the dead.
He is the Firstborn of every creature.
He is the Firstfruits of them that slept.
He is the Foundation.
He is the Friend of publicans and sinners.
He is the Gift, and the Unspeakable Gift.
He is the Giver of rest.
He is God with us.
He is the Good Shepherd.
He is the Great Shepherd.
He is the Head of the church.
He is the Head of the corner.
He is the Helper.
He is the High Priest.
He is the Holy One.
He is the Holy Thing.
He is our Hope.
He is our Hope of Glory.

There are many more that I could name. You can see all 160 Names of the Lord Jesus Christ, by ordering **BFT #1529** at **1-800-JOHN 10:9**.

When a preacher says that he has no more sermons to preach, do not believe him. He is a lazy man. The things of Christ are unsearchable. If he is preaching the Word of God he is going to find the unsearchable riches of Christ in that Bible. You never run out of things to say. You never wonder what you are going to do next. That is why I stick to Bible books and Bible preaching verse by verse. I know what I am going to do next. Even though I do not know exactly how I am going to say it, I know where I am headed. That is why I stick to the books, and I do not get sidetracked. I do occasionally give illustrations, but they are still explaining the verse. The *"unsearchable riches of Christ"* are there to all who will listen.

Ephesians 3:9

"And to make all *men* see what *is* the fellowship of the mystery, which from the beginning of the world hath been hid in God, who created all things by Jesus Christ" Paul was a preacher preaching *"the unsearchable riches of Christ"* to all men. He wanted all men and women, boys and girls to see what salvation in Christ was all about. The Lord Jesus Christ is the Creator. This verse says that God the Father *"created all things by Jesus Christ."* The last three words, *"by Jesus Christ,"* show us that Jesus is the One through whom the Father created all things. Do you know that those last three words are left out of the new versions of our day? You do not have *"by Jesus Christ"* in the New International Version, the New American Standard Version, the Revised Standard Version, the New Revised Standard Version and many more modern perversions. Do you know why they left it out? The manuscripts that the translators used, "B" (the Vatican) and "Aleph" (the Sinai) left them out. Do you know why those manuscripts left them out? They left them out because the Gnostics in Egypt who doctored those Greek manuscripts did not believe that the Lord Jesus Christ was the Creator. They took out the words *"by Jesus Christ"* because of doctrinal error. The booklet, *Gnostic Heresies Invaded the Critical Text* by Dr. Thomas Strouse, **(BFT #1997)** explains why this happened.

Do you know why these texts are different? Do you know why the Textus Receptus text is different from the Westcott and Hort text which underlies these new versions? It is different because the heretical Gnostics changed the New Testament manuscripts that they had in their hands. They did not alter all the texts because they did not have all of them in their hands. These were Egyptian heretics who denied the deity of Christ, His bodily resurrection, and His miracles. They also denied that Christ was one Person with two natures, deity and perfect humanity. They separated the divine Christ from the human Jesus, making them two Persons rather than One. They denied that He was the Creator. They changed and altered the texts in their possession at every opportunity.

Differences in Greek Texts

There are 5,604 places in the New Testament where the Westcott and Hort (Nestle/Aland or United Bible Society) Greek texts of the NASV, NIV, and most other modern versions differ from the Traditional Received Greek Text which underlies our King James Bible. Many of these 5,604 places involve more than one Greek word.

Dr. Jack Moorman, missionary to London, England, is completing a study showing that these places of difference amount to over 8,000 Greek Words. That is the difference. Things that differ are not the same. Greek words are just dropped right out of the text in 2,886 places. There are three hundred and fifty-six passages that are important in their doctrinal content. This is one of those places. Dr. Jack Moormon has listed all 356 places of doctrinal changes in the NIV and other modern versions in a large hundred-page book that he has written. We carry it in the Bible For Today ministry. He shows why the Gnostic heretics doctored the Greek text. He shows the different doctrines that are omitted by the NIV, the NASV, and the other modern versions.

This is a battle. It is not just a pink tea party that we are in here. This is the Word of God. This is the Bible. There is a man by the name of Callwell who has written various things on the New Testament text. He said,

"The majority of the variant readings in the New Testament were created for theological or dogmatic reasons."

He also said,

"Most of the manuals and handbooks in print including mine will tell you that these variations were the fruit of perilous treatment which was possible because the books of the New Testament had not yet obtained a strong position as the Bible."

He even said that there was careless treatment of the manuscripts. He also said that the majority of the variant readings were doctrinal in import, and this is one.

All things were created *"by Jesus Christ."* He is perfect God. That is one thing that the Gnostic did not want to believe. They had two branches of Gnosticism. There were the followers of DOCETISM who believed that Christ was just an appearance or some sort of a spirit. They believed He was not real. He was not really a man. Then you had a second group called the ADOPTIONISTS. The Adoptionists believed that the Holy Spirit adopted Jesus at His baptism. They believe that Jesus Christ was not a Divine Person. They believed that Jesus was a man and that Christ was a principle. They said that the two got together at Jesus' baptism. These two views were part of the heresies of Gnosticism. I firmly believe that this is why 5,604 places (totaling over 8,000 Greek Words) were altered in certain manuscripts.

I counted all of the words that Westcott and Hort either added, subtracted or changed in some other way in the Greek New Testament. The totaled 9,970 Greek Words. That is thirty words short of ten thousand words. You might ask if ten thousand words are worth fighting for. Yes, they most certainly are!

Could there be errors of doctrine involved? Oh, yes! Why do all of these "major" fundamentalist institutions like Bob Jones University, Detroit Baptist Seminary, Central Baptist Seminary, and Calvary Baptist Seminary say that no doctrine is involved? I don't know which it is. I hope it is ignorance of the truth. I have done my best to convince everyone with whom I have talked that there are many doctrinal differences between the Received Text and the Revised Text.

These schools say that the differences between these two Greek texts take up less than one page in the Greek New Testament if put together. That is again false. If you write down these nine thousand nine hundred and seventy Greek words and put them end to end, you have forty-five point nine pages, almost forty-six pages of differences in these Greek texts. There are differences between the false Westcott and Hort Greek text and the Textus Receptus Greek text which underlies our King James Bible.

This is one of the verses where there has been a change. These words, "*by Jesus Christ*" are gone from the other text. When you have a cemetery that has no grave markers, you do not know if you are walking on a grave or not until you come up to the grave. When you come up to a version which is a perversion of the Scripture, whether it is the New American Standard Version or the New International Version or what ever modern version you choose, it is like coming up to a grave with flat markers. You cannot see it. You have to dig underneath it. When you read an NIV, it just simply says "*who created all things.*" It leaves out the words "*by Jesus Christ.*" When you read through the Bible, you do not even know what is missing. They do not put it in a footnote. They just simply take it out.

Ephesians 3:10

"To the intent that now unto the principalities and powers in heavenly *places* might be known by the church the manifold wisdom of God" It says here that the "*principalities and powers in heavenly places*" (which would probably be the angels) would be told "*by the church*" the "*manifest wisdom of God.*" The angels cannot understand redemption. They cannot understand all the things of God. The Lord never came to redeem angels. He came to redeem human beings who were sinners, lost, and bound for Hell.

The church is to manifest the "*manifold wisdom of God.*" That word, "*manifold,*" POLUPOIKILOS, means "*much variegated, marked with a great variety of colors*" The church is to be showing off God's wisdom to the inhabitants of Heaven. We who are saved are also to show other people the "*manifold wisdom of God.*" We are either walking testimonies or walking distractions to the "*manifold wisdom of God.*" We are either showing a bad tale of Christ, or we are showing something that is good. As it says in the book of 2 Corinthians 3:2 that we are an epistle "*known and read of all men.*" We must show the "*manifold wisdom*" of our God.

Ephesians 3:11

"According to the eternal purpose which he purposed in Christ Jesus our Lord" Paul's preaching of this mystery that the Jew and Gentile would be joint partakers of the Gospel and would be in one body was according to God's *"eternal purpose."* God was not surprised by Calvary. God was not surprised by the day of Pentecost. He was not surprised by anything that has happened in the church. It was all according to His eternal purpose. God is not time-oriented or time-bound. He is the God of eternity. There was no beginning and there is no ending with our God.

God's eternal purpose was to send a Saviour to die for the sinners that Adam and Eve made because of their sin. Adam and Eve propagated sin by passing on the sin nature to all mankind. The Lord Jesus Christ was the *"lamb slain from the foundation of the world"* (Revelation 13:8) in order to take away this sin. This was the *"eternal purpose"* of God which He *"purposed in Christ Jesus our Lord."*

Look at the last words in this verse, *"our Lord."* There is a battle today over the teaching of *"lordship salvation."* John MacArthur has it wrong. He believes you cannot be saved until you make Jesus the Lord of your life, your words, and your talk. How can a sinner lost in sin make Jesus his Lord? How can we live like this before we are saved. It is not lordship and then salvation. It is first salvation and then lordship. When Paul was saved and converted on the road to Damascus, in Acts 9:6, he asked, *"Lord, what wilt thou have me to do?"* He could not do a thing before he was saved, and you and I cannot do a thing before we are saved. Our works are foolishness with God, and there is nothing good about them. After we are saved is the time that we must make Jesus Christ our Lord.

That Greek word for *"Lord"* is KURIOS. It means *"he to whom a person or thing belongs."* If you are saved and trusting Christ as your Saviour, you belong to the Lord Jesus Christ. There is a second part of that definition which says, *"about which he has power of deciding."* Our Lord has the power to decide what we do. If he does not, then He is not our Lord, and quite possibly, we are not one of His people. I realize you can be saved without making Christ your Lord, but it seems illogical for a Christian to be saved and want to make himself lord of his own life rather than the Lord Jesus Christ. This is very inconsistent.

This word *"Lord"* means *"the owner."* If you are saved, the Lord Jesus Christ is your owner. If you have a car, you are the owner of that car. The Lord Jesus, if He is our Lord, is our Owner. He has bought us with a price. He is the one who has *"control of the person."* It is part of the definition. Paul wanted the Lord Jesus Christ to be in control of him. Are you that type of a Christian?

Do you want the Lord Jesus Christ to be in control of you? That is an important and vital decision. Do you want your own way? The Lord Jesus wanted to be controlled by His Father's will at all times. He said *"not my will, but thine, be done"* (Luke 22:42). He prayed in the garden, *"if it be possible, let this cup pass from me; nevertheless not as I will, but as thou wilt"* (Matthew 26:39). We have a great Saviour, and we can preach *"the unsearchable riches of Christ."* That is what we seek to do here in our Bible For Today Baptist Church. We want to build up the saints of God and, by God's grace and mercy, have them be made just like Christ is in faith and in purpose.

Ephesians 3:12

"In whom we have boldness and access with confidence by the faith of him" This phrase, *"in whom,"* refers back to the Lord Jesus Christ. It is He Who alone gives us both *"boldness and access."* If we are not in Christ, we have no *"boldness."* We have no *"access,"* and we have no *"confidence."* We can have access unto the Father and into Heaven itself only through saving faith in the Lord Jesus Christ.

Boldness is a scarce commodity these days. Many people are timid. Elmer Blurt was a salesman from long ago who would go house to house and try to sell his products. He would knock on the door and say, *"I hope nobody is home. I hope I hope."* He was timid and shy. That is the way it is with many of us when we go knocking on doors trying to tell people about the Lord Jesus Christ. God gives us *"boldness."*

Here are some verses on boldness.
- **Proverbs 28:1**
  The wicked flee when no man pursueth: but **the righteous are bold as a lion**.

The righteousness of Christ can make us bold.
- **Acts 4:13**
  Now **when they saw the boldness of Peter and John**, and perceived that they were unlearned and ignorant men, they marvelled; and they took knowledge of them, that they had been with Jesus.

Peter and John told their audience about Christ. The Lord Jesus gives us boldness to speak the truth about salvation and grace.
- **Acts 4:29**
  And now, Lord, behold their threatenings: and grant unto thy servants, that **with all boldness they may speak thy word**,

This is what the apostles prayed for in this prayer meeting.

- **Acts 4:31**
 And when they had prayed, the place was shaken where they were assembled together; and they were all filled with the Holy Ghost, and **they spake the word of God with boldness.**

These men were beaten many times. They were under threat of death if they were to speak anymore in the name of Jesus.

- **Ephesians 6:19**
 And for me, that utterance may be given unto me, **that I may open my mouth boldly,** to make known the mystery of the gospel,

Preachers, missionaries, and pastors need boldness to preach the Word of God. Some preachers seem to be afraid of their own shadow. They have deacons and choir leaders that do not agree with them. They are afraid to death to preach the Bible because of some influential people in their church who do not believe the Bible, or do not like them or so not like the way they preach. We need to be bold in the proclamation of the Scriptures. We must not go beyond the Scriptures, but we have to preach the truth of the Word of God boldly without fear or favor.

That is the problem with many large churches. I am glad we have a small church. When you get a big flock and a big church, you have to have a big building. Then you have to pay for it. When you have to pay for it, you have to be careful not to step on this person's toes or the other person's toes. Otherwise they will not give money, or they will go away to some other church. In that situation, the pastor is often concerned about who is in attendance, and that makes him afraid of his own shadow. When we are preaching the truth of the Word, people who want to hear the truth will come to hear it preached. That is my feeling. God can give us boldness. That is what Paul wanted.

- **Philippians 1:20**
 According to my earnest expectation and *my* hope, **that in nothing I shall be ashamed, but *that* with all boldness**, as always, *so* now also Christ shall be magnified in my body, whether *it be* by life, or by death.

Paul wrote this when he was in his first Roman imprisonment.

- **Hebrews 4:16**
 Let us therefore come boldly unto the throne of grace, that we may obtain mercy, and find grace to help in time of need.

In Christ we have boldness and access through faith in Christ.

- **Hebrews 10:19**
 Having therefore, brethren, boldness to enter into the holiest by the blood of Jesus,

The Old Testament Hebrews did not have access to the throne of God. Only the high priest could enter that Holy of Holies. Leviticus 16 tells about it. First, he had to have a blood offering of a bullock for his own sins. Then he had to sacrifice a goat for the sins of the people. He could enter that holy place only once a year. When the Lord Jesus Christ died on Calvary, that veil which separated the holy place from the most holy place was rent in two from the top to the bottom. Now, those of us who are redeemed have access to the very presence of God in Heaven by the blood of the Lord Jesus Christ.

- **Hebrews 13:5-6**
  Let your conversation *be* without covetousness; *and be* content with such things as ye have: for he hath said, I will never leave thee, nor forsake thee. **So that we may boldly say, The Lord *is* my helper, and I will not fear what man shall do unto me.**

I hope we can boldly say that. God gives us "*boldness.*"

We also have "*access*" through the Lord Jesus Christ.

- **Romans 5:1-2**
  Therefore being justified by faith, we have peace with God through our Lord Jesus Christ: **By whom also we have access** by faith into this grace wherein we stand, and rejoice in hope of the glory of God.

- **Ephesians 2:18**
  For **through him we both have access** by one Spirit unto the Father.

Access means that we can go before God the Father at any time. If we are God's children, He lets us come to Him and enjoy fellowship.

Ephesians 3:13

"Wherefore I desire that ye faint not at my tribulations for you, which is your glory" Paul did not want the Ephesian Christians to faint. This is a negative prohibition in the present tense. There are two types of prohibitions in the Greek language. One is with the aorist tense, and the other is with the present tense. The aorist tense means do not even begin to do something. This present verb is in the present tense which means to stop an action already in progress. These Christians here at Ephesus were fainting and shaking in their boots. Paul says, "Stop it." He says, "Quit your worrying." We should not be worn out and exhausted because of our tribulations.

This was written from a Roman prison. Paul was a prisoner of Jesus Christ. He was not a prisoner because he had done anything wrong. He had not robbed a bank, killed anybody, committed adultery, or done anything else that was wrong. He was a prisoner because he was a faithful servant of the Lord Jesus Christ. I do not understand completely how Paul's tribulations could be their "*glory*," but somehow it did work out for their benefit. Maybe part of the "*glory*" that they are getting is that he is writing to them.

Ephesians 3:14

"For this cause I bow my knees unto the Father of our Lord Jesus Christ" Paul did not want these Ephesians to faint because he was a prisoner and going through tribulation. He had boldness and access to God. He bowed his knees unto the Father. This is one of the attitudes of prayer, the bended knee. Sometimes they prayed standing in the Old and New Testaments. Sometimes they prayed kneeling. Sometimes you and I may pray lying in our beds as well as in these other positions.

Anyway you want to pray is correct. Sometimes we talk about our prayer bones being tired. Sometimes your knees do hurt. It is not wrong to pray in your bed or sitting. Have you ever fallen asleep while you are praying? Sometimes while I am praying, I do not remember what I am saying, and I fall asleep. Remember the disciples in the garden of Gethsemane. They fell asleep while they were praying. Jesus said to them, "*What, could ye not watch with me one hour?*" (Matthew 26:40)

Notice the One to Whom the prayer is directed. It is directed unto God the "*Father.*" There are what I consider to be unscriptural hymns which talk about praying to the Holy Spirit. Pentecostals and Charismatics often pray to the Holy Spirit. There are some who pray to Jesus, and that, too, has no foundation in the Scriptures. I know that God understands these things, but we are to pray to God the "*Father*" in the Name of the Lord Jesus Christ. We sing a chorus each Sunday in our church that says, "*Thank you Jesus for all you've done.*" When we sing that, we are not praying to Jesus. We are thanking Him.

There is nothing wrong with thanking Jesus or the Holy Spirit, but our prayer is to the Father through His Son the Lord Jesus Christ. Over and over in the book of John it says, "*Whatsoever ye shall ask the Father in my name, He will give it you*" (John 16:23). I think it is important that we get the right perspective on prayer. As I said, there are some hymns that are written to the Holy Spirit, but you find that there is not a single place in the Old or New Testament that shows we are to pray to the Holy Spirit. Prayer is always to the Father through the Son. If we know that something is Scriptural, we ought to do it. Regardless, the main thing is to pray.

Ephesians 3:15

"Of whom the whole family in heaven and earth is named" This is speaking about the "*family*" of those who are saved. I believe that the Lord Jesus Christ knows us by name. The Bible teaches this. "*He calleth His own sheep by name*" (John 10:3).

The word, "*named,*" ONOMAZO, means "*to make mention of the name.*" I believe the Lord is praying for everyone of His blood-bought children. He is interceding for us. "*He ever liveth to make intercession for them*" (Hebrews 7:25). But suppose the "*family*" mentioned here is not the saved family only. That would indicate that the Lord Jesus Christ is interested in everybody in the whole world. He is praying that they may come to know Him by faith. This meaning seems also possible.

The question might be asked, "How could the Lord Jesus Christ name everybody who is saved in the whole world?" Is He not omnipotent? Is He not omniscient? Can He not do that? If computers can load so much material in their memory banks, then why cannot the omnipotent, omniscient Saviour name us? He is concerned about us and He names us before the Father.

Satan is concerned about us too. It says in the book of Revelation that Satan bears witness against the brethren and accuses the brethren everyday (Revelation 12:10). If Satan who is not omnipotent and not omniscient can accuse the "*brethren*" and possibly knows us by name, how much more can the Lord Jesus Christ, God the Son, know us by name. Although Satan has more power and wisdom than you or I have, he still is just a fallen angel with limited power.

The Lord is interested in us by name. Remember when the Lord was near the tomb after his resurrection. One of the women was standing there looking at Him supposing He was the gardener. He called her by name, "*Mary*" (John 20:16). He knew Lazarus by name also. He said, "*Lazarus, come forth*" (John 11:43). The name is important. The book of Revelation speaks of a "*new name written which no man knoweth*" (Revelation 2:17). The name is written in the Lamb's book of life. Our names are important to the Lord. They should be important to us. Where possible, we should know each other's name as well.

Ephesians 3:16

"That he would grant you, according to the riches of his glory, to be strengthened with might by his Spirit in the inner man"

Paul's prayer request in this verse is that the Ephesians and us today would be granted strength in the "*inner man.*" What is the source of this power? The source of this strength in the inner man is "*according to the riches of His glory.*" We do not get this strength from our bank account. It is according to God's unlimited riches of glory.

Many men and women spend a lot of money to be physically strong on the outer man. There are fitness centers everywhere. A new center opened up recently in Collingswood here. There are even fitness centers in motels for those who are traveling. When we were in a motel in Arizona, there was an exercise room that had about fifteen machines in one place. People use that equipment to get their bodies in shape and strong. There is nothing wrong with that, but God wants us to be *"strengthened with might by His Spirit."*

God does not want us to be weaklings. We need to be strong enough to do our jobs.

- **Psalms 27:14**
 Wait on the LORD: be of good courage, and **he shall strengthen thine heart**: wait, I say, on the LORD.

The heart is the inner man. God wants us to be strong from the Holy Spirit of God. This is Scripture.

- **1 Peter 5:10**
 But the God of all grace, who hath called us unto his eternal glory by Christ Jesus, after that ye have suffered a while, **make you perfect, stablish, strengthen, settle** *you*.

All over the world, there are people who are as weak as water spiritually. They need to be strengthened with might and God's power.

We are coming into a day that is not going to be easy! We could be persecuted for our faith. Many countries, such as Liberia, West Africa, have suffered. Pastor St. Solomon Joah is still preaching the Word in Liberia. He is on three radio stations there. Pastor Joah is being *"strengthened with might by His Spirit in the inner man."* God is also strengthening the Liberians who are following Pastor Joah. Many of them are weak in the body because they do not have any food, but God is strengthening them internally.

- **Ephesians 6:10**
 Finally, my brethren, **be strong in the Lord, and in the power of his might.**

The Word of God will strengthen us and make us bold. The Bible tells us in 1 Timothy 4:8 that *"bodily exercise profiteth little."* There is nothing wrong with physical exercise, but, more importantly, we must be built up in the inner man. What will happen if we are strong? What can we do? We will be able to do a lot of things for the Lord that we could not otherwise do. One thing we could not do if we were not strengthened in the inner man is start a church like our Bible For Today Baptist Church. We would say, "Who is going to come?" Somebody told us that nobody would come to a house. That is what they told me. Well, the Lord just let us begin. God can give us great faith. When God strengthens us by *"His Spirit in the inner man,"* we can work effectively for Him. We can pray, we can witness, and we can live to please our Saviour.

Ephesians 3:17

"That Christ may dwell in your hearts by faith; that ye, being rooted and grounded in love"

"That Christ may dwell in your hearts by faith" These Ephesian Christians had Christ dwelling in their hearts. *"Dwelling"* has the idea of a person settling down and making oneself at home. That is what the Greek word means. I know that the New Testament usually mentions that it is the Holy Spirit of God Who indwells the born-again Christian. But in John 14:23, it says that the Father and the Son will make their abode in the Christian.

- **John 14:23**
  Jesus answered and said unto him, If a man love me, he will keep my words: and **my Father will love him, and we will come unto him, and make our abode with him**.

Because God is omnipotent, it is possible to have the Father, Son, and Holy Spirit abiding in every saved Christian.

Here Paul says to the Ephesian Christians *"that Christ may dwell in your hearts by faith."* You can live in a house and not be welcomed. Am I right? You perhaps have been in somebody's house where you felt that you were not welcomed. You may be in a house physically, but being welcomed and making yourself at home is a different situation. The Lord Jesus Christ may be in your heart by faith, but He may not be settled down and feel welcomed. That is what God wants in everyone of our hearts and lives. He wants to be free to use us to His glory. He wants to be free to make Himself available to us. He wants to have us comfortable with Him there. You know that the Lord Jesus is not comfortable in the heart-house of one who is walking out of fellowship with the Lord.

One of Paul's prayer requests was that *"Christ may dwell in your hearts"* in a real settled way. Are you glad that the Lord Jesus Christ has saved you? I hope you are glad. Are you glad that the Holy Spirit of God indwells you? I hope you are glad. Are you glad that the Father and the Son indwell you as Scripture teaches? I hope you are glad.

When a person whom you want to please is in your house, you do not do certain things that would be a shame to that person. Am I right? Though it should not be so, there are some things that people do not do when the preacher comes or when the Chaplain comes. Did you know that? People might be cursing a blue streak in the military, but when they see the Chaplain coming all is quiet. There are certain things you do not do in front of a preacher. We also expect a preacher to speak and act in a different way from those who do not know the Lord. The Lord Jesus Christ is dwelling in and making His home comfortably in us. He wants to guard us against wicked thoughts, wicked words, and wicked deeds. Will you permit Him to do this?

"that ye, being rooted and grounded in love" We are to be rooted like a plant with roots that go down deep. This is very important indeed. This word, *"rooted,"* RHIZOO, means *"to strengthen with a root, to render firm, to fix, establish, cause a person to be thoroughly grounded."* This is a plant illustration.

We are also to be *"grounded in love."* This is a building illustration that refers to a foundation of a building. *"Love"* is to be our foundation.

- **Proverbs 10:12**
Hatred stirreth up strifes: but **love covereth all sins**.
- **1 Peter 4:8**
And **above all things have fervent charity** among yourselves: for **charity shall cover the multitude of sins**.

We do not justify sin, but love does enable us to get around strife. We have all kinds of problems, I am sure. If we were to name all of them publicly, we would probably have many fights and troubles. We might not agree with one another on many non-Biblical things, but love covereth a multitude of differences of opinions.

Ephesians 3:18

"May be able to comprehend with all saints what *is* the breadth, and length, and depth, and height"

"May be able to comprehend with all saints" If we are born-again, we are called *"saints"* in the Bible. It is not just canonized Roman Catholic people who are saints. Every saved believer is a *"saint"* of God. Scriptures says we are holy ones and set apart.

"what *is* the breadth, and length, and depth, and height" By using the words, *"breadth, and length, and depth, and height,"* Paul is speaking about the love of Christ. These are the four dimensions of Christ's love which is mentioned in the next verse (19).

1. The Breadth of Christ's Love.

The love of Christ is wide enough for all classes of people all over the world. He will take them all in if they repent of their sins and turn to the Lord Jesus Christ as their Saviour and Redeemer. It is not as the hyper-Calvinists have taught that God's love is limited to the elect rather than to extend to every person who ever lived or who ever will live in this world. God's love is universal. It includes the entire world as John tells us so clearly. Yet salvation

only for those who trust in the Saviour Who has loved them.
- **John 3:16**
  For **God so loved the world**, that he gave his only begotten Son, that whosoever believeth in him should not perish, but have everlasting life.

2. The Length of Christ's Love.

The length of Christ's love is forever. He will never stop loving us. His love is *"everlasting."*
- **Jeremiah 31:3**
  The LORD hath appeared of old unto me, saying, Yea, **I have loved thee with an everlasting love:** therefore with lovingkindness have I drawn thee.

3. The Depth of Christ's love.

There is no sinner who is so low that Christ cannot reach him, love him, and raise him up. Christ's love can reach down to the lowest man on skid row. Christ can reach any man, woman, boy, or girl who has committed the most heinous sin. The love of Christ can handle that.

Christ loved Zacchaeus who was a tax collector who stole money from hundreds of people.

Christ loved the woman at the well who had five husbands, and the man that she was living with was not even her husband. He loved her and gave her water, everlasting water, that would not pass away.

Christ loved the thief at Calvary who said, *"Lord, remember me when thou comest into thy kingdom"* (Luke 23:42). There is no end to the depth to which the love of Christ can go.

Christ loved the publican who was at the temple praying beside the Pharisees. The Pharisee stood up and said with a loud voice, *"God, I thank thee, that I am not as other men are, extortioners, unjust, adulterers, or even as this publican"* (Luke 18:10). But the publican was so low that he did not even look up. He just smote his breast and said, *"God, be merciful to me a sinner"* (Luke 18:13). The love of God goes down to the lowest depths of degradation.

4. The Height of Christ's Love.

Christ's love reaches to the highest sinners. Christ's love even reaches to those who are up and out. Jesus Christ's love went to Nicodemus, a ruler of the Jews. Christ's love went to Felix, a governor; Festus, a governor; and Agrippa, a king. His love goes to presidents, kings, rulers, and queens. His love reaches even to the President of the United States as well as to all the lesser officials in our nation. The love of Christ has no height impediments. He is for everyone. Nobody is too high whose needs cannot be met by the Lord Jesus Christ. There is nobody that is so high that he does not need the salvation that Christ can give.

Ephesians 3:19

"And to know the love of Christ, which passeth knowledge, that ye might be filled with all the fulness of God"

"And to know the love of Christ" Paul prayed that these Ephesians might know the full dimensions of the love of God. What would make the Lord Jesus, the God-Man, the God of all eternity leave that pleasant place of Heaven in order to come to this wicked earth? What would make that possible? What would make anybody leave their wonderful surroundings and go into a place of dirt, filth, disaster, and sin? The motivation of the Lord Jesus Christ was His love for sinners.

"which passeth knowledge" How can you know something that passes what you know? It seems to be a contradiction. To know Christ and His love goes beyond what we do know. It passes all human understanding and human knowledge. It is only comprehended by spiritual discernment.

"that ye might be filled with all the fulness of God" Paul then prays that they might be filled with all the fullness of God. People say that they do not want to be filled with the fullness of God. They say they would rather be filled with money, intelligence, or possessions. But Paul said, I want you to be *"filled with the fullness of God."* God has some *"fullness"* that He wants to give to us. God's fullness wants to fill our minds and our bodies if we are saved. *"Be filled with the Spirit"* is a command in Scripture (Ephesians 5:18). That means to be controlled by the Spirit of God so that He can use us for His ministry and to His glory. We need to be filled with all of the fullness of God so that God can control us. That was Paul's prayer for these Ephesian Christians. We need to know the love of God which passeth knowledge. We need to be filled, not with the things of earth, time, or space, but with the things of eternity.

Ephesians 3:20

"Now unto him that is able to do exceeding abundantly above all that we ask or think, according to the power that worketh in us"

"Now unto him that is able to do exceeding abundantly above all" That is quite a marvelous verse. It is used many times by pastors for benedictions. It is a good benediction. The "*now unto him*" probably refers to God Himself in all three Persons, God the Father, God the Son, and God the Holy Spirit.

I believe that there is a five-level picture here.

1. Level #1

First of all, we have to realize that God "*is able.*" He has power to do anything He wants. No man on earth, no angel in Heaven or in Hell can match His power. He is able. He is able to do things and not just think. Many people say they are going to do this or do that. That is just talk, and talk is cheap.

2. Level #2

The second level is that He is able "*to do all.*" There is nothing in the world that He is not able to do.

3. Level #3

The third level is He is able to do "*above all.*" This is at a level that is "*above*" the preceding "*all*" should anyone question the thoroughness and all-encompassing nature of this love.

4. Level #4

The fourth level is He is able to do "*abundantly above all.*" His abundance has no end.

5. Level #5

The fifth level is He is able to do *"exceeding abundantly above all."* The five levels are ability, all, above all, abundantly above all, and exceeding abundantly above all.

I do not know if you could pile any more adjectives or adverbs on that situation. It is saying that the Lord Jesus Christ, God the Father, and God the Holy Spirit are all omnipotent. I remember when I accompanied a little bishop from India to meetings in Canada. He used to sing that little chorus like this in his broken English, *"God can do 'anyting, anyting, anyting.' God can do 'anyting' but fail."* This is true, and he knew, it even though there were tough times in India. Are times tough for you today? God is able to do anything but fail.

Have you ever been asked if there is anyting too big that God cannot lift? People sometimes ask questions like this to get you on edge. Well, God is able to lift anything. Can God create something so big that He cannot lift it? No, He cannot. That is a contradiction. The Lord who is able and who is omnipotent is exactly that. He *"is able to do exceeding abundantly above all that we ask or think."*

"that we ask or think" Notice there are two divisions after that. He not only can do all that we *"ask,"* but he also can do all that we *"think."* He can do what we ask. Sometimes people do not ask because they do not think God can do it. The Lord says, *"Call unto me, and I will answer thee, and shew thee great and mighty things, which thou knowest not"* (Jeremiah 33:3).

He can also do what we think. We have concepts in our minds. How amazing that God is able to do just what we think even though we have not even asked for it. He can read our minds. He knows our thoughts (Psalm 139:2). These car makers are making cars of the future. Men are always dreaming up things. Look at all these inventions. All of the televisions and radios and flights to the moon and aircraft started with thoughts in the mind. God is *"able to do exceeding abundantly above all that we ask or think."*

No matter what people construct, God is able to do above all of that. God is the One who made us. God is the One who put us together as human beings. We never should forget that. The trouble with the unsaved man bound in sin is that he does not even believe that there is such a person as God. They certainly do not believe the Lord Jesus Christ can be their Saviour. It is a sad thing.

"according to the power that worketh in us" How is He able to do exceeding abundantly above all that we ask or think? He can do it through His *"power that worketh in us."* Where is the power? It is the power of the Holy Spirit of God. Can you see the Holy Spirit? No. He is invisible.

Can you see air? No. You can feel air if somebody blows at you. You can smell air if it is bad breath or if it is perfume, but you cannot see air. Can you see electricity? No. Can you see radio waves? No. You cannot see them, but you can hear, feel, and sense them when they come out of a radio. The Holy Spirit of God has power in the believers.

In the first century and the apostolic times, the Holy Spirit demonstrated great power. The apostles could have removed mountains if they met the conditions. They were great evangelists and great preachers. Paul the Apostle by the Spirit of God was able to go on three missionary journeys. Has God's power stopped? Has God's power ceased? Is He no longer able to work in us who are saved? He still has that power. The Holy Spirit of God is not shackled. We just have to release that power and be sure that we are walking with Him. He is able to do "*exceeding abundantly above all that we ask or think.*"

I realize that the charismatics and the Pentecostals in many places emphasize the Spirit of God in an unscriptural way. Some of the Presbyterians, Episcopalians, Lutherans, and Baptists diminish the power of the Holy Spirit of God. That is why they are so dead and non-missionary. We do not want to go to excesses with the Spirit of God, but we must realize that it is the Spirit of God which can give us power to serve the Lord Jesus Christ. He is the One that can empower us. He is the one that can empower our church. If the Spirit of God is not empowering us as we preach, sing, listen, and pray, then it is worthless. God works in the Spiritual realm. There is a power that works in the Devil's people too.

- **Ephesians 2:1-2.**
 And you *hath he quickened*, who were dead in trespasses and sins; Wherein in time past ye **walked according to the course of this world, according to the prince of the power of the air**, the spirit that now worketh in the children of disobedience:

What makes those that follow the occult go into trances? It is the power of Satan. God wants us to love Him and serve Him rather than Satan and his devilish "*power.*"

Ephesians 3:21

"Unto him *be* glory in the church by Christ Jesus throughout all ages, world without end. Amen"

"Unto him *be* glory in the church by Christ Jesus" The churches should glorify the Lord Jesus Christ. Churches should not glorify themselves, their preacher, their people, their deacons, or anything else but the Lord. You say why are so many churches falling into apostasy? They are falling into apostasy because they have stopped glorifying the Lord Jesus Christ.

They say that Christ is not deity. They do not believe that Jesus is God the Son. They say that he is simply a man. The glory is not there in those churches.

"throughout all ages, world without end. Amen" How long should churches glorify the Lord Jesus Christ? They should glorify Him throughout all ages!

- **Revelation 4:11.**
  Thou art worthy, O Lord, to receive glory and honour and power: for thou hast created all things, and for thy pleasure they are and were created.

These are the twenty-four elders who give praise to the Lord in Heaven throughout all ages.

- **Revelation 5:11-12**
  And I beheld, and I heard the voice of many angels round about the throne and the beasts and the elders: and the number of them was ten thousand times ten thousand, and thousands of thousands; Saying with a loud voice, **Worthy is the Lamb that was slain to receive power, and riches, and wisdom, and strength, and honour, and glory, and blessing**.

This is speaking of the Lord Jesus Christ. The Lord Jesus Christ is worthy. I pray that God would answer this prayer of Paul in our Bible For Today Baptist Church and other churches as well. I pray also that we may be strengthened with God's might by the Spirit of God in the inner man. I pray that we may know His power and exceeding grace in this wicked world in which we live. *"Unto him be glory in the church by Christ Jesus throughout all ages, world without end. Amen."*

Ephesians Chapter Four

Ephesians 4:1

"I therefore, the prisoner of the Lord, beseech you that ye walk worthy of the vocation wherewith ye are called"

"I therefore, the prisoner of the Lord" Paul talks about himself being a *"prisoner of the Lord."* Paul was not a prisoner because he shot somebody or robbed somebody. He was a *"prisoner of the Lord."* He was imprisoned because he preached Christ. Paul was in that dark, dank prison house in Rome, Italy, as a prisoner for the Lord Jesus Christ. This is only the second time that he has mentioned that he was a prisoner. He does not mention this very often. He is not complaining. He is not having crying fits or having a pity party.

"beseech you that ye walk worthy of the vocation wherewith ye are called" He is beseeching these Ephesians to live right. Every believer who is regenerated by the Holy Spirit of God has a *"calling."* You have been called by God through faith in Christ. Now, Paul says *"walk worthy"* in him. If we are saved, we are to walk in a worthy manner that would not besmirch that wonderful name of Jesus. Many believers, I am sad to say, are not *"walking worthy"* of that Name. If we say we are believers and walk as if we are not believers, it is a shame and a contradiction. Unbelievers see this, and they know it and measure it. It is a sad thing. God wants us to *"walk worthy."*

Ephesians 4:2

"With all lowliness and meekness, with longsuffering, forbearing one another in love"

"With all lowliness" How are we to walk? We are to walk with lowliness. *"Lowliness"* is translated from the Greek word, TAPEINOPHROSUNE, which means *"having a humble opinion of one's self, a deep sense of* one's [moral] littleness." We should not be puffed up toads and "know it alls." We are to walk in a lowly manner. We could not create the world. We are just sinners saved by grace through faith.

"and meekness" We are also to walk in "*meekness*," not weakness. "*Meekness*" is translated from the Greek word, PRAOTES, which means "*gentleness, mildness.*" We are to have a gentle spirit. We are not to be like a bull in a china shop, as the saying goes.

"with longsuffering" We are to walk with "*longsuffering.*" That word is an interesting word. It is made up of two Greek words. One word is MACROS which means "*remote, distant, far off.*" The other word is THUMOS which has the idea of "*boiling up.*" "*Longsuffering*" means that your boiling point is still a long way off.

"*Longsuffering*" has to do with people as compared to patience which has to do with things. You have heard of the "*patience of Job*" (James 5:11) and all the things that were against him. He suffered the loss of family, the loss of servants, and the loss of possessions. "*Longsuffering*" is putting up with people. People sometimes can agitate you more than things. People can get under your skin sometimes even more than adverse circumstances. MAKROTHUMIA says, in effect, "*I don't care what people might do to me. They can agitate me and agitate me, but my boiling point is still afar off.*"

"forbearing one another in love" We are to walk forbearing one another in love. My mother, Helen Peirce Waite, always used to talk about the two "bears" that you must be aware of and take heed to in order to get along well in life. They are "*bear*" and "*forbear.*" She was right. "*Forbearing*" in the Greek is ANECHOMAI which means "*to hold up, to hold one's self erect and firm.*" When we are holding ourselves up firm, we are able also to sustain and bear up others who are weak and are ready to bow down. That is what "*forbearing one another in love*" means.

We all are not all equally strong in the Lord. We are different people, and we all have different strengths. There are many who are just about ready to stumble. We must forbear and stand tall so that we can lift up others who are beside us and who are about to stumble.

Ephesians 4:3

"Endeavouring to keep the unity of the Spirit in the bond of peace"

"Endeavouring to keep the unity of the Spirit" We cannot always keep the unity of the Spirit, but we endeavor to do so. The Greek word for endeavor is SPOUDAZO which means "*to exert one's self, endeavor, give diligence.*" We are to give diligence to have "*unity.*" Our church is a small church, but is getting bigger. Though small, we still have to exert ourselves to *"keep the unity of the Spirit and the bond of peace."* Perhaps one of the unifying things in the early churches was the fact that they had no church buildings as such.

"Endeavor" is in the continuous present tense. We must continue to *"keep the unity of the Spirit in the bond of peace."* We are unified on our Bible. We use and defend the King James Bible. Nobody is fighting or arguing about bringing their New International Versions or their New American Versions. We are unified in being independent Baptists. We are united against apostasy and unbelief and agree with our Church's doctrinal position.

What are you going to do with churches that are split? I do not know what to do, but the Lord has to do something. Have you ever been in a church which has split into three or four different factions? One wants this, and one wants that so that you do not know which direction you are going. We must always continue to endeavor to be unified. If we do not, somebody might come and try to create disunity.

"in the bond of peace" A *"bond"* is that which bound Paul in the prison. We have a bond which binds us together in peace. The Greek word for *"bond"* is SUNDESMOS which speaks *"of ligaments by which the members of the human body are united together."* The ligaments in our body connect the bones and hold the organs in place.

The word for *"peace,"* EIRENE, in the Christian sense is *"the tranquil state of a soul assured of its salvation through Christ, and so fearing nothing from God and content with its earthly lot, of whatsoever sort that is."* That is the peace which the Lord Jesus Christ can give to us. We are to keep that unity *"in the bond of peace."*

Ephesians 4:4

"There is one body, and one Spirit, even as ye are called in one hope of your calling"

"There is one body" Here are seven unities. First, there is *"one body."* There are different figures of speech for the church. In other places the church is referred to as a building, but here those who are saved are called a *"body."* Sound, Biblical local churches are "bodies" with a small "*b*," but there is only one Body of Christ.

"and one Spirit" There is also one Holy Spirit of God. There is also a spirit of the Devil, but that is not the Holy Spirit. If we are saved, we have been born again and regenerated by the Holy Spirit.

"even as ye are called in one hope of your calling" There is also *"one hope"* of our calling. What is that *"one hope"*? That *"one hope"* is the hope that got Paul arrested in Jerusalem. The people were all stirred up because Paul preached about the *"hope"* of the resurrection (Acts 23:6). We have a hope of a resurrection. The resurrection of the Lord Jesus Christ is a fact. He was raised from the dead, and because He lives so we who are saved shall live also. The *"blessed hope"* is that we will be caught up in the rapture to be with Christ forever, receiving resurrected bodies. Another *"hope"* is that we will be with Him in Heaven. That is a *"hope"* that our bodies will be changed one day and will be made like unto His glorious body.

- **1 John 3:2**
  Beloved, now are we the sons of God, and it doth not yet appear what we shall be: but we know that, **when he shall appear, we shall be like him**; for we shall see him as he is.

That is a hope.

- **Titus 2:13**
  Looking for that blessed hope, and the glorious appearing of the great God and our Saviour Jesus Christ;

I am glad that someone asked to sing another stanza of the hymn, "When the Trumpet of the Lord Shall Sound." That is the time when the resurrection will occur. That could be at any moment. That is what we call the imminent, at any moment, return of Christ. There is no prophecy that says certain things must be fulfilled before the rapture of the believers occurs. It could be today. It could be now.

Ephesians 4:5

"One Lord, one faith, one baptism"

"One Lord" The *"one Lord"* is the Lord Jesus Christ. Lord means *"master, sovereign, or possessor."* If you are saved, then the Lord Jesus is your Lord. The word for Lord in the Greek is KURIOS which means *"he to whom a person or thing belongs, about which he has power of deciding; master, lord, one who has control of the person, the master."* The question is have we made Him our Lord and our Master? A servant simply does the will of another. Does He possess us? Do you let the Lord Jesus Christ make your decisions. Or do you say, "I am doing pretty well on my own, and I'll just take care of myself." God wants us to have the Saviour as our Lord, Master, and Possessor of all that we have and all that we are.

I would rather have the Lord Jesus Christ be my *"Master"* than any individual human beings. Would you not? A lot of slaves have masters. We are considered by God as being slaves and bondmen of Christ. He is our Master and our Lord. Paul found that out immediately.

Some people wonder how long it takes for a Christian to make Jesus Christ their Lord? It did not take Paul two seconds. The Lord Jesus Christs appeared to Paul on the road to Damascus when he was on his way to kill Christians. The

Lord blinded Paul with a light that was brighter than the sun. Paul addressed Jesus immediately as *"Lord,"* KURIOS. He said, *"Lord, what wilt thou have me to do?"* (Acts 9:6). That could be your decision as well as soon as you are saved.

Many Christians say, "I am saved. I have a Saviour, but I don't know if I am going to make Him Lord. I'll just think about that." Let us make Him our Lord, our Master, and our Sovereign. Let us read His Word and then, like in the Marine Corps, when the officer gives an order and says to jump, we just reply *"How high?"* That is all. There should be no question.

"one faith" I believe that *"faith"* is the body of doctrine found in the Old Testament and the New Testament. It is unfortunate that some interpret things differently from others. There are all different types of interpretations of *"one faith."*

We need to make sure that we get our faith from the right Bible which in the English language is the King James Bible. In other languages make sure that Bible conforms to the Hebrew Masoretic text and the Greek Textus Receptus text. The problem with these new versions and perversions is that they have another *"faith."* There are separate faiths and doctrinal errors.

At the Bible For Today we have a one hundred-page book available that shows where there are 356 doctrinal errors in the New International Versions and other modern versions that follow the Westcott and Hort false New Testament Greek text. There are 5,604 places where the Greek text which underlies these false versions is different from our King James Bible's Greek text which is the Textus Receptus. Doctrine is involved in no less than 356 places. If you have the wrong Bible, you have some places where false doctrine is found.

Unfortunately, today there is not one doctrine, but there are many doctrines.

- **John 6:47**
  Verily, verily, I say unto you, He that believeth **on me** hath everlasting life.

That is Bible doctrine. That is *"one faith."* Everlasting life comes through believing on the Lord Jesus Christ. The New International Version and the New American Standard Bible leave out the important two words *"on me"* because they follow the false Greek text of Westcott and Hort. They follow this Gnostic heretical text from Egypt. The NIV says, *"I tell you the truth, he who believes has everlasting life."* They omit *"on me."* The Gnostics did not believe that Christ was necessary for salvation. If you are going to have *"one faith,"* you better have the right underpinning to that faith. It does not matter what language you are talking about. Whether it is German, French, Italian, Spanish, Chinese, or Japanese, you need to make sure your Bible is accurately translated from the right Greek and Hebrew texts.

"one baptism" Recently I baptized one of our church friends. That was water baptism. I practice baptism by immersion of saved people, symbolizing their death, burial and resurrection with the Lord Jesus Christ. I believe that the baptism mentioned here is referring to the baptism of the Holy Spirit.

- **1 Corinthians 12:13**
  For by one Spirit are we all baptized into one body, whether *we be* Jews or Gentiles, whether *we be* bond or free; and have been all made to drink into one Spirit.

There is only "*one baptism*" by the Holy Spirit. This "*baptism*" is not to be confused with speaking in tongues which occurred on the Day of Pentecost (Acts 2:4). Nor is it to be confused with the filling of the Holy Spirit (Ephesians 5:18). There can be many fillings for power, but only "*one baptism*" by the Holy Spirit at conversion.

Water baptism is an emblem or a shadow of the true baptism, the baptism of the Holy Spirit. The baptism of the Holy Spirit joins us to Christ our Head and also joins us to other saved people.

Ephesians 4:6

"One God and Father of all, who *is* above all, and through all, and in you all"

"One God and Father of all" I think this is speaking to all the Christian believers. God is the Father of all believers who are born into his family through faith in Jesus Christ. He is not the Father of all people. That is the distinction between truth and error in our modernistic and liberal churches. These churches say that God is the Father of all people, Christian and non-Christian.

The context of this passage clearly indicates that God is the Father of all believers. He is speaking to the Ephesian Christians. He is not speaking of the universal Fatherhood of God or the universal brotherhood of man. That is the doctrine of the Devil. The Devil wants everybody to be ecumenical. God is not the Father of an unsaved person, Satan is. This is taught very clearly in John when the Lord Jesus Christ was speaking to the Pharisees.

- **John 8:44**
  Ye are of *your* father the devil, and the lusts of your father ye will do. He was a murderer from the beginning, and abode not in the truth, because there is no truth in him. When he speaketh a lie, he speaketh of his own: for he is a liar, and the father of it.

The Lord Jesus was talking to the Pharisees, the religious Jews. They had the right theology up to a point, but they added to it and changed it by their rules, regulations, and traditions. The Lord Jesus Christ believed in two fatherhoods. The *"Father"* in this verse is God, the Father of all believers.

"who *is* above all, and through all, and in you all" Notice that God is *"above all."* He is above all spatially, located in Heaven, but He is also above us in His power and in His might. He is *"through all."* That means that the Father is dispersed among all believers all over the world because of His omnipresence. He is also *"in you all."* This is God's indwelling in the saved people.

- John 14:23
  Jesus answered and said unto him, If a man love me, he will keep my words: and my Father will love him, and **we will come unto him, and make our abode with him**.

In His omnipresence, the entire Godhead--Father, Son, and Holy Spirit--indwells all those who are redeemed and saved by God's grace. Because God is omnipotent and omnipresent, He can do that.

Ephesians 4:7

"But unto every one of us is given grace according to the measure of the gift of Christ" This is talking to the Christians there at Ephesus, but it could be said of us who are believers today. God gives gifts according to the *"measure of the gift of Christ."* Every saved person has been given a *"gift"* from Christ. God gives you some special thing that you can do that no one else can do. This is not a natural gift. It is a supernatural gift.

What is your gift? Maybe you have two or three gifts. That is all right, too. Have you found your gift? Are you using it for the glory of Christ? We all have been given the gift of *"grace."* It has been given by *"measure."* The word *"measure,"* METRON, is *"an instrument to measure something."* There are all kinds of gifts which are spoken of in 1 Corinthians chapter twelve, Ephesians chapter four, and Romans chapter twelve. What is your gift?

Once you have your gift, exercise it. Do not just let it sit idly by. Whether it is your gift of giving, or your gift of praying, or your gift of ministry, or the gift of helping, use it! I cannot figure out for the life of me why my wife writes so many notes and letters. It takes a lot of time, paper, and ink. I have just decided that apparently that is her *"gift."* She just writes and comforts people. She gets letters back, and they thank her for the comfort that she has given them. Half of the time she does not even remember what she wrote. That is a gift. We need to use what God has given to us. We should not say "Why are you doing this?" when somebody is using the gift that they believe Christ has given to them.

We should always say "as the Lord leads" before we go ahead and do anything, even when we use our spiritual gift for the glory of God. How do we know the leading of the Lord? The leading of the Lord is always according to Scripture. It is never contrary to Scripture. It is according to what God has laid on our heart. God sometimes uses other mature Christians who really know the Word of God to guide us.

Ephesians 4:8

"Wherefore he saith, When he ascended up on high, he led captivity captive, and gave gifts unto men." The Bible teaches that the Lord Jesus Christ *"ascended"* bodily into Heaven. It was a miracle of all miracles which occurred after the resurrection miracle. When the women came to the tomb, they did not find the body of the Lord Jesus. The angel told them, *"He is not here: for he is risen, as he said. Come, see the place where the Lord lay"* (Matthew 28:6).

After His bodily resurrection, He had a bodily ascension to Glory. This is what Paul is speaking of here. In that bodily ascension, Jesus defied all the laws of nature. He defied the law of gravity. He went up without a rocket. He also defied the law of heat and cold because He did not freeze to death as He went up into the cold. His resurrected body was able to do that. He defied the law of oxygen needed for sustaining our present life. There is no oxygen higher up in the atmosphere. He defied the speed of light and of sound. He was instantaneously in Heaven. Do you realize how many light years it would take to go to Heaven under the laws we know today?

The Lord Jesus *"ascended up on high"* and *"he led captivity captive, and gave gifts unto men."* We are going to see the different views of what that means in the next verses.

Ephesians 4:9

"Now that he ascended, what is it but that he also descended first into the lower parts of the earth?" The Lord Jesus Christ *"descended"* before he *"ascended."* Others have different views on what the *"lower parts of the earth"* means than I do. Let me just give to you what I believe this verse is talking about. I believe the Lord Jesus Christ did descend into the lower parts of the earth where Sheol or hades is.

Luke 16 reveals that before the resurrection there were two compartments in the place of departed spirits. The righteous went to a place called *"Abraham's bosom."* The ones who rejected God's love and grace were in a place of torment. The rich man went to the tormented section, and Lazarus, the poor man, went to Abraham's bosom. Before the cross and Christ's bodily resurrection, there seems to have been two sections in the place of departed spirits. Now, there is only one section in that place of departed spirits.

The one section that remains after Christ's resurrection is for those who are lost and waiting to be cast into eternal fire. These are the ones who are in the tormented section that the rich man went to. The upper section, the blessed section, or Abraham's bosom section is no longer there in the lower parts of the earth. The Lord Jesus removed that whole section and took them to Glory. All the Old Testament saints who are saved are no longer in that blessed section of the departed spirits, but they are with the Lord. That is what the Lord Jesus meant when He said to the thief on the cross and told him, "*Today shalt thou be with me in paradise*" (Luke 23:43).

2 Corinthians 12:2-4 tells us that Paul was caught up into the third Heaven, into Paradise. That is Heaven. Paradise was removed from the lower parts of the earth and carried up into Glory so that now the saints are with Christ which is far better. I believe this is what it means when it says that "*he led captivity captive.*"

Those who were in "*Paradise*" which was the blessed and believing section of sheol, the place of departed spirits, were captives there. They could not go to be with Christ until the price of their redemption had been paid. It was not until the resurrection had taken place that those captives were freed. The spirits and souls of saved people now go directly to Heaven. If you have ever played Monopoly, you know that sometimes you do not pass "Go," but you go directly to jail. They were in jail. They were in bondage. They were captives, and God through His grace and through the Lord Jesus Christ has now taken them to Heaven.

Ephesians 4:10

"He that descended is the same also that ascended up far above all heavens, that he might fill all things"

"He that descended" The Apostle's Creed has this phrase in it: "*He descended into Hell.*" Many people have asked the question, "Did Christ descend into Hell?" In the Greek language of the Apostle's Creed, that Greek word is not GEHENNA but is HADES which is the unseen world. The Lord Jesus Christ did descend into that paradise section of hades in order to remove those captives, empty it, and then return into Glory.

"is the same also that ascended up far above all heavens, that he might fill all things" The Lord Jesus Christ is in Heaven today. There are three heavens. Paul said he was caught up into the third Heaven (2 Corinthians 12:2). Fourteen years before, Paul was stoned at Lystra and dragged out of the city (Acts 14:19). They supposed that he was dead. Personally, I think that he was dead. I think the Lord took him home to show him glory. If there is a third Heaven, that means there is a first and a second heaven. The first heaven is the aerial heaven, the sky where the clouds are. The second heaven is the sidereal or starry heaven. The third Heaven is the

Heaven of God. The Lord Jesus Christ is up there in Glory at the Father's right hand. What is He doing? He is praying that the sinners who are saved by God's grace might live holy lives. He is also praying that those who sin would sin no more. He is our great High Priest.

Ephesians 4:11

"And he gave some, apostles; and some, prophets; and some, evangelists; and some, pastors and teachers" These are the gifts that the Lord Jesus Christ gave. We believe that the gifts of *"apostles"* and *"prophets"* were foundational gifts. They were for the times before the Bible was completed. There were twelve apostles. I believe that Paul took the place of Judas who was a traitor and not saved.

The *"prophets"* were those who gave the Word of God before the Scripture was complete. We do not believe that there are prophets now. Some people interpret prophets as those who send forth the Word of God, like preachers. *"Prophet"* comes from PRO, *"before,"* and PHEMI, *"to speak."* It means to speak beforehand the Word of God and give the Scriptures. We do not have a need for that now since the Scriptures are completed.

There is no need for these revelatory gifts after God's revelation was completed in the Bible. There are Charismatics and others who are wild about this gift of prophecy. They stand up on the platform and give these prophetic words. I believe that is false. I believe that is unscriptural. I believe the gift of prophecy, speaking the Words of God, is no longer a gift in the church since the Scripture has been completed.

- 1 Corinthians 13:8
  Charity never faileth: but **whether *there be* prophecies, they shall fail**; whether *there be* tongues, they shall cease; whether *there be* knowledge, it shall vanish away.

We believe that the *"evangelists"* are still with us today. They are the ones who preach and proclaim Christ. We are sorry that some evangelists are unscriptural. We are sorry that Billy Graham who started out one way has ended up another way. He is an example of an unscriptural evangelist. He has Roman Catholic priests up on the platform with him. He has unsaved people praying for him. He refers the people who walk the aisle back to lost churches. He appeared twice on Robert Schuller's program. On that program he said that everybody is in the "Body of Christ" even if they have not even heard of Jesus Christ. That is absolutely false, and it goes against anything that he has ever preached.

Today we have evangelists. May they be true Biblical evangelists saying that all men are lost until they come to Christ by faith. May they bring forth the good news that we are sinners and that the Lord Jesus Christ died for our sins and that we can receive salvation by grace through faith. If you need Christ as your Saviour, trust Him and accept Him. That is evangelism.

Dear old Dr. Lewis Sperry Chafer, the founder of Dallas Theological Seminary and my teacher for four years, said in our course on true evangelism, "*Men, you haven't preached the gospel until you've given them something to believe.*" The thing to believe first of all is that you are lost with no hope of being saved yourself. The second thing to believe is that Christ died for you and your sins. The third thing is you must repent of your sins and trust the Lord Jesus Christ as your Saviour. That is something to believe. Then God gives you His righteousness.

"*Pastors and teachers*" are still here. Some combine those two. What is a "*pastor*"? He is the one who shepherds the flock. He is to shepherd those God has given him for care. The Lord Jesus Christ is our Shepherd. We are His sheep, but the preachers and undershepherds are in charge of the local church which is their flock.

The duties of a shepherd are many. There are five tasks of a Middle Eastern shepherd. These are the same tasks that I have as a Pastor of this church.

Five Tasks Of A Shepherd

✔ **First, they are to watch for enemies trying to attack the sheep.** We have to watch for enemies. Sometimes I name the enemies. If you do not name the enemies, how do the sheep know that they are an enemy to watch out for?

✔ **Second, they are to defend the sheep from attackers.** I do not want attackers to get any of you.

✔ **Third, they are to heal the wounded and sick sheep.** We have some wounded and sick sheep who are not spiritually mature. We need to heal the wounded and the sick sheep.

✔ **Fourth, they are to find and save lost or trapped sheep** who are out of the fold and do not know where to come in. We must seek them and bring them in.

✔ **Fifth, they are to love the sheep.** Love covereth a multitude of sins. When a pastor looks out at his people in the pews, he sees them and loves them even with all their failings. Do you not love your children even though some of them are wayward? The shepherd is to love them and share in their lives and so earn their trust.

During World War II, a pilot who guarded and guided a disabled plane back to the aircraft carrier was called a shepherd. This shepherd-pilot flew alongside the disabled plane always maintaining visual contact. Some of the wayward sheep have to have the Pastor fly along side of them to bring them back to safety. That is the job of a Pastor who is called of the Lord and who is doing his job for the Lord Jesus Christ.

Ephesians 4:12

"For the perfecting of the saints, for the work of the ministry, for the edifying of the body of Christ"

"For the perfecting of the saints, for the work of the ministry" These gifts were given for the "*perfecting of the saints for the work of the ministry*" and for the edifying of the saints. God wants pastors to perfect the saints. Does that mean to make them perfect? Notice he uses the word "*saints*" again, meaning "believers." "*Perfecting*" means "*to complete or to equip*" the saints. That is why pastors preach the Word of God so that they can equip the believers that are gathered. You do not want to have an imperfect saint go out and serve the Lord. You want to perfect the saints so that they can have the best ministry possible. Any Christian, even those who are newly-born, can go out and serve the Lord. These gifts were given to make whole the body of Christ.

"for the edifying of the body of Christ:" They were also given to edify or to build up "*the body of Christ*." A little baby is weak. A little baby is small and needs to be built up with nourishment and proper exercise. The word, "edifying," is OIKODOME. It means "*the act of building up or the act of one who promotes another's growth in Christian wisdom, piety, happiness, and holiness.*" That is the purpose of these gifts: to edify and to build up the saints.

Ephesians 4:13

"Till we all come in the unity of the faith, and of the knowledge of the Son of God, unto a perfect man, unto the measure of the stature of the fulness of Christ" These gifts have to be here until we come to "*the unity of the faith*." There are all kinds of disunity. When we get to Glory, we will be completely unified. We will then come to the complete "*knowledge of the Son of God*."

The church's end and goal is to become a "*perfect man*." The word is ANER which means "*of a male*." God in Scripture refers to the complete body of Christ as a male and not as a female.

I realize that the feminists will not like that. They are making gender-neutral versions of the Bible. They have different readings in the hymn books. They talk about the Mother-Father God. When the Bible uses the word, *"brethren,"* the gender-neutral Bible changes it to *"brothers and sisters."* No, the Lord Jesus was a man. I am not against women, but I do not like the women feminists who want to take over the churches and everything else.

I am not against women, but God has ordained that men and not women are to be in the pulpit preaching and having the Biblical leadership in the church. I know that the Roman Catholics have women reading Scriptures. I know the Methodists, Episcopalians, the Lutherans, and some of the Baptists have women deacons and women preachers. A woman preacher is out of place. God has never called a woman to be a preacher. They should confine their ministry, if requested by the Pastor, to children. I do not believe women should ever teach men, for example, in mixed Bible school classes or in any other capacity. These should be taught by Biblically-qualified men.

The *"perfect man"* is male. There is masculinity in the Scripture that we cannot avoid. When we come into the Bible and translate, we must translate what God has put there. We must not make every gender word feminine or neutral in a translation like the self-proclaimed lesbian, Virginia Molenkott, did. She believes that the Lord Jesus was androgynous, that is, half man and half woman. That is what she wrote. Believe it or not, but this lesbian woman was trained at a good school, Bob Jones University, and is now teaching at Patterson College in New Jersey. The word androgynous comes from two words, ANER which means male and GUNE which means female. No matter what man may say, God is not a male/female. He is referred to as a male. That is the language of Scripture.

Ephesians 4:14

"That we *henceforth* be no more children, tossed to and fro, and carried about with every wind of doctrine, by the sleight of men, *and* cunning craftiness, whereby they lie in wait to deceive"

"That we *henceforth* be no more children" *"Be no more children"* is in the present tense. Remember, there are two different kinds of prohibitions in the Greek language. One is the present tense prohibition, and the other is the aorist tense prohibition. The aorist tense prohibition means to not even begin to do something. Here it is the present tense prohibition which means to stop doing something that you are doing. He is saying, "Stop being children!" That word for *"children"* is NEPIOS which is *"an infant, or a little child."*

That is why I entitled this message, "Stop Being Infants." God does not want us to be babies. There is nothing wrong with being a baby if you are a baby. In our spiritual life we start out as babies, but we are to stop continuing to be babies and infants. You have to grow up.

"tossed to and fro" Notice the dangers here. There is a danger of being "*tossed to and fro.*" That word for "*tossed*," KLUDONIZOMAI, means "*to be tossed by the waves.*" Have you ever been on a ship? You are tossed by the waves. When I was a Navy Chaplain, I went from Brooklyn, New York, to Bremerhaven, Germany and Southampton, England. Those Atlantic Ocean waves just tossed the large ship back and forth. You have seen the different waves right here in the ocean where we live. This verse says stop being children that are tossed back and forth just like a wave! The Bible says that the wicked are like the waves of the sea.

- Isaiah 57:20-21
  But **the wicked are like the troubled sea**, when it cannot rest, whose waters cast up mire and dirt. *There is* no peace, saith my God, to the wicked

"and carried about with every wind of doctrine" He says "*stop being carried about.*" That word for "*carried about*" is PERIPHERO. PHERO means "*to carry some burden,*" and PERI means "*about*" like a periscope turns all the way about. So the word means that which makes you look three hundred and sixty degrees around. Paul says stop being children tossed about and carried and moved about with every wind. This word for "*wind*" is ANEMOS which is a "*wind, a violent agitation and stream of air.*"

We have all kinds of false "*doctrines.*" Do we not? We have Christian Science and all the other cults. We have the modernist doctrines as well as the Jehovah Witness doctrines. We have John MacArthur with his heresy on the blood of Christ. We have Arminians who do not believe you can be saved for eternity and who believe that you can lose your salvation. We have Preterists who believe that everything in the book of Revelation is past and that there is no future or resurrection of the body. With all these doctrines, Paul says, "Stop being babies, and grow up!"

One of the most important doctrines is the doctrine of the Bible, the Word of God. Let me just point that out right now. You have some Christians that seem to know what the Bible is and have been using it for years. But now they stopped using it. A church here in our area had used the King James Bible for one hundred years. Then all of a sudden, those people voted ninety per cent to change that Bible to something else. They moved away from their hundred-year position. This is a change of doctrine.

What are we? Are we little babies? Are we children or are we men, women, boys, and girls who are strong and growing up in the things of the Lord? Are you "*carried about with every wind of doctrine*"?

"by the sleight of men" That word for "*sleight,*" is KUBEIA. It means "*dice playing*." These people who have sleight of doctrine role the dice and try to see what is going to happen. Sometimes they cheat. We do not want to be carried away by the deception of men because the doctrinal dice players are like dice players who sometimes cheated and defrauded their fellow players.

"*and* cunning craftiness, whereby they lie in wait to deceive" The methods of the Devil lead one astray. He uses a lot of cunningness. People would not be hog wild for false doctrine unless there were something that was sweet like a juicy delectable bit of strawberry in that doctrine. These doctrines have a come-hither smell like perfume which get people to follow them. Paul says stop being babies, grow up, and do not follow the winds of doctrine which are wrong.

Ephesians 4:15

"But speaking the truth in love, may grow up into him in all things, which is the head, *even* Christ" "They were told to "*grow up*" and get stronger in the things of the Lord. That is what Paul is wanting these baby Christians to do. While growing up, they must learn to "*speak the truth in love*." This "*truth*" is found in the entire Bible. The "*speaking*" of this "*truth*" does not always find a ready reception in the ears and lives of those to whom it is spoken, sad to say. Yet this "*truth*" is necessary for believers to "*grow up*" in maturity before the "*Head*," Who is the Lord Jesus Christ. This is why Pastors must "*preach the Word*" (2 Timothy 4:2) faithfully and constantly.

Ephesians 4:16

"From whom the whole body fitly joined together and compacted by that which every joint supplieth, according to the effectual working in the measure of every part, maketh increase of the body unto the edifying of itself in love"

"From whom the whole body fitly joined together and compacted by that which every joint supplieth" The Lord Jesus Christ, the Head of the Body, is the One from Whom the saved ones are all "*joined together*" as believers by the Holy Spirit of God. We are held together and "*joined together*" by every supporting ligament, each individual member of the Body of Christ. There is not a single "*joint*" in the Body of Christ that is not necessary. There is not a single "*joint*" in our local church that is not necessary. We are "*compacted*" together.

"according to the effectual working in the measure of every part, maketh increase of the body unto the edifying of itself in love" God wants the believers to *"increase,"* grow stronger, and more mature. He wants us to be more perfected unto the Lord Jesus for His glory. May we stop being infants! We all need growth, and if we are on the path that the Lord has for us, we will grow up in the knowledge of the Lord Jesus Christ. This can be done by the *"effectual working"* in *"every part"* of the *"body."* This building up or *"edifying"* is done *"in love."*

Ephesians 4:17

"This I say therefore, and testify in the Lord, that ye henceforth walk not as other Gentiles walk, in the vanity of their mind" In this part of this chapter, there are what I call *"stop signs."* That is, there are seven uses of the Greek present tense prohibition which means to stop an action that is presently going on.

Seven Stop Signs

Stop Sign #1. In verse 17, Paul says to stop walking *"as other Gentiles walk, in the vanity of their mind."*

Stop Sign #2. In verse 26, Paul says *"Be ye angry"* but stop sinning when you are angry..

Stop Sign #3. Also in verse 26, Paul says to stop letting *"the sun go down upon your wrath."*

Stop Sign #4. In verse 27, Paul says to stop giving *"place to the devil."*

Stop Sign #5. In verse 28, Paul says *"Let him that stole"* stop stealing any more, *"but rather let him labor, working with his hands the thing which is good, that he may have to give to him that needeth."*

Stop Sign #6. In verse 29, Paul says to stop letting *"corrupt communications proceed out of your mouth, but that which is good to the use of edifying, that it may minister grace unto the hearers."*

Stop Sign #7. In verse 30, Paul says to stop grieving *"the holy Spirit of God, whereby ye are sealed unto the day of redemption."*

Before considering these verses before us, let me tell you about an incident that took place recently Do you remember that terrible fire in a dormitory at Seton Hall? Three freshmen on the third floor died and sixty-two were injured. One of the commentators reported that there was a freshman student on the third floor who cried out two words, *"Save me!"* This may have been one of the three who died. Who knows? She knew that she was near death. The fire was there. That is what everyone who is lost and unsaved needs to know. They need to know that there is a Hell beyond and that without Christ's salvation they are in serious danger. We have to cry out just like Peter did when he was sinking in the Sea of Galilee, *"Lord, save me"* (Matthew 14:30). This is an illustration of the imperative nature of being saved today. We need to be saved, not from the fire in this life, but from the eternal fire of Hell.

"Walk not as other Gentiles walk, in the vanity of their mind." This is the first thing that Paul said they were not to do. *"Stop walking as other Gentiles walk."* That is a prohibition in the Greek present tense. Each believer must check up on his or her life. We are not to walk around like the other Gentiles are walking in the *"vanity of their mind."*.

That word translated *"vanity"* is MATAIOTES which means *"what is devoid of truth and appropriateness, perverseness, depravity, frailty, want of vigor."* We have to watch and guard our *"minds"* so that they are not *"devoid of truth or frail."* The word for *"mind,"* NOUS, means *"the mind, comprising alike the faculties of perceiving and understanding and those of feeling judging, determining."* We need to guard our *"minds"* from *"vanity."*

The Ephesians were told by Paul to stop walking as the other Gentiles. We must also stop walking as other Gentiles. If the other Gentiles do that which is evil and displeasing to the Lord, then we believers ought not to walk in that direction. We need to stop it. The Ephesians were doing it, and Paul calls them into account for it.

Ephesians 4:18

"Having the understanding darkened, being alienated from the life of God through the ignorance that is in them, because of the blindness of their heart" These Gentiles were walking with their understanding darkened. They were *"alienated"* from God's life. The word translated *"alienation,"* APALLOTRIOO, means *"to be shut out from one's fellowship and intimacy."* Those who are walking as the Gentiles have no intimacy with God. There are so many people today who are walking without that close fellowship with the Lord Jesus Christ.

That word translated *"blindness"* is POROSIS which means *"the covering with a callus."* It is a hardening. When the mind is hardened, it cannot see. That word also means *"the mind of one that has been blunted."*

Think of Ahithophel and Hushai, the counselors to Absalom. Absalom followed Hushai's counsel (2 Samuel 17:6-7,14), but had he followed Ahithophel's, advice David would have been killed. When Ahithophel realized that his counsel had not been taken, he went home and hanged himself (2 Samuel 17:23). If that is not blindness and stubbornness of heart, I do not know what is. I always remember that. I say to myself, "*Lord, deliver me from that kind of stubbornness.*" Many times people do not take the right counsel that we give them. Do not get all upset over it. Just say, "*Well, maybe they'll take my advice another time.*" Do not be so stubborn.

The "*heart*" is the center of the physical and spiritual life. That is why the heart is a terrible thing to have blinded. Those who are unsaved have blinded hearts.

- **2 Corinthians 4:3-4**
  But if our gospel be hid, it is hid to them that are lost: In whom **the god of this world hath blinded the minds of them which believe not**, lest the light of the glorious gospel of Christ, who is the image of God, should shine unto them.

There is a blinded mind, and here in Ephesians 4:18 is a blinded heart.

Ephesians 4:19

"Who being past feeling have given themselves over unto lasciviousness, to work all uncleanness with greediness."

"Who being past feeling" These Gentiles were "*past feeling.*" They ceased to feel pain. They had been anesthetized. They were just like a person who is "*dead drunk*" as they say. They're "*feeling no pain.*" These people had no feeling about their sins. They were calloused, insensitive, and apathetic.

"have given themselves over unto lasciviousness" They had given themselves over to the power of "*lasciviousness.*" We have Gentiles all around us who have also "*given themselves over unto lasciviousness.*" The word for "*lasciviousness*" is ASELGEIA which means "*unbridled lust, excess, licentiousness, wantonness, outrageousness, shamelessness, insolence.*"

"to work all uncleanness with greediness" "Uncleanness" is "*moral impurity or lustful, profligate living.*" This is not only what was happening in the Ephesian's day, but this is what is happening today. Many of those who are lost have been anesthetized from pain and have given themselves over lock, stock, and barrel to "*uncleanness.*" The Lord Jesus wants us who are believers to be giving ourselves over to Him. We should be saying like Paul, "*What wilt thou have me to do?*" (Acts 9:6). These unsaved Gentiles were giving themselves over to lust and darkness. "Greediness" is that Greek word,

PLEONEXIA, which means a *"greedy desire to have more."* Some define greed as *"the itch for more."* A greedy person will say, *"If only I had a little more."* A millionaire is not satisfied because he wants another million. A billionaire wants another billion. There is no end to greediness. The Bible says, *"Be content with such things as ye have: for he hath said, I will never leave thee, nor forsake thee."* (Hebrews 13:5)

Ephesians 4:20

"But ye have not so learned Christ" The Lord Jesus Christ does not teach us *"greediness."* He does not teach us *"lasciviousness."* He does not teach us about *"blindness of heart"* or being *"alienated from the life of God."* He teaches us things that are decent and proper.

- **Matthew 11:28-29**
  Come unto me, all *ye* that labour and are heavy laden, and I will give you rest. Take my yoke upon you, **and learn of me**; for I am meek and lowly in heart: and ye shall find rest unto your souls.

We learn of Him as we read His Word. We have to learn of Christ.

- **2 Timothy 2:15**
  Study to shew thyself approved unto God, a workman that needeth not to be ashamed, **rightly dividing the word of truth**.

The Word of Truth has been wrongly divided so many times and in so many places. All of the modern versions and perversions are wrongly dividing God's *"Word of Truth."* We have to be *"rightly dividing."* We need, like a surgeon with a scalpel, to be cutting in a straight line. We have to be skilled in these matters.

Some people say they are Christians; but when you look at their lives, they are living like the Gentile's live. One of two things is true. They are either lying about being born-again Christians, or they are walking contrary to God's Word. *"But ye have not so learned Christ."*

Ephesians 4:21

"If so be that ye have heard him, and have been taught by him, as the truth is in Jesus" If you have been taught by the Lord Jesus Christ, you do not walk arm and arm with the world. You might say *"Well, I'm comfortable walking with the world, and I'm comfortable being a Christian."* Those things do not go together. You cannot be comfortable in both worlds. As the Lord Jesus said, *"No man can serve two masters"* (Matthew 6:34). You have to choose. There are people who say that they are just trying to live a little bit of the Christian life. They want to live "sort of" a

Christian life. They do not want to be too religious. They do not want to be fanatical.

Well, what is fanatical? What does that mean? We get the word, *"fan"* from this term. This is not talking about the fan that blows air on a hot summer day but about the *"fan"* that eagerly goes to see or participate in an activity like baseball, football, or golf.

Was Paul a fanatic? I suppose many people would call him a fanatic. What person in the twenty-first century would recommend that you should go on three missionary journeys all over the known world without getting paid for it. Paul worked his fingers to the bone as a craftsman making tents. He preached the gospel and underwent many adverse conditions. He was beaten with rods and almost killed. In fact, he was killed one time with stones and dragged out of the city of Lystra (Acts 14:19). Would not people today call him a fanatic?

Does not the Lord Jesus Christ want us to follow Him as Paul did? Would not they call the Lord Jesus Christ a fanatic? Although He knew everything (omniscient), had all power (omnipotent), and was everywhere present (omnipresent), He only had a little band of twelve people. After preaching fervently for three and one-half years, all He had, as apostles, were twelve men, and one of them was a traitor. Would not Jesus be considered somewhat of a fanatic? Only John and Peter were at His trial, and the only apostle at the cross was John. He was the only apostle who witnessed that terrible scene.

I hope that you do not disappoint the Lord Jesus Christ. Be strong for Him, and follow Him no matter what. I remember in June of 1945, that I gave the salutatorian address to my high school class. In my speech I gave a testimony for the Lord Jesus Christ. Mrs. Waite also gave a talk that gave a good gospel message. We were saved and in tune with the Lord. I remember one of the things that I said that day about the Lord Jesus Christ being a teacher. It was a poem entitled "By the Waters of Galilee." It was given to me first by my High School janitor, Uncle Charles Allen, who led me to Christ in 1944.

Ephesians 4:21

"By the Waters of Galilee"

"Behold, a Teacher went forth to teach
Some two thousand years ago,
Before the age of the telegraph,
The car or the radio.
He had no books, and no magazines
And held no scholastic degree,
But men still ponder the things He taught
By the waters of Galilee.

He knew!--the people didn't, that the earth was round
That water was H2O,
The fourth dimension was still unknown
In Jerusalem and Jericho.
But His soul was stirred by the urge to break
All fetters and make men free.
God's will--He shed His precious blood on Calvary
By the waters of Galilee.

We know full well that the earth is round,
That water is H2O,
The fourth dimension has lost its kick,
There's little we do not know,
But it's not mechanics this old world needs
But rather, to make men free,
More teachers to teach the Master's Will,
About His "Finished Work" on the hill
By the waters of Galilee."

      By A. J. Dunlap

We have been taught of Him. We have to be founded on the Lord Jesus, Who is the Truth (John 14:6).

Ephesians 4:22

"That ye put off concerning the former conversation the old man, which is corrupt according to the deceitful lusts" God wants us to "*put off*" our "*old man*" behavior. We are to put it off just like we would take off our greasy mechanics clothes when we come into our house. We need to put them off and throw them away. Some people do not want to throw them away. They want to keep the old sins around a little bit. God wants us to set them aside. These former things that we did before we were saved are "*corrupt*." They are depraved, so we who are saved must put them off.

The Holy Spirit of God can help us put them off. We cannot put them off ourselves, but He can help us overcome these "*deceitful lusts.*" "*Deceitful lusts*" are "*the desire for things which are forbidden.*" God is not pleased with the former path that we were on before we were saved.

Ephesians 4:23

"And be renewed in the spirit of your mind" God wants us to have a "*renewal.*" Some churches talk about renewal when they need revival. Renewal means to take something that is already there and make it right. God wants us to be "*renewed in the spirit of the mind.*"

The mind is capable of many things. The mind can invent. The mind can think, but also the mind can devise things that are very dangerous and deadly. They can devise computer viruses that can completely shut down computers. Why would a mind want to do that? That is a question I have never been able to understand. Do they just want to prove that they are smart enough to beat a computer? Do they just want to ruin people's programs all over the world?

We need our minds "*renewed.*" The old mind just will not do. We need the new mind that is created in Christ Jesus. In order to have a godly mind, we have to feed on godly things. A mind can see wickedness in its eye-gate. It can hear wickedness in its ear-gate. The mind itself can think wickedness. Wickedness can be in our hearts. We have to throw out the old and let God the Holy Spirit renew us.

How often does that take place? It ought to take place everyday.

- **Lamentations 3:22-23**
  It is of the LORD'S mercies that we are not consumed, because his compassions fail not. **They are new every morning**: great *is* thy faithfulness.

God's mercies are "*new*" every morning. The Lord Jesus prayed in the disciple's prayer, "*Give us this day our daily bread*" (Matthew 6:11). Something that is daily is something that is fresh. You do not want second day bread. For spiritual things this will not do. We have to have something that is fresh from the Lord each day.

Ephesians 4:24

"And that ye put on the new man, which after God is created in righteousness and true holiness"

"And that ye put on the new man" We are to put off the old and *"put on the new man."* We are to put on the clothing of the *"new man,"* the Lord Jesus Christ. God says that you are to clothe yourself with the *"new man."* We are to put it on as we would put on a new suit of clothes.

This new man is the new nature.
- **2 Corinthians 5:17**
Therefore **if any man be** in Christ, **he is** a new creature: old things are passed away; behold, all things are become new.

"which after God is created in righteousness and true holiness" God created the worlds, but He also *"created"* a new person in the believer. If you are saved, you are a new creation. God created the *"new man."* It did not evolve. It is *"created in righteousness and true holiness."*

The new nature cannot sin, but the old nature can sin. We have these two people inside of us, the *"old man"* and the *"new man."* They are in a fight. The one you feed the most is the one that is going to win out. This is just like the two dogs in the fight. The one who is fed is the stronger and wins the fight. We need to feed the *"new man"* so that he wins the fight.

Recently Mrs. Waite and I looked at a nature show on television about elephants. I was glued to that thing. It told us how many muscles elephants had in their trunk and how many pounds of food they ate every day. It takes them eighteen hours to eat every day. They are consumed with eating daily for eighteen hours. Needless to say, they do not get much sleep. Those elephants have one thing on their mind during their waking hours, and that is food. In spiritual things we have to have one thing on our minds. That is *"putting on the new man"* which is *"created in righteousness and true holiness."*

On television you see these people who are made-over for a "before-and-after" picture. First, you see a man looking all disheveled and uncouth before he is made-over. Then, you see him coming out looking wonderful. God is not interested in make-overs that are on the outside. Putting on the *"new man"* is a make-over that is on the inside. To coin a phrase, God is interested in make-unders instead of make-overs. He is interested under the surface, in the inner man. That is the thing which God has *"created in true righteousness and holiness."*

We are to put on that *"new man."* Yes, we have the *"new man"* and the *"old man."* Yes, we have a battle within us if we are born again, but the Holy Spirit of God can manifest His fruit (Galatians 5:22-23). We do not need the works of the flesh which are manifested and mentioned in Galatians 5:19-21.

Ephesians 4:25

"Wherefore putting away lying, speak every man truth with his neighbour: for we are members one of another"
There were apparently some liars in the Ephesian church. Do we have any liars here present? I do not know. I cannot read your heart. Only God knows your heart. Is *"lying"* anything big? It is in the Bible, so it must be big. This is one of the illustrations of putting away the old nature.

What is *"lying"*? Lying is not telling the truth, the whole truth, and nothing but the truth. That is the phrase that we put in the answer to that book, *From the Mind of God to the Mind of Man.* God wants us to speak truth.

Now, I realize that if you do not want to answer a question it would be truthful to say, *"No comment."* Harry Truman did that all the time. I remember when Captain Kirk of the original Startrek, William Shatner, was being interviewed recently. They asked him about the death of his wife who had died of an over dose of drugs. He said, *"I can't answer at this time, no comment."* He did not lie. He just did not comment. It is nobody's business. There are some things you do not have to tell. That is not lying.

That does not mean you have to voice your opinions all the time. When someone asks how they look, you do not have to tell them that they look bad. When they smell bad, you do not have to tell them that they smell bad. When they are ugly, you do not have to tell them that they are ugly. That is not lying. That is just *"shutting up"* and making no comment at all.

By all means, *"put away lying."* That word for *"lying"* in the Greek is PSEUDOS. Our English word, *"lying,"* means *"conscious and intentional falsehood, in a broad sense, whatever is not what it seems."* Lying is anything that is not true. Lying in English usually involves a motivation to deceive. If I lie to somebody, I have a motive to deceive. The Greek word for *"lie,"* PSEUDOS, speaks of an untruth that is not a fact whether it is purposeful or not. Anything that is untrue is a lie in the Greek whether you mean it or not.

Teachers need to beware because they will receive the greater condemnation if they teach wrong (James 3:1). God holds us accountable if we preach the Word of God wrongly. Sometimes you may not be sure when you teach. Well, then say that you are not sure. Then you are not lying. If you say something that you are not sure of and present it as fact, you will be held accountable for that. We need to speak the *"truth."* The Lord Jesus is *"the way, the truth, and the life"* (John 14:6). He is Truth. God's Word is truth.

"*Sanctify them through thy truth: thy word is truth*" (John 17:17).

When it says "*we are members one of another*," it is referring to the body. We have two arms and two legs which are parts of our bodies, so we ought to be careful to speak the truth so we do not offend other Christians who are part of the same spiritual "*body.*"

Ephesians 4:26

"Be ye angry, and sin not: let not the sun go down upon your wrath"

"Be ye angry, and sin not" Here is stop sign number two. "*Be angry.*" In other words, "*be aroused against sin.*" That is what this means. The Lord Jesus was provoked, emotional, and "*angry*" when He dealt with the Pharisees in Matthew 23. He called them names. He called them "*whited sepulchres*" (Matthew 23:27). He was "*angry*" when He cleansed the temple of the wicked moneychangers who were selling doves for profit (Matthew 21:12). He was "*angry*" against sin.

Some people say that we should never be angry or never be emotional about anything. God says, "*Be ye angry and sin not.*" That verb for "*sin*" is in the present tense as a negative prohibition. It means to stop an action already going on. It means to "*stop sinning.*" They were angry, and they were sinning. They let their anger get to the sinning stage. This says, "*Stop your sinning when you are angry.*" Be very careful. Do not cross the line.

"let not the sun go down upon your wrath" The last part of this verse is a third stop sign. The first word used for "*anger*" is ORGIZO. This word means "*to be provoked to anger, be angry, be wroth.*" The word used here for "*wrath*" is PARORGISMOS. This word means "*indignation, wrath, or exasperation.*" This is "*extreme and uncontrolled wrath.*" Do not let the sun go down on that kind of wrath. Cool down before you sleep. Stop letting the sun go down on this kind of wrath. That is what they were doing.

Ephesians 4:27

"Neither give place to the devil" This is just a short verse, but it is stop sign number four. It is a present tense prohibition, and it means "*stop giving place to the devil.*" Giving place is like giving him a room. Do not give any room for Satan, but give room to the Lord Jesus Christ. The hymn, "Have You Any Room for Jesus," speaks about this. Do not give Satan any wiggle-room. Do not let Satan in through the eye-gate, the ear-gate, the mouth-gate, the foot-gate, the hand-gate, and by no means the heart-gate. Do not let Satan in at all. If you do, you will be in trouble. Do not let his foot get into the door because when his foot gets in the door, his whole body will come through. Do not give any "*place to the devil.*" He doesn't belong in your life if you are saved by Christ.

You have heard the expression, *"Don't let the camel into the tent because once the nose comes in, the whole camel comes into the tent and the tent will be gone."*

There is a sign in one of our rooms concerning temptation which reads:

Avoiding Temptation

"Avoiding temptation is next in importance to resisting temptation. For the lust of the eye is fearfully apt to begin the lust of the flesh. We met this in Matthew Henry's Commentary the other day, 'Do not approach the forbidden tree unless you would eat forbidden fruit.' It reminds us of old Thomas Fuller's quaint saying, 'If you do not wish to trade with the Devil, keep out of his shop.'"

A. J. Gordon

Here is a good definition of who the Devil is.

The Devil

"He is the prince of demons and the author of evil. He is persecuting good men, estranging mankind from God and enticing them to sin. He is afflicting them with diseases by means of demons and taking possession of their bodies at his biding."

Satan is party to all of this. You cannot give him any place lest he take over. God says stop it. These Christians at Ephesus apparently were doing this.

Ephesians 4:28

"Let him that stole steal no more: but rather let him labour, working with *his* hands the thing which is good, that he may have to give to him that needeth"

"Let him that stole steal no more" There were apparently some thieves in this Ephesian church. Earlier Paul told the liars to stop lying, and now he speaks about the thieves here at Ephesus.

As a young boy before I was saved, I was a petty thief. I used to take candy bars from one of our drug stores now and then. I would put them in my pocket and go out and eat them. That was a very wicked thing to do, and I am ashamed of it. Don't any of you young people go out and steal. That is horrible. I have not stolen another candy bar since, nor will I ever. God says quit it! Stop your stealing.

It is stealing when you do something else on company time other then what the company is paying you to do. Give full measure. When you work for someone, make sure you are not stealing their time.

" **but rather let him labour"** That *"labour"* is *"difficult, tiring, exhausting, and toilsome labor."* That is what the Greek word, KOPIAO, means. *"To labor with wearisome effort, to toil."* Let them toil. A friend of ours works painting indoors. He was painting in apartments that had no heat. He was there all day long painting in the cold. That is toilsome labor.

"working with *his* hands the thing which is good, that he may have to give to him that needeth" There is nothing wrong with working with our hands. People often distinguish between a blue collar worker and a white collar worker. Some look down on those who are working with their hands. God says to labor and to work with your hands. The Lord worked with His hands. The heavens are the works of His hands. The Lord Jesus worked with His hands as a carpenter's son. I am sure that He helped Joseph in the carpentry shop. Paul worked with his hands. He was a tent-maker. Some of us work more with our hands and others of us work more with our minds. Some do both.

Some of us who work with our hands do not need to use our minds as much. Some of us who work with our minds could not work with our hands even if we tried. Whatever our situation, we need to labor instead of stealing so that we can *"give"* to others who are in need. Instead of *"stealing"* from somebody in greed, let us *"give"* to some fellow Christian who is in need.

Ephesians 4:29

"Let no corrupt communication proceed out of your mouth, but that which is good to the use of edifying, that it may minister grace unto the hearers"

"Let no corrupt communication proceed out of your mouth" Here is stop sign number six. Apparently these Ephesian Christians were foul-mouthed also. Paul said "Stop it!" This is a prohibition in the present tense which means stop something that is already in progress.

If you look at the television at all, you see many things that are corrupt. Last night there was a whole show on homosexuality. It was horrible. Using God's name in vain is in vogue all over. You cannot go anywhere without hearing God's name used in vain. This is a horrible thing. There are filthy words which are common street terms spoken on television all the time now.

There used to be a law against this. Some of you old-timers remember when curse words were blanked out of television programs.

Stop letting "*corrupt communication*" come out of your mouth. What if you don't think you can keep quiet, and think you just have to say something. Don't say it! Just shut your mouth. Keep your teeth together and nothing "*corrupt*" will come out of your mouth. You do not have to have wickedness coming out of your mouth.

"but that which is good to the use of edifying, that it may minister grace unto the hearers" God wants us to use our mouths to edify. The Greek word for "*edify*" is OIKODOME. It means "*the act of building up, the act of one who promotes another's growth in Christian wisdom, piety, happiness, holiness.*" God wants us to promote growth. Instead of corrupt communication coming out of our mouth, let us be building up instead of tearing down.

You might think that Christians do not use "*corrupt communication.*" Some who call themselves Christians do. Believe it or not, even some preachers use foul language. Dr. Peter Ruckman, for instance, uses very strong language, even at times what we would call swear-words when he preaches. He uses bad language and writes bad language in his books. God said not to let "*corrupt communication*" come out of your mouth. Let your words be gracious.

Ephesians 4:30

"And grieve not the holy Spirit of God, whereby ye are sealed unto the day of redemption"

"And grieve not the holy Spirit of God" Here is the seventh stop sign. We are to stop grieving the Holy Spirit of God. Apparently these Ephesian Christians were grieving the Holy Spirit. God says stop it! The word, "grieve" is LUPEO which means "*to make sorrowful, to afflict with sadness, cause grief, to throw into sorrow, to make one uneasy.*"

The Holy Spirit of God is a Person. If we are born again, the Holy Spirit of God is indwelling our bodies. He is a Person. Do you want to be cruel or inhuman to your friend or your spouse? Do you want to be obnoxious and grieve them and cause them sorrow, sadness, and grief? You certainly do not. Then why do we do it to the Holy Spirit of God? We ought to be able to say that the Holy Spirit is not grieved.

According to Dr. Lewis Sperry Chafer, the founder of Dallas Theological Seminary and my teacher for four years, there are three things that are prerequisites for the filling, empowering, and controlling of the Holy Spirit of God. He writes about this in his book *He That Is Spiritual*. Two are negative, and one is positive. Here are the three commands:

Ephesians 4:30

Three Requirements For The Holy Spirit's Filling

1. We must not "*quench*" the Spirit by saying no to the will of God. (1 Thessalonians 5:19)
2. We must not "*grieve*" the Spirit by having known unconfessed sin in our life. (Ephesians 4:30)
3. We must "*walk in the Spirit*" with a moment by moment dependence on the Holy Spirit. (Galatians 5:16)

Walking in the Spirit of God is something that believers should do continuously moment by moment. Quenching the Spirit is saying no to the will of God which causes Him not to burn brightly. Grieving the Spirit is living with known, unconfessed sin in our lives.

Known unconfessed sin grieves the Holy Spirit of God. If we do not know we have sinned, that is one thing. But when we sin knowingly with our body, our lips, our mouth, our mind, and do not confess to God, that grieves the Holy Spirit of God. It makes Him sorry and sad. Paul says stop grieving the Holy Spirit of God.

This is why Christians are not on the victory side. The Spirit of God that is within saved people wants us to have all the fruits of the spirit: love, joy, peace, longsuffering, gentleness, goodness, faith, meekness, and temperance (Galatians 5:22-23). Instead of possessing our possessions, we are just wandering out in the wilderness. We are just as sad as can be and have no victory because we are grieving the Spirit of God. The Spirit of God wants to bestow on us all nine aspects of His fruit.

"whereby ye are sealed unto the day of redemption"
Once we are saved, we are always saved. That is a Bible truth. There it is. He has sealed us until "*the day of redemption.*" That is until we get our new glorified bodies.

There are two things that a "*seal*" does. One, it shows ownership. A "*signet*" and a "*seal*" show ownership. Two, it shows security. They tried to "*seal*" the tomb of the Lord Jesus Christ, but they could not keep Him in there. The angels rolled away the stone so that the people could get inside, not so that Jesus could get out. He did not need anyone to roll away the stone. They sealed the tomb so that no one would steal His body. A "*seal*" shows ownership and security.

Once we are saved, we are *"sealed"* by the Holy Spirit of God until *"the day of redemption"* when we get our new bodies. When Jesus saves us, we come out of the kingdom of darkness, Satan's kingdom, into the kingdom of light, God's kingdom (Colossians 1:13). The Lord Jesus Christ is now our Saviour, and God is now our Father. The Holy Spirit seals us showing that we are owned by Him lock, stock, and barrel. If He owns you, why do you not let Him use you?

Ephesians 4:31

"Let all bitterness, and wrath, and anger, and clamour, and evil speaking, be put away from you, with all malice:"
Notice the word, *"let."* You cannot do it by the flesh. You cannot remove the *"bitterness."* The Lord must do it through you. There is a valuable poem on this written by my mother-in-law, Gertrude Grace Sanborn, in 1944. It points out the great dangers of born-again Christians (and even the unsaved) being filled with that sin of the flesh, *"bitterness."* Only God the Holy Spirit can remove completely this sin from the life as we yield to His control over us.

Ephesians 4:31

OH BITTERNESS!

Oh Bitterness!
Thou doest lie in wait to do thy work in Christians
And with great activity spring to life
At sound of strife or strain.

Calling forth each carnal impulse--
Urging, luring, leading on
To conclude that life is vain.
Dark thou art and cruel and so unloving.

Nor forgives, forgets, art blind, 'tho ever hears.
Troubles all who bow before thy scepter,
Giving freely days and nights of scalding tears.
Ne'er content thou art to trouble only one heart;

But unawares will steal upon another,
And swiftly bear desires to the earth.
Wrath, and anger, clamor, evil speaking
Join the fray as flesh presides and rules.

Holding court and thriving in the desert,
Oh Bitterness!
Self and unforgiveness are thy tools;.
Binds around with incoherent thinking.

Bears one off to dungeons of despair,
Feeds us there on memory's little morsels
With retaliation guarding everywhere.
Oh Bitterness!
            By Gertrude Grace Sanborn

You cannot on your own get rid of the passion of anger or wrath.

"*Clamour*" is "*yelling or screaming out.*" You need the Lord to help you remove this as well.

"*Evil speaking*" is speaking evil about the Lord.

That word, "*let,*" makes it clear that you do not do it. This is just like when you are driving a car. You may steer your car, but you do not make that car move. You have a gas engine. It is running, and the wheels are turning. You just have your foot on the pedal and hands on the steering wheel. You just let that car's engine do the work. If you are going to let go of bitterness, wrath, anger, clamour, evil speaking, and malice, you have to "*let*" it happen. The word, "*let,*" shows passivity. You do not do it. You are not the one in charge of putting behind you bitterness, wrath, anger, or clamor. It is the Lord Jesus Christ and the Holy Spirit Who let us put these away. Let it happen.

Ephesians 4:32

"And be ye kind one to another, tenderhearted, forgiving one another, even as God for Christ's sake hath forgiven you"

"And be ye kind one to another" Put away the wrath and evil, and just be "*kind.*" Kindness is an art that seems to be slipping away in Christian circles. If you do not agree with somebody, they might be unkind to you. Can we not have disagreements and still be thought of as being "*kind*"?

I have many people who disagree with me, and I disagree with them. I try to be "*kind*" with them and to them. As you know, I have a disagreement with some of John MacArthur's teaching. I was attending a nearby church when a representative of John MacArthur was at the church. When we met, I said hello to him, and he would not even shake my hand. Even though we differ, he should still have been kind to me. I think of another example of this lack of kindness when I met a missionary from ABWE (Association of Baptists For World Evangelism) with whom I differ. I greeted him with a hello, and he would not even speak. He turned the other way. That is so strange. Could he not have been "*kind*"?

I can be "*kind*" to all these people whom I name as false teachers. I do not have to agree with them, but I can speak to them kindly. Kindness is a missing link in the Christian community.

"tenderhearted, forgiving one another" "*Tenderhearted*" is "compassion one to another." We should be praying for our fellow-believers.

The Greek word for "*forgiving one another*" is CHARIZOMAI which means "*to do something pleasant or agreeable to one, to do a favor to, to show one's self gracious, kind, benevolent.*" Have you ever sinned and needed somebody to "*forgive*" you? Have you ever needed to forgive someone else?

"even as God for Christ's sake hath forgiven you" The greatest pardon that anybody could receive is the forgiveness and pardon of his sins. God gave us His righteousness.

- **Romans 5:1**
  Therefore **being justified by faith**, we have peace with God through our Lord Jesus Christ:

He has declared us righteous and He has forgiven us all trespasses. Since He has done this for us, let us do it for one another.

We often get in each other's way. We are too often angry at each other. We need to say that we forgive one another. Paul says to make sure that you have forgiveness one to another in church. Walk together as brethren, and be kind and tenderhearted. You may not agree with certain things, but kindness and tenderheartedness will cure anything that is troublesome in any local church.

Ephesians Chapter Five

Ephesians 5:1
"Be ye therefore followers of God, as dear children"
"Be ye therefore followers of God" In view of all that has gone before and since the Holy Spirit of God is not to be grieved by our actions, we are to be continuously *"following"* God as dear children. A number of verses instruct us about this.
- **Matthew 4:19**
  And he saith unto them, **Follow me**, and I will make you fishers of men.
- **Mark 8:34**
  And when he had called the people *unto him* with his disciples also, he said unto them, Whosoever will come after me, let him deny himself, and take up his cross, and **follow me**.
- **John 10:27**
  My sheep hear my voice, and I know them, and **they follow me**:
- **1 Peter 2:21**
  For even hereunto were ye called: because Christ also suffered for us, **leaving us an example, that ye should follow his steps**:

We need to follow the Lord and be imitators of the Lord *"as dear children."* Once we are saved, we become *"children of God"* by faith in Christ.
- **Galatians 3:26**
  For **ye are all the children of God by faith** in Christ Jesus.

We are all children, but that is not enough. God wants us to be *"dear"* children. That word, *"dear,"* is the Greek word, AGAPETOS, which means *"beloved, esteemed, dear, favored."* It also means *"worthy of love."* God loves us. He will love us no matter what we do, but we should be worthy children and be worthy of His love. Let us be sure that we are worthy.

Ephesians 5:2

"And walk in love, as Christ also hath loved us, and hath given himself for us an offering and a sacrifice to God for a sweetsmelling savour"

"And walk in love, as Christ also hath loved us" To *"walk in love"* is to walk in love with Christ, in love with truth, and in love with one another. We are to continue *"to walk in love, as Christ hath loved us."* In other words we are to love others in the same way as Christ has loved us. How did He love us? He loved us when we were sinners. He loved us when we were lost. He loved us when we were in darkness and in sin. That is the type of love that we should have one to another.

"and hath given himself for us" He not only loved us, but He *"gave Himself for us."* It was one thing to leave Heaven's Glory and to come to this wicked world. That was hard enough for our Saviour who had no sin in Him and had been with the Father for all eternity. But He also *"gave Himself for us"* on the cross of Calvary. He took in His own body all of our sins, all the garbage and filth of the sins of the entire world. He *"gave Himself."* He did not send an angel or even several angels to die for us. They could not have done it. He did not send someone else. It had to be *"Himself."* That is why it is so important that we have a Saviour who died in our place.

He died *"for us"* which means *"for our benefit."* There are two words for *"for"* in the Greek language. There is ANTI, which means *"instead of, for, or in place of."* Then there is HUPER, which is what this word is. It means not only *"in place of and instead of"* but also *"for the benefit of."* He died for the benefit of us as well as in our place.

"an offering and a sacrifice to God for a sweetsmelling savour" He died as *"an offering and a sacrifice to God"* which was a *"sweetsmelling savour."* In the first five chapters of Leviticus, there are five different offerings. The first three are *"sweetsmelling"* offerings, and the last two are non-sweetsmelling offerings. The *"sweetsmelling"* offerings are the burnt offering, the meat or meal offering, and the peace offering. The non-sweetsmelling offerings are the sin offering and the trespass offering which were for sin and wickedness.

This verse declares that the Lord Jesus Christ gave Himself as a *"sweetsmelling"* offering. In the Old Testament, the Lord was pleased with the fragrance of these offerings. We do not need any more offerings like the Old Testament Jews had. The Lord Jesus Himself is the only sacrifice that we need. He was a sacrifice of a *"sweetsmelling savour"* to the Lord. The Lord is completely pleased with His sacrifice.

Ephesians 5:3

"But fornication, and all uncleanness, or covetousness, let it not be once named among you, as becometh saints" Here is our first stop sign in this chapter. *"Named"* is a verb in the present tense. This is a present tense prohibition. It means to stop an action that is already in progress. The Ephesians were *"named"* and cataloged as those who were fornicators, unclean, and covetous. Paul says for them to stop it. If anyone who reads this is guilty of these things, God says stop it. Stop letting it even once to be *"named among you."*

"Fornication" is used primarily to describe sexual relations on the part of those who are unmarried. This sin is rampant today not only among non-Christians but also among professing Christians. This is a deed spoken about and practiced in our day and age. It is often called "Christian fornication"! Let me tell you, there is nothing "Christian" about it. It is sin! We see out-of-wedlock pregnancies galore. I would like to know when is it going to stop? There are at least four important passages which refer to this.

- 1 Corinthians 6:13
  Meats for the belly, and the belly for meats: but God shall destroy both it and them. Now **the body *is* not for fornication, but for the Lord**; and the Lord for the body.
- 1 Corinthians 6:18
  Flee fornication. Every sin that a man doeth is without the body; but he that committeth fornication sinneth against his own body.
- 1 Corinthians 7:2
  Nevertheless, **to avoid fornication**, let every man have his own wife, and let every woman have her own husband.
- 1 Thessalonians 4:3
  For this is the will of God, *even* your sanctification, that **ye should abstain from fornication**:

Many of the new versions do not even use the word *fornication*.

Uses of the Word, Fornication

King James Bible	32 times.
New King James Version	12 times.
New American Standard Version	4 times.
New International Version	0 times
New Century Version	0 times

God wants His born-again people (and all people) to abstain from the sin of *"fornication."* Our young people ought to be controlled. Our children ought to be monitored. Our children ought to be supervised on these so called "dates" that they have. One way of avoiding the temptation to commit the sin of fornication by young people (and even older people) is for them not to pair-off privately. If you have some other solution to this temptation, I would be interested to know it. Our churches have to worry about that. It is not only the young people who have a problem with this but it is also the older people. Those who are older must also watch out for the sin of *"fornication."* These Ephesian Christians were fornicating, and that was a serious sin.

"Uncleanness" is the word for AKATHARSIA. It is the *"impurity of lustful, luxurious, profligate living."* Paul says to stop letting *"uncleanness"* even once be named among them. They were living like the prodigal son did in Luke 15.

"Covetousness" is the word for PLEONEXIA. It is the *"greedy desire to have more."* Paul says to stop coveting. Stop wanting extra things. Covetousness is put in the same category with fornication and uncleanness.

Ephesians 5:4

"Neither filthiness, nor foolish talking, nor jesting, which are not convenient: but rather giving of thanks." These are things that believers are to stop, also. These three sins are a continuation of the list of things that are not to be *"once named among you"* in verse four. These are sins of speech.

The first sin is *"filthiness."* This is referring to *"obscenity, a dirty mouth, or dirty talking."* Apparently this is what they were doing at the Church of Ephesus. Paul says stop it. Let it not continue to be *"named among you."*

The second sin is *"foolish talking."* It is the Greek word MOROLOGIA. The first part of that word is MOROS which is a *"fool."* It means *"speaking or acting like a fool or a moron."*

The third sin is *"jesting."* This probably refers to *"low jesting"* which would include *"filthy dirty joking around."*

Sins of Speech
1. Dirty talk
2. Foolish talk
3. Filthy talk

Instead of using our mouths for these sins, we ought to thank the Lord for what we have. That is just like the chorus that we sing *"Thank You Jesus For All You've Done."* We no not need to have these wicked sins on our lips, but we need to be thankful.

Ephesians 5:5
"For this ye know, that no whoremonger, nor unclean person, nor covetous man, who is an idolater, hath any inheritance in the kingdom of Christ and of God"

"For this ye know, that no whoremonger, nor unclean person, nor covetous man, who is an idolater" The three sins in this verse, *"whoremonger," "unclean person,"* and *"covetous man"* go back to verse three.

The word translated *"whoremonger"* is PORNOS. It refers to *"a male prostitute, a man who indulges in unlawful sexual intercourse."* This behavior would characterize the homosexual lifestyle which is rampant today throughout the world.

The word for *"unclean person"* is AKATHARTOS. This means *"in a moral sense: unclean in thought and life."*

The word for *"covetous person"* is PLEONEKTES. It refers to *"one eager to have more, especially what belongs to others."*

Covetousness is here equated with *"idolatry." "Idolatry"* means *"to look at and to worship that which is seen."* An idolater is like covetous people. They want to worship that which is seen. When they see a house, they want it. When they see another person's husband or wife, they want them. When they see money, they want that. They want anything that is material, and that is *"idolatry."*

"hath any inheritance in the kingdom of Christ and of God" Those who are continuously whoremongers, those who are continuously unclean, and those who are continuously covetous have no inheritance in the kingdom of Christ and of God. I want you to know that the verb *"hath"* here is in the present tense and shows a continuous action. You may fall into some of these sins. But if you continue in them, God says that you are not saved and are not a part of His kingdom.

- Luke 6:43
  For **a good tree bringeth not forth corrupt fruit**; neither doth a corrupt tree bring forth good fruit.

Ephesians 5:6

"Let no man deceive you with vain words: for because of these things cometh the wrath of God upon the children of disobedience" Here is the second stop sign in this chapter. It means to *"stop being deceived."* The verb, *"deceive,"* is in the present tense. It is a negative prohibition in the present tense which means to stop an action already in progress. These Christians were being deceived with *"vain"* and empty words. Paul says for them to stop it. Do not be any longer deceived with such *"vain"* and empty words.

The *"wrath"* of God comes because of these six sins which are mentioned: *"fornication, uncleanness, covetousness, filthiness, foolish talking, and jesting."* The *"wrath"* of God comes on those who continuously disobey God and practice these sins. Some people say that God is not a God of *"wrath,"* but He is a God of love. Well, He is a God of love, but He is also a God of righteousness, holiness, and *"wrath."* *"Wrath"* against sin is a part of God's nature. It is His holy, measured, predictable reaction against sin.

Here are ten passages describing God's wrath.

- **Matthew 3:7**
  But when he saw many of the Pharisees and Sadducees come to his baptism, he said unto them, O generation of vipers, **who hath warned you to flee from the wrath to come**?

There is going to be a *"wrath to come"* in Hell. Modernists and unbelievers do not believe this, but it is there.

- **John 3:36**
  He that believeth on the Son hath everlasting life: and he that believeth not the Son shall not see life; **but the wrath of God abideth on him.**

Can you imagine that? All unsaved people have *"the wrath of God"* resting right on their shoulders.

- **Romans 1:18**
  For **the wrath of God is revealed from heaven against all ungodliness and unrighteousness** of men, who hold the truth in unrighteousness;

- **Romans 5:9**
  Much more then, being now justified by his blood, **we shall be saved from wrath through him.**

If we are saved, we are saved from the *"wrath"* of the fires of eternal Hell. It is a wonderful privilege to be saved from *"wrath."*

- **Romans 13:4**
  For he is the minister of God to thee for good. But if thou do that which is evil, be afraid; for he beareth not the sword in vain: for **he is the minister of God, a revenger to** *execute* **wrath upon him that doeth evil.**

That is what government should do against evil people.

- **Ephesians 2:3**
  Among whom also we all had our conversation in times past in the lusts of our flesh, fulfilling the desires of the flesh and of the mind; and **were by nature the children of wrath**, even as others.

Before we were saved, we were children destined to *"wrath."* We were headed for Hell.

- **1 Thessalonians 1:10**
  And to wait for his Son from heaven, whom he raised from the dead, *even* Jesus, which **delivered us from the wrath to come.**

If we are saved, we came to the Lord Jesus Christ Who *"delivered us from the wrath to come."* He is a deliverer from Hell.

- **1 Thessalonians 5:9**
  For **God hath not appointed us to wrath**, but to obtain salvation by our Lord Jesus Christ,

- **Revelation 6:16**
  And said to the mountains and rocks, Fall on us, and **hide us from** the face of him that sitteth on the throne, and from **the wrath of the Lamb:**

These are people during the Tribulation period who are lost. The Lord Jesus Christ will be a *"Lamb"* with holy *"wrath"* against sin. The great day of His *"wrath"* is coming.

- **Revelation 14:10**
  The same shall drink of the wine of the wrath of God, which is poured out without mixture into the cup of his indignation; and he shall be tormented with fire and brimstone in the presence of the holy angels, and in the presence of the Lamb:

Hell is eternal. It is a serious thing.

This verse says stop being deceived with these empty words. Do not be deceived. The *"wrath"* of God is coming on the children of disobedience because of these sins. I am glad that we can escape His *"wrath"* by being in Christ.

When Moses went up on the mount to get the law of God, no one else could touch Mount Sinai. The animals could not even touch the mount. If anyone touched it, they would die. When Moses went up the mountain to talk to God, he was so close to the glory of God that his face shone (Exodus 34:29). He had to put a veil over his face when he came down and read the commandments to the people of Israel. When he went back up the mount to meet with the Lord, he took off his veil. He could not see God. He only saw the back parts of God (Exodus 33:23). God put him in a narrow opening in the rock where God hid him and protected him (Exodus 33:22). We have a Saviour who died for us and protects us from God's "*wrath*" against sin.

Ephesians 5:7

"Be not ye therefore partakers with them" This is stop sign number three in this chapter. Stop being "*partakers with them.*" This is a present tense prohibition that means to stop an action that is already in progress. If it were in the Greek aorist tense, it would mean do not even begin doing something. The present tense here indicates that they were being partakers with those who were unclean and fornicators. Paul says, "Stop it!"

I am sure that when the Ephesians got this letter they did not like being accused of this. Nobody wants to be accused of doing wrong, but it was necessary in their case. Paul said to stop being partakers with these evil people. He said to cease being in joint fellowship with them. Believers are to be "separated" people. Biblical separation is both positive ("**unto**" someone and some things) and negative ("**from**" some people and some things). Christians must be "separated" **unto** the Lord Jesus Christ and that which pleases Him; and be "separated" **from** sinful people and all the sins of this world.

We cannot go out anywhere in the world and not be around sinners, but we do not have to be in close fellowship with them. That is what this word implies. We cannot help being around wicked people, but we do not have to have them as our closest companions and friends. Paul says stop being joint-partakers in their ventures and filthy lifestyle. We do not have to do this. We should separate ourselves from their evil.

Ephesians 5:8

"For ye were sometimes darkness, but now are ye light in the Lord, walk as children of light"

"For ye were sometimes darkness, but now are ye light in the Lord" All of us who are saved were one time in "*darkness.*" It was just as black and dark as the darkness of the night when there is no sun, moon, or stars in the sky. We were in filthiness and in sin.

Now, if we are born-again and saved, there is a difference. God says that we are "*light.*" The Lord Jesus Christ said, "*I am the light of the world: he that followeth me shall not walk in darkness, but shall have the light of life*" (John

8:12b). You cannot say that you are following the Lord Jesus and be walking in darkness. You cannot do it. You are either walking in darkness or following the Lord Jesus Christ.

"walk as children of light" If you are redeemed, you should walk like you are supposed to walk. As it says in 1 John 1:5, *"God is light, and in Him is no darkness at all."* We cannot have fellowship with Him and walk in darkness. God wants us to be what we are. If we are saved, we are *"children of light"* and God expects us to walk in that way. It is a sad thing when people who profess to be in *"light"* are walking in *"darkness"* and fellowshipping with darkness. It just does not add up.

It is more honest to profess to be in darkness and walk in line with your profession. When you say you are *"light"* and then walk like the Devil, then everyone knows it. The Christians know it, and the unsaved world knows it. The worldlings are laughing at you. If I make a profession to know Christ and then walk like the Devil, everybody knows it.

Ephesians 5:9
"(For the fruit of the Spirit *is* in all goodness and righteousness and truth)"

Remember the fruit of the Spirit.
- **Galatians 5:22-23**
  But the fruit of the Spirit is **love, joy, peace, longsuffering, gentleness, goodness, faith, Meekness, temperance**: against such there is no law.

The *"fruit"* of God's Holy Spirit is not to participate in evil but in *"goodness, righteousness, and truth."* That is the *"fruit"* of God's Holy Spirit. Now, if the Holy Spirit has saved us and given us new life, He has taken up His abode in our bodies. If we are saved, our bodies are the temple of the Holy Spirit which is in us. We are not our own. We are bought with a price (1 Corinthians 6:19-20). Never forget it. Our bodies do not even belong to us.

There are three things that we need to be aware of if we want to let the Holy Spirit produce His *"fruit"* in our life. The Holy Spirit of God can fill us and control us if we let Him. Without an understanding of these three requirements (two negative and one positive), there cannot be the filling of God the Holy Spirit in the saved person. As I look over the current status of born-again Christians that I have observed, I see altogether too many believers who are walking after their flesh, bearing various *"works of the flesh"* (Galatians 5:19-21) instead of the *"fruit of the Spirit"* (Galatians 5:22-23). Why is this? It is without doubt due to the fact that there is a woeful lack on the part of these saved ones to make full use of God's power working through them. The following three requirements are a helpful key for success in this matter.

> ## Three Requirements For The Spirit's Filling
> 1. We must not *"quench"* the Spirit by saying no to the will of God. (1 Thessalonians 5:19)
> 2. We must not *"grieve"* the Spirit by having known unconfessed sin in our life. (Ephesians 4:30)
> 3. We must *"walk in the Spirit"* with a moment by moment dependence on the Holy Spirit. (Galatians 5:16)

If we conform to these three actions, then God the Holy Spirit can fill us, can control us, and can produce His fruit in us. In so doing, He will eliminate in our lives the *"works of the flesh"* (Galatians 5:19-21).

We have a choice if we are saved. We have the flesh, the old nature inherited from Adam, which is wicked and sinful, but we also have God the Holy Spirit Who indwells us. We have a choice. We can walk in the Holy Spirit and enjoy His *"fruit,"* or we can walk according to the flesh and manifest the *"works of the flesh."* God does not want us to manifest the *"works of the flesh"* or walk closely with those who do. We are to manifest all *"goodness, righteousness, and truth."*

Ephesians 5:10

"Proving what is acceptable unto the Lord" That word, *"proving"* is translation of the Greek word, DOKIMAZO, which means *"to test, examine, prove, scrutinize [to see whether a thing is genuine or not], as metals."* It is like the testing of metals.

There is another word for testing which means to test with the hope that you will fail the test. When Satan tested or tempted the Lord Jesus in the wilderness, Satan hoped that Jesus would fail the test. What Satan forgot was that the Lord Jesus Christ is Deity. He was perfect God and perfect Man. Jesus could not fail that test.

The word here for "test" has the idea to test with the hope that you are going to pass the test. It is like the parachute that you make yourself when you are a paratrooper. You always have an extra parachute, but you always pack your own parachute. You put that parachute to the "test" to make sure that it will work. It certainly is not a test that you hope will fail. That is what this word means.

We should *"prove"* or "test" what is *"acceptable unto the Lord"* and what is acceptable unto people. If you seek what is acceptable to people, you are going to be a people-pleaser. I heard a politician interviewed on C-SPAN recently. He said that many people say and do things to please the people. It is hard to go against what people think.

You might please the people so that you will not stand out in a crowd. Shadrach, Meshach, and Abednego stood out in a crowd. Everybody else bowed down, and they were the only ones left standing. They were not going to worship a false God. *"Proving what is acceptable unto the Lord."* May we ask, *"Lord, what wilt thou have me to do?"* (Acts 9:6)

Ephesians 5:11

"And have no fellowship with the unfruitful works of darkness, but rather reprove *them*"

"And have no fellowship with the unfruitful works of darkness" Here is stop sign number four in this chapter. *"Have no fellowship with the unfruitful works of darkness."* This is a present tense prohibition in the Greek structure which says to stop an action already in progress. These Ephesian Christians were having close fellowship with the *"unfruitful works of darkness."* This was an action already in progress. God says "Stop it!" God does not want us to have *"fellowship with the unfruitful works of darkness."*

Someone asked me a question the other night about 1 John 2:15-17. The question was, *"To what extent are we not to love the world?"* Obviously, we are in the world that God created. But this refers to the wicked world of sinners. We are to be separated from the things of the world that are evil. We are to separate from *"the lust of the eyes, the lust of the flesh, and the pride of life"* because these are all a part of this world system (1 John 2:16).

"but rather reprove them" This also tells us an action that we are to do. This is in the present tense which shows a continuous action. The Greek word for *"reprove"* is ELEGCHO. It means *"to convict, by conviction to bring to the light, to expose, generally with a suggestion of shame of the person convicted."* We are to *"reprove the unfruitful works of darkness"* by bringing them to light.

When we lived in Texas and Florida, we had a lot of dealings with cockroaches. Whenever you turned the lights on, those critters would scurry away and hide so that you did not even know that they were there. That is what we have to do with the *"unfruitful works of darkness."* We need to shine the light on them so that they will be *"reproved,"* rebuked, and exposed for what they are.

We need to name them. We ought to reprove the evil works of darkness. We need to reprove people whose lives are out of kilter with the Lord. We need to reprove the churches and groups that are wrong and walking in the wrong path by fellowshipping with the unfruitful works of darkness. We are to oppose them and expose them.

Ephesians 5:12

"For it is a shame even to speak of those things which are done of them in secret" God said that we should not even *"speak"* about the wicked things that are done *"in secret."* We talk about this sin or that sin, but we do not have to speak about the details because *"it is a shame."* The wicked people who are living for the world, the flesh, and the Devil are doing shameful things. God does not want us to continuously speak about the things that they do in secret.

If you talk about the wicked details of sin, some Christian people may think that it sounds pretty good, and they might be tempted to go out and do that thing. This is just what happens when bomb-making manuals are printed and published on the Internet. Evil people get curious and experiment and end up in the news headlines. When you continuously talk about the secret vile deeds of evil people, others will learn about these sins and perhaps will start copying those evil things.

Ephesians 5:13

"But all things that are reproved are made manifest by the light: for whatsoever doth make manifest is light" This is almost a definition of the word *"reprove."* To *"reprove"* is to bring things right out in the open or make them visible. That is what that word *"manifest,"* PHANEROO, means. It means *"to make manifest or visible or known that which has been hidden or unknown, to make manifest, whether by words or deeds, or in any other way."*

When you *"reprove"* evil things, you bring them out into the light. Remember that *"men loved darkness rather than light because their deeds were evil"* (John 3:19). Those that do evil deeds do not like to come into the light because the light will reveal their deeds. That is why fornication and adultery often are done at night.

- **Proverbs 7:8-10**
  Passing through the street near her corner; and he went the way to her house, **In the twilight, in the evening, in the black and dark night**: And, behold, there met him a woman with the attire of **an harlot**, and subtil of heart.

That is why thievery is often done at night. That is why gambling and the wicked things of the world are done at night. They think that the darkness will hide them. In Atlantic City, New Jersey, and other places, they don't even wait until the darkness to do their gambling. They do it all day and all night as well.

What they do not realize is that there is no darkness with God. He can see through the whole patch of lies and wickedness. He can see everything. There is no way we can flee from the Lord. *"Whither can I go from thy presence?"* (Psalm 139:7) There is no way that you and I can escape the all-seeing, all-knowing, all-powerful eye of God. There is no way the sinner can escape from God either. The wicked do not seem to know this. They think they can just turn off the lights and everything will be fine and their sin will be hidden.

It might be fine with the world, but it is not fine with the Lord. What makes things *"manifest is light."* If our deeds, our words, our thoughts, or our actions cannot stand the *"light"* of day, then we ought to change our deeds, our words, our thoughts, and our actions. If we are saved, we will one day stand at the judgement seat of Christ where all things are going to be revealed before the Lord. We have to be sure that our lives are in line.

- **John 16:8**
  And when he is come, **he will reprove the world of sin, and of righteousness, and of judgment**:
- **2 Timothy 4:2**
  Preach the word; be instant in season, out of season; **reprove, rebuke, exhort** with all longsuffering and doctrine.

If we are not *"preaching the Word,"* we would not touch most of these subjects. There are many preachers who do not talk about these things, but we believe that when the Bible talks about it we should, too. We must preach about these things. This is God's Word.

This is His love letter to us. But within His love letter, there are warnings of danger for us, too. When the Sunshine Bridge in St. Petersburg suddenly collapsed, it sent many unsuspecting cars into the water where the passengers perished. All of this happened because they did not know that the bridge was out. They had no warning. God gives us warnings in His Word. We must heed these warnings or suffer the consequences.

Ephesians 5:14

"Wherefore he saith, Awake thou that sleepest, and arise from the dead, and Christ shall give thee light"

"Wherefore he saith, Awake thou that sleepest" Here is a call to action. I am sorry to say that many Christians are asleep. I do not mean physically, but spiritually. Speaking of sleeping, one lady told me that she worships every Sunday morning at the shrine of "Saint Mattress." But this verse is speaking of people who are sleeping spiritually.

What do we do when we sleep? We have no conscious idea of what is going on. God wants us to be *"awake."* When I was taking chemotherapy for

Hodgkin's Disease (cancer of the lymph glands), I used to get sleepy when the drugs were being put into my arm. I used to try to do my work, but I finally just gave up and slept. I know what it is to be sleeping when you do not want to sleep. God says wake up to those who are sleeping. We are not to be sleeping. We are to be *"awake"* so that we can do the work of God.

"and arise from the dead, and Christ shall give thee light" This is spiritual death. We are to arise from spiritual death. These Ephesians had no real life. Paul says *"arise"* from your death. Be saved and then live for the Lord Jesus Christ. Christ is our *"light"* and our life, and He is the one who can give us purpose in what we do.

- John 8:12
  Then spake Jesus again unto them, saying, **I am the light of the world**: he that followeth me shall not walk in darkness, but shall have the light of life.

I do not think that too many people want to be *"dead."* Some people seem to get a strange "high" from taking so much heroine that they are almost dead. They say that is the best high. Sometimes they accidentally kill themselves by doing this. Suicide is also on the rise. I was told one day about a man who wanted to jump off a building because his business collapsed. His wife told me that he thought seriously about jumping off of the high rise building where he lived because his business failed. Some do want to die, but we are to rise from the dead spiritually, and Christ will give us life.

Ephesians 5:15

"See then that ye walk circumspectly, not as fools, but as wise" Paul says we are to *"walk circumspectly."* That is a good word. That is exactly the translation of this Greek word PERIPATEO. PERI has the idea of *"around,"* and PATEO has the idea of *"walk."* Thus, it means *"to walk around."* The English word *"circumspect"* comes from the Latin word, *"circum,"* which means "around," and *"spect,"* which means "to see." Thus, it means *"to see all around."* Incidently, other translations take the word PERIPATEO and translate it *"live."* We are to *"walk around"* like a periscope. A periscope comes from PERI, *"around,"* and SCOPEO, *"to see."* You can see in all three-hundred and sixty degrees of the compass with a periscope. By using a periscope you can see if there is a destroyer coming after you to kill you. That is how God wants us to walk.

When we look behind us we can see what is there. Psalm 23:6 says: *"Surely goodness and mercy shall **follow** me all the days of my life."* That is what is behind us. When we look ahead of us, we are to take *"the shield of faith... and the sword of the spirit"* (Ephesians 6:16-17). All of our weapons are offensive for the enemies who are in front of us.

When we walk, we are to walk looking in all directions. God wants us not only to look ahead but also to look and walk *"circumspectly."* People who threaten to kill you say, "Watch your back." *"Wherefore let him that thinketh he standeth take heed lest he fall"* (1 Corinthians 10:12). That is why we have to *"walk circumspectly."* God says *"walk looking in all different directions."*

If the Devil cannot trip you up in a straight attack, he will trip you up from the rear, the right, or the left. If you are only looking for opposition from the front, you are in trouble. Be assured of this. The world, the flesh, and the Devil will trip you up one way or another. These opposing forces are sneaky. The world is sneaky. Your own flesh is sneaky. The Devil is sneaky. Walk circumspectly. Get your periscope out and look all the way around the horizon. Do not walk as *"fools"* but as *"wise."*

Ephesians 5:16

"Redeeming the time, because the days are evil"

"Redeeming the time" "Redeeming" is from the verb, EXAGO-RAZO. It means *"to buy up, to buy up for one's self, for one's use."* Redemption is a purchase. When the Lord Jesus redeemed us with His precious blood, He made a down payment on His purchase of our souls. We do not use the word *"redeemed"* too much. If you go into a pawn shop and sell something for some instant cash, you can get the item back by redeeming it. You have to go back into that pawn shop and buy that item back for a price.

To *"redeem the time"* means *"to make sacred use of every opportunity for doing good."* It is as if our zeal for doing well is the purchase money by which we buy back the time and make it our own. To buy back the time is to *"redeem"* it. It is to make good use of that time.

How many hours in one day do you have in your life? You have twenty-four hours in that day which is the same amount of time as I have. How many hours in one day does the Devil have? He has twenty-four hours. The world also has twenty-four hours a day. What are we doing with our time? Some people fritter away their time. They don't seem to care. God says that saved people are to *"redeem"* the time. He says to take every opportunity and make it count for eternity.

I am trying in the last few years of my life to *"redeem the time"* by preaching the Word of God here in our Bible For Today Baptist Church. I am trying to make good use of that time. I am trying to study and to learn all I can for the Lord. I do not know how many years I have left. In 1985, I seemed doomed to death. I had Hodgkin's Disease which is cancer of the lymph glands. The Lord has spared my life so far. From that day to this, I have been trying to buy up the opportunities. You never realize the beauty of life and the value of life until you are looking death right in the eyes. That is what was before me.

God interceded. He made a difference. He raised me up from that deadly disease. I appreciate that, praise God for that, and I want to live the remainder of my life, as before, to please the Lord Jesus Christ, *"redeeming the time."*

"because the days are evil" All of us are living on "borrowed" time. We could die right now for any reason, so we are to make good use of our time. Why? *"Because the days are evil."* These days could not be much more evil than they were in the days of Lot in Sodom and Gomorrah or in the days of Noah when the flood came. These days are as evil as we could possibly think. Much on television is evil. Much on the Internet is evil. Much on radio is evil. Many books are filthy today. One of our friends told us that it is difficult in his work situation. He is in with evil people. He works as a waiter and, it is tough for him because of the sin all around him.

Ephesians 5:17

"Wherefore be ye not unwise, but understanding what the will of the Lord *is*"

"Wherefore be ye not unwise" Here is stop sign number five in this chapter. This is a negative prohibition in the present tense which tells us to stop an action already in progress. Stop being *"unwise!"* The Christians at Ephesus were being *"unwise."* Paul said "Stop it!" Somebody who is not wise is a fool. They are senseless and foolish. They are stupid, *"without reflection or intelligence. They are acting rashly."* That is what the Greek word for *"unwise"* means. It is APHRON.

"but understanding what the will of the Lord *is*" On the contrary, these Ephesian Christians are not only to avoid being *"unwise,"* but they are also to be *"understanding."* They are to be continuously *"understanding what the will of the Lord is."* Some of us have great *"understanding"* about the things of the secular world. Some people understand the things of time and space, but do not know very much about *"what the will of the Lord is."* If we are saved, God wants us and expects us to know *"what the will of the Lord is."* We must not *"quench the Spirit"* (1 Thessalonians 5:19) by saying "no" to the will of God. My mother-in-law, Gertrude Grace Sanborn, always used to quote William Pettingill who said, *"Full knowledge of God's will is found in full knowledge of God's Word."* This is very true.

We have to read, study, and live the Word of God. We must use the right English Bible to do this (if we are English-speaking people). This is our King James Bible. I believe that every Christian should read his or her Bible through from Genesis to Revelation at least once each year, asking God to give understanding as to *"what the will of the Lord is."* This can be done at the rate of only 85 verses per day. We have to know *"what the will of the Lord is,"* and we have to *"redeem the time because the days are evil."* We trust that we will learn not to be fellowshipping with evil things and people, but we will "*reprove them*" and be awakened from our "*sleep*" so that we can serve the Lord and please Him in all that we do.

Ephesians 5:18

"And be not drunk with wine, wherein is excess; but be filled with the Spirit"

"And be not drunk with wine, wherein is excess" Here is another one of those stop signs. It is stop sign number six. This is the only stop sign in this passage. It is a present tense prohibition which means that the Ephesian Christians were to stop an action which is already taking place. This shows us what the Ephesian church was like. Many of them were possibly drunkards. They might have drunk too much wine and were intoxicated. Paul says for them to quit it. I know some people believe they can drink in moderation. Paul says to absolutely quit it.

To the contrary, they should be "*filled with the Spirit*" of God. Wine is an intoxicating drink and has an affect upon those who use it. It can control such people. It is the wine that is controlling people when they drink it. But God wants His people to be controlled by the Holy Spirit. There are a number of verses on wine in the Bible.

- **Proverbs 20:1**
  Wine *is* a mocker, strong drink *is* raging: and whosoever is deceived thereby is not wise.
- **Daniel 1:8**
  But **Daniel purposed in his heart that he would not defile himself** with the portion of the king's meat, nor **with the wine which he drank**: therefore he requested of the prince of the eunuchs that he might not defile himself.

The king's wine was probably loaded with alcohol. Wine in the Bible is always grape juice unless the context clearly indicates otherwise. Wine is usually just the fruit of the vine, but here it was no doubt strong, intoxicating wine.

- **Luke 1:15**
  For he shall be great in the sight of the Lord, **and shall drink neither wine nor strong drink**; and he shall be filled with the Holy Ghost, even from his mother's womb.

John the Baptist was a Nazarite and abstained from all wine.

- **Romans 14:21**
  It is good neither to eat flesh, **nor to drink wine**, nor *any thing* whereby thy brother stumbleth, or is offended, or is made weak.

That is God's rule.
- **1 Timothy 3:3**
  Not given to wine, no striker, not greedy of filthy lucre; but patient, not a brawler, not covetous;
- **1 Timothy 3:8**
  Likewise *must* the deacons *be* grave, not doubletongued, **not given to much wine**, not greedy of filthy lucre;
- **1 Timothy 5:23**
  Drink no longer water, **but use a little wine for thy stomach's sake** and thine often infirmities.

What does the apostle Paul mean? A little grape juice is not impure like water might be in areas where Timothy might have been ministering. If you have ever been to a foreign country, you know that the water is often impure. When we were in Liberia, we used boiled water because our bodies were not used to the bacteria that is in the Liberian water. The Africans did not get sick from drinking the water because their bodies were used to what was in the water. This was the case with Timothy in the city of Ephesus. It was not an excuse for Pastor Timothy to drink intoxicating wine.

- **Titus 1:7**
  For a bishop must be blameless, as the steward of God; not selfwilled, not soon angry, **not given to wine**, no striker, not given to filthy lucre;
- **Titus 2:3**
  The aged women likewise, that *they be* in behaviour as becometh holiness, not false accusers, **not given to much wine**, teachers of good things;
- **1 Peter 4:3**
  For the time past of *our* life may suffice us to have wrought the will of the Gentiles, when we walked in lasciviousness, lusts, **excess of wine**, revellings, banquetings, and abominable idolatries:

I was in the Naval Chaplain Corps on active duty from 1956 through 1961. When I served with the Marines in Okinawa, I was the only chaplain in the Third Marine Division, Third Marine Regiment, Third Marine Battalion who abstained totally from all alcoholic beverages. My regimental chaplain who was a graduate of Wheaton College said, *"Chaplain Waite, do you know you are the only one in the regiment who doesn't drink?"* I told him that I represented, at the time, the General Association of Regular Baptist Churches (GARBC), and it had in their Church covenants, at that time at least, that every local church member affiliated with them was to *"abstain from intoxicating drink as a beverage."* That was what our standard was. I said, *"Sir, I represent sixteen hundred churches where none of them drink. Am I as a chaplain going to violate what our churches stand for?"* In addition to this, I have a personal conviction against drinking any *"intoxicating drink as a beverage"* and would not do this no matter what other churches or people might do.

I am sorry to say that has changed. We have GARBC churches and pastors that do not have that standard any more of no drinking and abstaining from alcohol as a beverage. The Regular Baptist Press in Illinois has changed the word of the totally *"abstaining from intoxicating drink as a beverage"* from their covenants that they now sell. That specific wording is now completely left out. It does not specify that anymore (at least when I read it a few years ago).

The Greek word, NEPHALEOS, is from NEPHO. It means to *"totally abstain from alcohol in any form."* There are seven verses which use that Greek word in reference to various people in the local churches.

- **1 Thessalonians 5:6**
Therefore let us not sleep, as *do* others; but let us watch and **be sober**.

That word for be *"sober"* is NEPHALEOS. That is for every believer. That is not just for pastors or deacons.

- **1 Thessalonians 5:8**
But let us, who are of the day, **be sober**, putting on the breastplate of faith and love; and for an helmet, the hope of salvation.

- **1 Timothy 3:2**
A bishop then must be blameless, the husband of one wife, **vigilant**, sober, of good behaviour, given to hospitality, apt to teach;

The word *"vigilant"* is NEPHALEOS which again means to abstain from all alcoholic beverages.

- **1 Timothy 3:11**
Even so *must their* wives *be* grave, not slanderers, **sober**, faithful in all things.

- **2 Timothy 4:5**
But **watch** thou in all things, endure afflictions, do the work of an evangelist, make full proof of thy ministry.

The word, *"watch,"* is NEPHALEOS.

- **Titus 2:2**
That the aged men **be sober**, grave, temperate, sound in faith, in charity, in patience.

- **1 Peter 1:13**
Wherefore gird up the loins of your mind, **be sober**, and hope to the end for the grace that is to be brought unto you at the revelation of Jesus Christ;

These words in the Bible make abstaining from alcohol a duty of every born-again Christian. I am sorry to say that when I gave these seven verses to one Bible-believing pastor in this country, he did not receive them very well. He became angry because he takes some wine with his meals. His wife also takes wine with her meals. He says he has some stomach trouble and that this is necessary. The Bible says it is NOT necessary.

The verses are clear. The words, NEPHALEOS and NEPHO, do not simply refer to the preacher, the deacons, or the Sunday school teacher. They apply to all believers. I was glad to find that nugget in the Greek language of the Scriptures. You can check out those words in any dictionary, and you will see that this meaning is there.

"but be filled with the Spirit" We are to be *"filled"* or to be controlled by the Holy Spirit. Remember, as mentioned several times before in this book, there are three things that we are to do so that we can be filled.

Three Requirements For The Spirit's Filling

1. We must not *"quench"* the Spirit by saying no to the will of God. (1 Thessalonians 5:19)
2. We must not *"grieve"* the Spirit by having known unconfessed sin in our life. (Ephesians 4:30)
3. We must *"walk in the Spirit"* with a moment by moment dependence on the Holy Spirit. (Galatians 5:16)

I want you to notice that *"be filled"* is in the present tense. It means that we are to be continually filled. It is also in the passive voice. There is an active voice and a passive voice in the Greek language. We would literally translate that *"be being filled continuously"* because it is passive. We do not fill ourselves with the Spirit of God. It is God Who has to do it. We have to be filled by Him.

Ephesians 5:19

"Speaking to yourselves in psalms and hymns and spiritual songs, singing and making melody in your heart to the Lord" Did you know that God has some standards regarding music? All of this modern cacophony of the so-called Christian rock and contemporary Christian music (CCM) are not within God's standards. God has standards.

God says that we are to *"speak"* to ourselves in *"psalms."* That is striking the chords of musical instruments in music such as *"hymns."* *"Spiritual songs"* are songs which are honoring to the Lord Jesus Christ and His Word. We are to *"sing and make melody in our hearts to the Lord."*

I do not think that cacophony is *"melody."* Cacophony is dissonance and bad sounds. It is not a *"melody."* I realize that by saying this I am going contrary to many churches in our land. The charismatics are for contemporary Christian music. Even many of our fundamental Baptist churches have gone contemporary. It is a terrible thing.

Several friends of ours out in the West Coast are searching for a fine fundamental Bible believing church which uses the King James Bible. They want separated and fundamental preaching, and they also are looking for good music. If the music is not right, then it is not meeting the spiritual needs of the heart.

Our church pianist here is a master-musician. I am sure he is quite able to play all rock music. Although he is able to play it, he would not touch it with a ten-foot pole. That is not his style. He believes, as do I, in following the command of *"speaking to yourselves in psalms and hymns and spiritual songs, singing and making melody in your heart to the Lord."*

It is wonderful to hear our congregation sing as a group of people who love the Lord and want to be here. It is making *"melody in our hearts to the Lord."* That is why we always give you a chance to ask to sing your favorite hymns at church. The preacher is not the only one to pick and sing the hymns. The congregation should also be allowed to pick the hymns which are a blessing to their souls. God has standards for music.

Ephesians 5:20

"Giving thanks always for all things unto God and the Father in the name of our Lord Jesus Christ" Thankfulness is important in the Christian's life. That is one reason that I like so much the song that we sing every Sunday morning, "Thank You Jesus For All You've Done." Notice that the pattern in prayer for saved people is to speak unto the Father in the name of the Son. Throughout Scripture, that is God's standard. We do not talk to God the Holy Spirit. We do not pray to God the Son. We pray to God the Father through God the Son, the Lord Jesus Christ. We are to be thankful Christians in all things.

Ephesians 5:21

"Submitting yourselves one to another in the fear of God." There are a series of submissions in this context. We are going to take the wife's submission in this chapter. In the next chapter, we are going to see the children's submission. Then we will look at the servant's submission. This series has to do with our various human relationships.

There are some who teach "mutual submission" of husbands and wives in the family and in the home. They say this is so because verse twenty-one precedes verse twenty-two. They say that is why we have mutual submission in the home. In effect, they are saying that nobody is "in charge." Nobody is the "head" of the home. This is not Scriptural. But that is being taught in many fundamental churches all over the country.

God's order is wives are to submit to their husbands. The husbands are to love their wives. There is also an order for the children. The Bible says, "*children obey your parents.*" It does not say "*parents obey your children*" although that is the practice many times. In some homes, whenever the child cries, the parent jumps up and asks the child, in effect, "*What wilt thou have me to do?*" Our homes are in serious trouble. There is also a proper order for the servants. A servant is supposed to be obedient to his own master although sometimes, in practice, we see the reverse of this.

The act of "*submitting yourselves*" is simply the opening statement to these three different relationships of Christians: (1) wives and husbands, (2) children and parents, and (3) servants and masters. If we are obedient Christians, we are to be in submission as it applies to us in whatever relationship we find ourselves.

That word for "*submission*" is HUPOTASSO. It means "*to submit to one's control, to obey, be subject, to arrange under, to subordinate.*" It was a Greek military term meaning "*to arrange troop divisions in a military fashion under the command of a leader.*" In non-military use, it was "*a voluntary attitude of giving in, cooperating, assuming responsibility, and carrying a burden.*"

Ephesians 5:22

"Wives, submit yourselves unto your own husbands, as unto the Lord"

"Wives, submit yourselves unto your own husbands"

Part of the meaning of the word "*submit*" is "*obey.*" That word, "*obey*" is often left out of the marriage ceremony. All of the old-time marriage ceremonies had the word, "*obey,*" in the vows. The old three words for the bride to assent to were that she was to "*love, honor,* and *obey*" her husband. But in many (if not most) marriage ceremonies today the word, "*obey,*" has disappeared from the wedding vows. We have a real problem on our hands because obedience is not in the vows. Young women, if you are unmarried and are unwilling to submit to the man whom you are going to marry, do not marry him. Just stop right now. Do not even bother marrying him until and unless you can be obedient to this command. It must be properly understood and practiced. It is a vital part of a Christian marriage.

Notice that it says *"submit yourselves unto your **own** husbands."* No wife has to submit to other men. It says *"your own husbands."* There is to be a submissive attitude. Surely in marriage you talk things over. What do you do if there is a decision that has to be made? It has to be made by someone. God has put the husband in charge of making the final decision in order, if necessary, to break a tie vote between the wife and the husband. The husband breaks the tie if there is a tie. This is just like the Vice-President who breaks any tie vote in the United States Senate.

I do not know whether or not you are familiar with nautical terms. In every submarine there is what is called a *"conning tower."* It has been defined as *"a low observation tower on a submarine, serving also as an entrance to the interior."* The officer in charge of the vessel stays in the conning tower where he directs the movements of that sub. He is in control of that ship. He has the *"conn"* or command of that ship.

The marriage needs someone in the conning tower, too. To have a marriage without anyone in charge is to have confusion. Someone has illustrated what confusion really is. Picture a log floating down a river heading for a steep and dangerous waterfall. Then also picture on this log a million ants riding on that log. Finally, picture that every one of those million ants thinks he has the "conn." That is indeed confusion. In marriage, if both think they are in charge, then no one is in charge. A marriage has to have a leader. The Bible has given that leadership to the husband. God holds him responsible for the things that go on in that marriage. He is the head of that home.

"as unto the Lord" That implies that Christian wives are to have the same attitude of submission as they should *"unto the Lord"* Jesus Christ. That is another problem we have in our churches. We have Christian women who are unwilling to submit to their Saviour. They want to do their own will and go their own way. This is God's Word, *"wives submit yourselves unto your own husbands as unto the Lord.:* This is God's plan.

Ephesians 5:23

"For the husband is the head of the wife, even as Christ is the head of the church: and he is the saviour of the body"

"For the husband is the head of the wife, even as Christ is the head of the church" God calls the husband *"the head of the wife."* This is God's plan and His order. This is not my plan, my order, or the order of any other human being. Go back to the garden of Eden. Go back to the days when God made man. He made Adam from the dust of the ground.

- **Genesis 2:7**
  And the LORD **God formed man of the dust of the ground,** and breathed into his nostrils the breath of life; and man became a living soul.

After Adam looked over all the beasts created by God and named them, he noticed that there was not a *"help"* that was *"meet"* or suitable for him (Genesis 2:20). There was no suitable mate for Adam of all the animals. Therefore, God caused Adam to go into a deep sleep and from his rib God made Eve (Genesis 2:21). God brought her unto the man, and they became one flesh (Genesis 2:24). God performed the first marriage there in the garden of Eden. That woman was taken from Adam's rib. Preachers have often pointed out that woman was not taken from the foot of man to rule over her and knock her down but was taken from his side so that he could love, hold, and cherish her by his side.

The husband is *"the head of the wife"* as claimed by God. It was not an easy responsibility being the head of a race. It was Eve who got the whole race into trouble, but it was Adam that followed her stupid and foolish lead. Adam got the whole race into trouble, also. Even though Eve was the leader in the fall, God blamed Adam because Adam was the *"head"* of Eve. Adam should have never followed, but should have instructed his wife. *"By one man sin,"* Adam's, *"entered into the world, and death by sin"* (Romans 5:12). It is not always a life of happiness and joy being the head of a home. Adam found that out. God holds the husband, or the man in charge, responsible for that home. It is very serious indeed.

"and he is the saviour of the body" The *"saviour of the body"* speaks of man's role as a protector. He is also the bread-winner. He is the one who takes care of the affairs of the home. I think that this is the sense in which the husband is to be the "saviour of the body." He is to be the deliverer of that family. If the family goes broke, many times it is the husband's responsibility. I know there are some husbands who think that the wife should do all the work for them, and they should just sit around and relax. That is not God's order. In fact, God told Adam, *"In the sweat of thy face shalt thou eat bread, till thou return unto the ground, for out of it wast thou taken"* (Genesis 3:19).

Ephesians 5:24

"Therefore as the church is subject unto Christ, so *let* the wives *be* to their own husbands in every thing" This is where this matter breaks down. How does the church today act? Wives may say *"I'm going to look at the believers in the church. Are these saved people subject unto the Lord Jesus Christ or are they not?"* When wives look around at people who call themselves Christians, they see them committing all types of sin, all gradations of wickedness and corruption. The wives say, "*Oh, I just have to be in subjection to my husband as the church is in subjection to Christ. I can see that many of the women in our church are not too much in subjection to the Lord Jesus Christ, so I don't have to be too much in subjection to my husband either.*" Do you see the reasoning? This is God's analogy. "*As the church is subject unto Christ,*" "*so should the wives be to their own husbands in everything.*"

Notice again, it says their "*own*" husbands. This is a voluntary attitude. We have a women's liberation revolt on our hands, do we not? The women's liberation movement cannot stand this teaching of Paul that the wife is to be subject unto her husband. They just cannot stand it. In fact, when the Southern Baptist Convention came out with a proclamation saying that wives in Christian homes should be in subjection to their own husbands, the news media from around our country tore them apart in scathing denunciation. "*How dare those terrible Southern Baptists say that!*" Those Baptist leaders were just quoting the Scripture in what was a rather mild statement. We are in a battle today, but our children should know what the standards are in God's Book. Our children and our children's children should know this so that they will be brought up in the "*nurture and admonition of the Lord.*"

Ephesians 5:25

"Husbands, love your wives, even as Christ also loved the church, and gave himself for it" I believe that this command to the husbands is really more important than the command to the wives. Both are important, but I believe this one is more important. That is why I entitled this message "*Husbands Love Your Wives.*" In this command there is no looking around as to how the others in the church are loving their wives. This standard for husbands is set, and it is permanent. This standard for the husband is serious. The husband is to love his wife as Christ loved the church. There is no wiggle-room for husbands. There is no possibility that we can explain this command away and minimize it.

It says the husbands are to "*love their wives, even as Christ also loved the church, and gave Himself for it.* That is the standard for husbands to love their wives. They are to love their own wives, not somebody else's wife. Today we have all kinds of fornication, unfaithfulness, and adultery. God says that this "marital love" is limited to the husband's own wife, and no other woman. That is in the present tense which means that there is to be a continuing action of love flowing to the husband's wife. What if the wife is ugly? Love her anyway. What if she is mean? Love her anyway. What if she is sassy? Love her anyway. What if she hits you? Love her anyway. What if she spends too much money? Love her anyway. What if she wrecks the family car? Love her anyway. If you are her husband, you married her *"for better or for worse."* Love her anyway and *"until death you do part."* There is no wiggle-room in this love.

I believe it is more difficult being a husband than being a wife in this situation. All a wife has to do is relax, take it easy, and let her husband run things. But the husband has to continuously love his wife with the same standard of love that the Lord Jesus Christ has as He loves the church. What kind of love was that? *"Christ also loved the church and gave Himself for it."* That word for *"gave"* is PARADIDOMI. It means *"to deliver up one to custody, to be judged, condemned, punished, scourged, tormented, put to death."* That is what the Lord Jesus did for the sins of the entire world, including the sins of believers. That is the measure, and that is the standard given in the Bible as the measure by which Christian husbands must love their wives. That standard will never change. It is an infinite standard which can never be fully met by any husband who ever lived.

Men, you must love your wives to such an extent that you would be gladly willing to die for them, in their place, if necessary. If you are not willing to die for your wife, you are not loving your wife *"as Christ loved the church and gave Himself for it."* That is a tremendous standard, men. Since our marriage in August of 1948, Mrs. Waite and I have stayed together as husband and wife. At present, both of us have been asked to go to Hammonton, New Jersey from time to time. My wife is talking to the ladies about "husband-loving," and I am talking to the men about "wife-loving." Those younger people are learning some things from the old-timers who have been through the mill. Mrs. Waite and I know what it is to live together happily and sometimes unhappily as married people for over a half century. We are trying to help others to profit from the things the Lord has taught us during this time.

Ephesians 5:26

"That he might sanctify and cleanse it with the washing of water by the word"

"That he might sanctify and cleanse it" This is the purpose for Christ's death. This is why the Lord Jesus Christ died for the believers. He separated the Church of believers unto Himself so that He might *"sanctify and cleanse it."* He wants us clean. He does not want dirty Christians. He does not want filthy Christians. He does not want Christians with bad spiritual breath. He wants Christians with clean hands and pure hearts. That comes by properly confessing and forsaking our sins. *"If we confess our sins, He is faithful and just to forgive us our sins, and to cleanse us from all unrighteousness"* (1 John 1:9).

Ephesians 5:26-27   **161**

"with the washing of water by the word" That cleansing is by the *"washing of water by the Word."* The Word of God cleanses. That is the water of life. That is what the woman at the well needed. She was seeking for the physical water of this life (John 4:7). When we were in Israel in the 1980's, my wife and I visited what was labeled as "Jacob's well." It is a ninety- foot well with only twenty feet of water. When the guide dropped a coin down that well, it took quite a while before it hit the water and we heard the "plunk." That woman was out at that big well, and the Lord Jesus asked her if she wanted some water. He said that He would give her some water. The woman said that the Lord could not give her water because the well was deep and He did not have anything to draw the water with (John 4:11). Jesus was talking about the water of "everlasting life" that comes by faith in the Lord Jesus Christ. That is what the woman went away with, not simply the water of this life. This is what the Lord said.

- **John 4:14**
  But whosoever drinketh of the water that I shall give him shall never thirst; but the water that I shall give him **shall be in him a well of water springing up into everlasting life.**

She went away and brought the men of the city back telling them that she had found the Messiah. She told them: *"Come, see a man, which told me all things that ever I did: is not this the Christ?"* (John 4:29)

The word used here in Ephesians 5:26 for *"word"* is not LOGOS, which is commonly used. It is RHEMA, which is the spoken word. That is why God wants preachers to preach the word. In preaching, it is the spoken word that flows out of the mouth. As it is preached sound and straight from the right Bible (in English, being the King James Bible), we can experience the *"washing"* of the Scriptures.

Ephesians 5:27

"That he might present it to himself a glorious church, not having spot, or wrinkle, or any such thing; but that it should be holy and without blemish" The Lord Jesus wants the church to be presented to Himself. We are considered to be the bride, and Jesus is considered to be the bridegroom. In Heaven the saved ones are going to be presented as a glorious church. He wants us to be glorious on earth. He wants us not to have any *"spot, or wrinkle, or any such thing."* The church should be *"holy and without blemish."*

We have so many Christians today in the church that have *"spots and wrinkles"* all over them. I just do not mean in their foreheads. I mean spiritual wrinkles and spiritual spots. How do you get off a spot? You can wash it with soap and water. Sometimes you need spot remover. If you can get the spots out, that is what you try to do. God wants us to get our spots out.

That word for *"present"* is PARISTEMI means *"to place beside or near, to be present."* One day the saved ones are going to be with the Lord. He wants to *"present"* to Himself believers without any *"spot or wrinkle."* How do you get wrinkles out? That is a little tougher than getting spots out. Our new American flag is flying outside for the first time. It has some wrinkles in it because we just got it out of the box this morning. Some wrinkles are more difficult to get out than others. You have to get out the iron and iron them. That does the job. God intends for our spiritual wrinkles to get out as well as our spiritual spots. He will have us a glorious church when we are presented unto Him. He will have us to be holy and without spot, blemish, or wrinkles. He wants us to be that way. We should try to be that way here on this earth as well.

- 1 John 1:9
 If we confess our sins, he is faithful and just to forgive us *our* sins, and **to cleanse us from all unrighteousness**.

He wants to cleanse us if we are saved. John was writing to believers who were urged to *"confess"* their sins. *"Confess"* is from the Greek word, HOMOLOGEO. HOMO means the *"same,"* and LOGEO means *"to say."* So it means *"to say the same thing as another, i.e. to agree with, to assent."* It means to say the same thing about our sins that God says about it. God nails it down. Confession means *"to agree"* with God that what we have thought, said, or done is sin.

If we *"agree"* with God, He has promised to be *"faithful and just to forgive us our sins and to cleanse us from all unrighteousness."* He is *"faithful"* because every time we confess, He forgives. He is *"just"* because the Lord Jesus paid the penalty on the cross of Calvary for those sins. He also *"cleanses us from all unrighteousness."* There is not a single bit of unrighteousness that God cannot cleanse. There is not a single bit of unrighteousness that this old flesh wants to wallow in that God cannot cleanse. He is in the business of cleaning believers because we get so dirty as we walk along the way in this wicked world.

Ephesians 5:28

"So ought men to love their wives as their own bodies. He that loveth his wife loveth himself" The standard is that believing husbands are to *"love their wives"* as they love *"their own bodies."* Men, I do not think you or I have ever purposely harmed our body. Some men have abused their bodies by using alcohol, smoking, using drugs, or even having unhealthy eating habits (hopefully, if at all, before they were saved).

Normally, we want to help our body. If we are hungry, we feed our body. If we are thirsty, we drink so that our body is satisfied. If we are cold, we put on some warm clothes. If we are warm, we turn on the air conditioning. There is no man in his right mind who wants to hurt his own body. Then why would we want to hurt our wives? She is a part of us. God has made the two to become *"one flesh"* (Genesis 2:24; Matthew 19:5-6; Ephesians 5:31). This *"one flesh"* is not only in the sexual relationship (which it is), but also in every other sense both spiritual and physical. Our wives are part of us, and we ought to love them as we love our own bodies.

Ephesians 5:29

"For no man ever yet hated his own flesh; but nourisheth and cherisheth it, even as the Lord the church" If you do not believe that you nourish your own flesh, just look at yourselves, men. In this crowd, it looks to me like you are all pretty well nourished. If you are going to care for your wife, you must see that she is *"nourished"* also, physically, spiritually, and in every other way. The Lord Jesus Christ nourishes us spiritually. He wants us to *"grow in grace, and in the knowledge of our Lord and Saviour Jesus Christ"* (2 Peter 3:18). That word used for *"nourish"* is EKTREPHO. It means *"to nourish up to maturity."* The Lord Jesus wants His children to be brought up into maturity. That word for *"cherish"* is THALPO. It means *"to warm, to keep warm."* The husband is to keep the wife warm spiritually as well as physically. It says in Scripture that she is the weaker vessel (1 Peter 3:7). The wife is the weaker vessel, not that she is weaker in the brain, but she is weaker in physique and structure. We are to realize that we husbands are to *"nourish and cherish"* our wives even as the Lord does the church.

Ephesians 5:30

"For we are members of his body, of his flesh, and of his bones" This Greek verb for *"are"* is a present tense verb which means that this is a continuous action. If we are saved, we are continuously members of His body. There is no loss of our salvation. He will never disassociate Himself from us. We are members of His body, of His flesh, and of His bones. We are just as close to the Lord Jesus Christ as His own flesh and His own bones.

Ephesians 5:31

"For this cause shall a man leave his father and mother, and shall be joined unto his wife, and they two shall be one flesh" The Amish people in Lancaster County, Pennsylvania, believe that when a marriage takes place, the parents should put an addition on the house and move to that new addition, giving the main house to those newlyweds. They all live together. Our neighbors are the same way. They had to get special permission to put on an addition to their house. They put in a mother-in-law apartment. But the city of Collingswood, New Jersey, did not want two-family houses. I testified for them and said they were good neighbors and that I was sure they would take good care of their property. They have the older family and the younger family in one house. They received permission, but there had to be openings in the sections of the house so that it would be considered all one house.

To "*leave*" the father and the mother means usually leaving in geography, but it also means leaving in mind, in spirit, and in control. It means leaving the old ways of doing things. It is the leaving of the father and the mother. Some wives are too much connected to their mothers and want to be mother's children the rest of their lives. Some husbands are too much father's children and want to be with their fathers the rest of their lives. There is an undue influence that should not be. God wants us to be joined to our wives. We should not forsake our wives for any one else, whether another woman, or even our father or mother. We are not to disrespect our mothers and fathers or dishonor them. We are to leave them as far as our former relationships used to be. We are to be "*joined*" to our wives. The word is PROSKOLLAO which means "*to glue upon, glue to.*" You have no doubt all used some of this super glue which dries in a minute and is permanent. That is the way God intends for husbands and wives to be glued to their mate. The two should be one flesh and joined.

Ephesians 5:32

"This is a great mystery: but I speak concerning Christ and the church." This "*mystery*" between husbands and wives is a "sacred secret." Paul is writing this about wives being in subjection to their own husbands and husbands loving their own wives. There is eternal security with believers. There should be eternal security, so to speak, in our marriages. We should keep together until death parts us one from the other. Christ "*loved the church and gave Himself for it.*" This is a great picture for our families.

The modernists and liberals have taken away the Lord Jesus Christ both in His Person and in His Work. They question His deity, His bodily resurrection, His Virgin Birth, and all the Christological doctrines that we hold dear. They have also taken Christ from being King of Kings and Lord of Lords. Therefore, He is no longer an example in marriage. Therefore, the wives no longer can see that they are subject unto Christ. They say He is just a person whom we can disrespect and disobey. That is the world's picture of Jesus Christ, but not so with the Word of God. To those who are redeemed, the Lord Jesus Christ is still our Master, our Lord, our Saviour, and the One we are to obey and adhere to. That is the picture of a glorified, powerful, omniscient, omnipresent, omnipotent Christ who is the picture of our husband and wife relationship in our homes.

Ephesians 5:33

"Nevertheless let every one of you in particular so love his wife even as himself; and the wife see that she reverence *her* husband"

"Nevertheless let every one of you in particular" This sums up the entire passage of the husband and wife relationship. Notice that it says *"nevertheless let every one of you in particular."* He speaks to everyone individually. God seldom tells a group to do something. He speaks to individuals.

"so love his wife even as himself" Wives are sitting here and wondering what they are going to do because they have a husband that does not love them. Well, you just pray that he may be able to read that section in Ephesians and believe it and practice it sometime.

"and the wife *see* that she reverence *her* husband" There may be some husbands hearing this and thinking that they have a wife who does not "reverence" them. What do you do? You just pray that the Lord would make the wife understand the Scriptural position and put herself where God wants her to be.

The Scriptures are very clear about the relationship between the husband and the wife. Yet, there is a great slippage among human beings in attempting to apply these verses. I always say this. Talk it over. My wife knows that I am the head of the home. I know that she is my wife and that I love her. We discuss everything before a major decision of any kind is made. Sometimes, she has the better idea. I make the decision, but her idea sometimes prevails. I have still made the decision. When we talk things over and my way is the way to go, we go my way. She agrees that is the way to go, and the ship of marriage continues on its course.

God holds the man responsible. If the home falls apart, I believe God is going to punish the husband. Husbands have a tremendous responsibility. That is why many men these days do not want to be husbands. They just want to shack up with somebody. They do not want that responsibility. They shirk their responsibility. A lot of husbands want to get out of marriages. They cannot stand it. When making decisions in marriage, talk it over, and then the husband must break the tie if there is one to be broken. In all of this, the wife must be willing to take her Scriptural place with and to her husband.

Ephesians Chapter Six

Ephesians 6:1

"Children, obey your parents in the Lord: for this is right" The world does not believe this is the way to go. In homes all over the country, children are not *"obeying"* their parents. The *"parents,"* many times, are obeying their children. This is a sorry situation indeed! A little one who does not even know his left hand from his right hand is telling its parents what to do and how to do it. The child yells and screams, and the parent jumps to attention. It is a sad thing.

I was a teacher for nineteen years in the School District of Philadelphia. I have seen this very thing. The parents do not get obeyed so, of course, the children do not obey the teachers either. The children of our land are in need of learning to obey their parents.

- **Romans 1:30**
  Backbiters, haters of God, despiteful, proud, boasters, inventors of evil things, **disobedient to parents**,

These are the signs of the time in a wicked, heathen world.

- **Ephesians 2:2**
  Wherein in time past ye walked according to the course of this world, according to the prince of the power of the air, **the spirit that now worketh in the children of disobedience**:

- **Ephesians 5:6**
  Let no man deceive you with vain words: for because of these things cometh the wrath of God upon **the children of disobedience**.

- **2 Timothy 3:2**
  For men shall be lovers of their own selves, covetous, boasters, proud, blasphemers, **disobedient to parents**, unthankful, unholy,

This parental disobedience is a sign of the last times, and it looks like we have been in those times for quite a few years. God says *"children obey your parents."*

We have some *"children"* here in the audience. I am teaching you God's Word. This is not my idea. It is God's idea. If there is anything that the parents would tell you to do that is contrary to the Word of God, you are to obey God rather then man (Acts 5:29); but most parents won't do that. If your parents would tell you to kill someone, commit adultery, lie, or steal, it is not to be done or obeyed. The obedience is to be *"in the Lord."* It must be in line with the Word of God.

There are thousands of commands that parents give to their children that have nothing to do with Scripture. It is just Mom and Dad telling you what to do, and children are to "obey." We have five children. They are adults now. Through the years we have tried the best way we knew how to train them up in the way that they should go (Proverbs 22:6). They were obedient children. They are not born that way. You have to get them that way. They stray quickly.

This verb in this verse (*"obey"*) is in the present tense which means that there is to be a continuous obedience. You do not just *"obey"* one day a week, but all the time. If mom or dad say to mow the lawn, you mow the lawn. If mom or dad say to clean up your room, you clean up your room. That word for *"obey"* is HUPAKOUO. It is an interesting word. It is spoken *"of one who on the knock at the door comes to listen who it is."* That is the duty of a porter. As soon as that knock comes, he goes like lightning to the door and sees who it is. That is obedience. It also means *"to hearken to a command, to obey, submit to."* That is what children are to do.

God says *"this is right."* People wonder what is right and what is wrong. People are looking and wondering what is the right thing to do in this situation or that situation. Children: this is the "right" thing to do in all situations, *"obey your parents in the Lord."* Hearken to them. If you do not do what your parents say, you are sinning against the Word of God. You are disobedient against the Scriptures.

You might ask, "How long does this last?" I think that the children are to be obedient to their parents as long as the children are living under the parent's roof. When they leave the roof and are on their own and have their own families, that is different. It is my belief that as long as they are young children, living under your roof and eating at your table, eating your food, drinking your water, and enjoying the heat from your furnace, they should obey their parents continuously. If they are mature individuals, adults, living with their parents, they should *"honour"* their parents, though the relationship is changed somewhat. If they have jobs, I believe they should pay room and board to help their parents with the many extra financial obligations that are theirs due to their adult children living with them. There are families such as this that choose this lifestyle, though this is not as common as children leaving the home.

Ephesians 6:2

"Honour thy father and mother; (which is the first commandment with promise)" This is the first commandment with promise.

- **Exodus 20:12**
  Honour thy father and thy mother: that thy days may be long upon the land which the LORD thy God giveth thee.

The promise is that you may live long if you honor your parents. The Palestinian Covenant promised to Israel that they would stay in the land if they obeyed the Lord. This was a conditional covenant. It was one which was dependent upon obedience. This is a promise.

- **Deuteronomy 5:16**
  Honour thy father and thy mother, as the LORD thy God hath commanded thee; **that thy days may be prolonged, and that it may go well with thee**, in the land which the LORD thy God giveth thee.
- **Luke 18:20**
  Thou knowest the commandments, Do not commit adultery, Do not kill, Do not steal, Do not bear false witness, **Honour thy father and thy mother**.

To *"honour"* your parents is *"to esteem and to value"* them. Honor continues no matter how old you are, but I believe obedience only maintains itself as long as the children are under the roof. You still honor your mom and dad even after you move away. You are to honor and esteem your parents highly. We differ with Bill Gothard who has the opinion that obedience to your parents is for life. I am told that his father did not want him to marry, so for many years he did not marry. I was told on good authority from some who were close to the situation that when Bill Gothard's father was dying, he drew Bill Gothard to himself and told him not to marry for four more years. Perhaps he has married now, I don't know. Be that as it may, it is ironic that Bill Gothard has been a single bachelor who has been telling people for many years how to be married, yet he himself was not married. With his dying father's permission, will he now marry? It is ironic that he has been telling everyone how to raise children, when he has had no children.

We are to honor our parents for life, yes. But we are not to obey them for life, no. We have obedience only as long as the children are under the roof, but we honor them always. Remember that word *"honour"* means *"to esteem something of value or to place a value upon."* You must honor your mom and your dad. You must make sure you have treated them with proper respect throughout their lives, though your relationship as an adult is not the same as when you were a child "under their roof."

Ephesians 6:3

"That it may be well with thee, and thou mayest live long on the earth" God promised this long life to the Israelite people. I realize that this promise is to Israel and not fulfilled in the church; but this is a promise which is repeated and quoted. God said that honoring your mom and dad is one of the things which will show me that you will live long in the land. As you know, the Jews did not live too long in the land of Palestine. They had about twenty-one kings of the northern tribes and about twenty-one kings of the southern tribes. That was all.

After that, the northern ten tribes of Israel went into Assyrian captivity in about 700 B.C. Later, the southern two tribes went into the Babylonian captivity in about 600 B.C. The land of Palestine was not theirs any more because this was one of the commandments that they failed to keep. They did not "*honour*" their parents so the land was not theirs. Today, they have gone back to the land of Palestine but they are there in disobedience to the Lord and in unbelief in His only begotten Son, the Lord Jesus Christ. As we know, they are fighting and battling with the Palestinians and others who are opposed to them. One day the Lord Jesus Christ will reign and rule on this earth, and they will have peace in Palestine. It does not look like they are going to have peace now with all the chaos in that region.

Ephesians 6:4

"And, ye fathers, provoke not your children to wrath: but bring them up in the nurture and admonition of the Lord" Here again is one of our stop signs. It means "*stop provoking your children to wrath.*" This is a negative imperative prohibition in the present tense which means stop an action already in progress. This was what the situation was here. Apparently, the fathers were "*provoking their children to wrath.*" Paul says for them to stop it.

Let us take a look at the word, "*provoking.*" It is PARORGIZO which means "*to rouse to wrath, to provoke, exasperate, anger.*" The Lord is provoked many times by the sins of His people.

- **Deuteronomy 31:29**
  For I know that after my death ye will utterly corrupt *yourselves*, and turn aside from the way which I have commanded you; and evil will befall you in the latter days; **because ye will do evil in the sight of the LORD, to provoke him to anger through the work of your hands.**

Evil "*provokes*" the Lord to anger.

- **Deuteronomy 32:21**
  They have moved me to jealousy with *that which is* not God; **they have provoked me to anger with their vanities**: and I will move them to jealousy with *those which are* not a people; I will provoke them to anger with a foolish nation.
- **1 Kings 14:9**
  But **hast done evil** above all that were before thee: for thou hast gone and made thee other gods, and molten images, **to provoke me to anger**, and hast cast me behind thy back:
- **1 Kings 16:2**
  Forasmuch as I exalted thee out of the dust, and made thee prince over my people Israel; and thou hast walked in the way of Jeroboam, and hast made my people Israel to sin, **to provoke me to anger with their sins;**
- **1 Kings 16:33**
  And Ahab made a grove; and **Ahab did more to provoke the LORD God of Israel to anger** than all the kings of Israel that were before him.
- **2 Kings 17:11**
  And there they burnt incense in all the high places, as *did* the heathen whom the LORD carried away before them; and **wrought wicked things to provoke the LORD to anger:**
- **2 Kings 17:17**
  And they caused their sons and their daughters to pass through the fire, and used divination and enchantments, and sold themselves **to do evil in the sight of the LORD, to provoke him to anger.**
- **2 Kings 21:6**
  And he made his son pass through the fire, and observed times, and used enchantments, and dealt with familiar spirits and wizards: he **wrought much wickedness in the sight of the LORD, to provoke** *him* **to anger.**
- **Jeremiah 44:8**
  In that **ye provoke me unto wrath with the works of your hands**, burning incense unto other gods in the land of Egypt, whither ye be gone to dwell, that ye might cut yourselves off, and that ye might be a curse and a reproach among all the nations of the earth?

There are many more verses that speak of *"provoking to anger."*

What does it mean to *"provoke to anger"*? You must start early in disciplining your children. That is when they need it. When they get beyond a certain age, it is too late. When you spank your children, it is called applied psychology by using the *"board"* of education. I still have a little paddle that I used to use when needed. It is called "The Board of Education." It says *"Grip here firmly."* Then it says *"Apply the board of education to the seat of learning."* That is what you do and it works. It is a principle of the Bible to carefully and properly discipline your children. I believe there are at least two rules for this process: (1) Do it ONLY when they need it. (2) Do it ALWAYS when they need it.

This is Scriptural. In the days in which we live now, I realize that parents can be put in jail for doing this. It is a sad thing, but the Scriptures are clear. This is not going to hurt the seat. You must start early. This is what the Bible says.

- **Proverbs 29:15**
  The rod and reproof give wisdom: but **a child left *to himself* bringeth his mother to shame.**
- **Proverbs 13:24**
  He that spareth his rod hateth his son: but **he that loveth him chasteneth him betimes.**

"Chasten him betimes" is an Old English expression for *"early."* When you start "early," your children understand that you love them. They understand that when they do things wrong, they are spanked and are not provoked. If you wait too long when they are older, then all of the sudden you will see wrath.

What are you to do positively fathers and mothers? You are to *"bring them up in the nurture and admonition of the Lord."* There are two words here. *"Nurture"* is the discipline, which includes the spanking of the child. *"Admonition"* is the speaking and instructing the child as to what went wrong and how to correct it next time. When the children get older, you talk more and spank less. People say, *"Well, can you discipline a child when the child doesn't know why they are being disciplined?"* I say yes. The child seems to give you the excuse that he didn't know that a thing was wrong, regardless of the fact that you had told him about it many times. This is only an excuse. Do the disciplining first, and then do the explaining later. If you wait until you give the child a five hundred word explanation on what he did wrong and what you are doing, the child will get you so buffaloed that you will not be able to do anything. The Biblical order is *"nurture"* first and then *"admonition."* The order is right in this verse.

The Greek word for *"admonition"* is NOUTHESIA. It means literally *"to put something in the mind."* We have three older sons who are two years apart. My daughter was born three years later. Then our youngest son was born nine years after that. Those three boys really needed discipline. After I disciplined them, I always said, *"Daddy loves you and because I love you I have to do what?"* They would say with a tearful voice, *"Spank me."* They knew what was coming and why.

- **Proverbs 19:18**
 Chasten thy son while there is hope, and **let not thy soul spare for his crying.**

Sometimes before you even spank the children, they cry. Is that a preemptive strike? Is that so you will not spank them? Children are very smart and very wise when it comes to avoiding pain.

You do not wound them or harm them. The Lord has made the seat very strong and well-padded. That is the way to go. The Lord does not agree with hitting children which results in giving them permanent damage. Unfortunately, this is what the world is seeing and wrongly calls it "spanking." That is not what we are talking about. If a teacher sees these kinds of things, that teacher should report this. This is child abuse. It is a sad thing when you see this kind of thing. The Lord must give us great wisdom with our children.

Ephesians 6:5

"Servants, be obedient to them that are *your* masters according to the flesh, with fear and trembling, in singleness of your heart, as unto Christ"

"Servants, be obedient to them that are *your* masters according to the flesh, with fear and trembling" Paul now takes up a third area of submission. He is talking to *"servants."* They had slaves in the New Testament times. This is what this word, DOULOS, means. It means *"one who does the will of another."* These Christian servants are to act in a certain way to please the Lord Jesus Christ. They are to be obedient just like the children are to be obedient. It is the same word, HUPAKOUO. As I said before, it is used *"of one who on the knock at the door comes to listen who it is."*

How do you apply this today? If you are working for someone, you are a *"servant"* to that person. If they are paying your salary, you are to do as they want you to do *"as unto Christ."* If your *"masters"* are instructing you to do something that is wicked, wrong, or against the Bible, you do not "obey." You *"ought to obey God rather than men"* (Acts 5:29). But in all other things we are to obey our *"masters"* who are over us. It must be done also *"with fear and trembling,"* that is, taking this work very seriously rather than making a joke of it. It should be considered by you as serious business.

"in singleness of your heart, as unto Christ" We are to obey just as if it were the Lord Jesus Christ who was giving us the commands. We are to be obedient to those who are over us *"in singleness of your heart."* That word for *"singleness"* is HAPLOTES. It means *"singleness, simplicity, sincerity, mental honesty, not self seeking, openness of heart manifesting itself by generosity."* We are to treat our bosses just as if the Lord Jesus Christ were giving us our orders.

Put yourself in any work situation. If you are a teacher, you have to obey your principal. One of my principals in a high school that I taught at in center city Philadelphia believed in stand-up teaching. As a teacher you were not allowed to sit down while you were teaching. That is an unusual command, but you either obey that rule or you do not teach in that school. So, I got some good heavy shoes and I stood up while I taught. Wherever you work, there are certain rules. When the manager tells you to do something, you do it even if the master is unsaved. That is what God wants us to do. Whomever we are under, it is as if we were under the Lord Jesus Christ.

Ephesians 6:6

"Not with eyeservice, as menpleasers; but as the servants of Christ, doing the will of God from the heart"

"Not with eyeservice" Our obedience is not to be done with *"eyeservice."* That is a good word. It comes from OPHTHALMODOULEIA. It has *"ophthalmology"* in the first part of it and *"doulos"* or *"slave"* in the last part of it. It means *"service performed [only] under the master's eyes."* You are not supposed to do the service only when the boss is looking at you. You should do it all the time. The master's eye usually stimulates the servant's diligence. If you are a Christian, you understand this. When I was a student at Dallas Theological Seminary, I worked in a cotton gin manufacturing company. It was the John E. Mitchell company. This company had big steel punch presses. I operated a 150-ton punch press. My job was to take long steel pieces, put them gradually into the press as it came down to make about 15 finger-like extrusions in each piece. I had to do that all day for eight to ten hours. It was quite a boring job. Every once-in-a-while I could talk to the other machine operator who had a 300-ton punch press for heavier jobs next to me. I remember the superintendent would call my name when I would go over and talk to the other machine operator. I was not on my job. The job was as boring as anything, but my job was to stay on my machine. That is what he was paying me for. We are not to work only when the boss is looking. We are to work all the time.

"as menpleasers" That is *"working to please men."* When we are working for someone, we are to serve them as the best possible employee. If you are a waiter or a waitress, you have to do what you are told to do in the serving business. We are certainly not to do things that are wrong or wicked. If your boss would ask you to steal, or do something else contrary to the Bible, of course you would not do that.

"but as the servants of Christ, doing the will of God"
It is hard for us to put ourselves in that place. When we work for someone else,

we are being just like "*servants of Christ.*" When looking at our work in this way, a common, ordinary task is made great, spiritual, and heavenly. We are "*servants of Christ doing the will of God from the heart.*" The "*will of God*" is that "*servants, be obedient to them that are your masters.*" The "*will of God*" is that "*children, obey your parents.*" The "*will of God*" is that "*wives, submit yourselves to your own husbands.*" The "*will of God*" is that "*husbands, love your wives.*" These are some things that are the "*will of God.*"

"from the heart" You and I both know the difference between doing something "*from the heart*" and doing something from the head. Some things, but not all, you do "*from the heart.*" You do them because you want to do them. Nobody has forced you to come to the church service here today. It is "*from the heart.*" You want to be here. Nobody has forced me to be your Pastor and to preach and teach God's Words in our church. It is "*from the heart.*"

There are certain things that we do "*from the heart*" because we love the Lord Jesus Christ. Parents, there are certain things that you do "*from the heart*" for your children because you love them, even though often they do not appreciate what you do for them. Husbands and wives do certain things "*from the heart*" because they love their spouse. You do not do things for the people you love because they have a whip over you. You do things for them because you love them. Remember, you are serving the Lord Jesus Christ and doing "*the will of God.*" He will reward you for that service. Be patient and wait for His "*well done.*"

Ephesians 6:7

"With good will doing service, as to the Lord, and not to men" The Lord Jesus Christ is the Person to Whom we belong if we are believers. He is our Lord. He is our owner and has control of us. He bought us with His precious blood on Calvary's cross. That word for "*service*" is DOULEUO which means "*to be a slave, serve, do service.*" It is the physical slave-type of obedient service "*to the Lord.*" Now, the obedience to the Master is not a question of obeying an earthly master. It is obedience to the Lord Jesus Christ, our heavenly Master, and "*not to men.*" He will reward us for our "*service.*"

Ephesians 6:8

"Knowing that whatsoever good thing any man doeth, the same shall he receive of the Lord, whether *he be* bond or free" The Lord will reward us for faithful service. You might say that the man or the woman for whom you work does not seem to appreciate you. They do not give you raises. They do not say thank you. They are gruff. We all have our bosses. Whatever situation that we are in has to be unto the Lord. No matter what our lot, we must do our service *"as unto the Lord."* He will reward us at the judgment seat of Christ.

- **2 Corinthians 5:10**
  For we must all appear before the judgment seat of Christ; that every one may receive the things *done* in *his* body, according to that he hath done, whether *it be* good or bad.

Ephesians 6:9

"And, ye masters, do the same things unto them, forbearing threatening: knowing that your Master also is in heaven; neither is there respect of persons with him."

"And, ye masters, do the same things unto them, forbearing threatening" This refers to a master-servant relationship where the *"master"* is saved. Notice that it says *"your master also is in heaven."* Do *"masters"* who are saved have to follow Scriptural rules also? Yes, they do. Just because you are saved, it does not mean that you are free to treat your servants in a roughshod manner.

God has a certain way that you are to treat your servants. We are to be *"forbearing threatening."* That word, *"forbearing,"* means *"omitting it or stopping it."* You as a *"master"* must not *"threaten"* your servants. You do not say, *"If you don't do this I will fire you."* Some bosses do that, and they make you look very bad. You must give up the idea of *"threatening"* those who are under you, but you can certainly reprimand *"servants"* who are not doing what they are supposed to be doing.

The taskmasters in Egypt were *"threatening"* to the Israelites who were building for Pharaoh. The Israelites were told that they would no longer have straw to help them make their bricks (Exodus 5:7-8). Yet, they had to make the same amount of bricks. If they were supposed to make a thousand bricks in one day, they still had to make a thousand bricks even though they were not given the straw. They had to find their own straw. The taskmasters were *"threatening"* the Israelites.

"knowing that your Master also is in heaven" Saved masters have a *"Master also in heaven."* Is anybody working under your orders? If you are in a home, you perhaps have workers under you. There is always somebody under you just as you are always under somebody else. No matter who we are under or who we are over, there is One Who is over us and that is our *"Master in heaven."* It is not the "Honorable Master" of the Masons. It is not the man whom the Indians worship in the happy hunting grounds. It is our *"Master,"* the Lord Jesus Christ. He is our *"Master."* Several times in the New Testament He is called the *"Good Master"* (Matthew 19:16; Mark 10:17; and Luke 18:18). "Teacher" is another word for *"Master."* The Spanish word for "*teacher*" is "*maestro*" which is similar in sound to "*master.*"

What is the Lord Jesus doing in Heaven? He is praying. He is praying for those who are saved. He is praying that we not sin against Him. If we do sin, He is interceding that we may be put back together and shaped up (Romans 8:34; Hebrews 7:25). He is praying for lost sinners who are not saved.

He is in Heaven waiting to make his enemies his footstool (Mark 12:36). When the last soul is saved on this earth, the Lord will rapture His church (1 Thessalonians 4:16-17). Then the Great Tribulation will occur until He will return to establish His Millennial reign. The Lord Jesus is in Heaven waiting.

He is in Heaven waiting for us to receive us when we die. When a person was stoned, they were put in a pit so that they could not run away. Then the executioners threw these huge boulders on top of the person. The person would bleed and his bones would break bone by bone. When Stephen was being stoned to death in Acts, chapter seven, he looked up when he was about to die and saw the Lord Jesus standing at the right hand of the throne of God. Jesus was waiting for His martyr, Stephen. Jesus was waiting for His one who had served Him well.

Yes, the Lord Jesus, our Master in Heaven, is doing a number of things. He is interceding on our behalf. He is praying for us. He is also waiting for those of us who die and go home to be "with Christ which is far better" (Philippians 1:23). We do not know when that day is. Not a single person in this world knows. When our time comes, He will be there to receive us if we are believers.

"neither is there respect of persons with him" The Lord does not play favorites like the rest of us do many times. He has no partiality. Let me quote a reference which explains this phrase "*respecter of persons.*" It means:

"*The fault of one who when called on to give judgment has respect of the outward circumstance of man and not to their intrinsic merits, and so prefers, as the more worthy, one who is rich, high born, or powerful, to another who does not have these qualities.*"

That is a "*respecter of persons.*" God is not that way. When we meet Him in Heaven, there will be no excuses. He does not have any "*respect of persons.*" We are either saved or we are lost.

Ephesians 6:10

"Finally, my brethren, be strong in the Lord, and in the power of his might" We are to be "*strong in the power of His might.*" There are eleven passages on "*power*" to which I would like to refer as we look at this verse.

- **Zechariah 4:6**
  Then he answered and spake unto me, saying, This *is* the word of the LORD unto Zerubbabel, saying, **Not by might, nor by power, but by my spirit**, saith the LORD of hosts.

The spiritual "*power*" is the power that God is interested in.

- **Acts 1:8**
  But **ye shall receive power, after that the Holy Ghost is come upon you**: and ye shall be witnesses unto me both in Jerusalem, and in all Judea, and in Samaria, and unto the uttermost part of the earth.

The "*power*" of God, the Holy Spirit, came upon the disciples.

- **Romans 1:16**
  For I am not ashamed of **the gospel of Christ: for it is the power of God** unto salvation to every one that believeth; to the Jew first, and also to the Greek.

- **Romans 1:20**
  For the invisible things of him from the creation of the world are clearly seen, being understood by the things that are made, **even his eternal power and Godhead**; so that they are without excuse:

- **1 Corinthians 1:18**
  For **the preaching of the cross** is to them that perish foolishness; but unto us which are saved it **is the power of God**.

- **1 Corinthians 2:45**
  And my speech and my preaching *was* not with enticing words of man's wisdom, **but in demonstration of the Spirit and of power:**

That is where the "*power*" is. It is in the Scriptures, the Words of God.

- **2 Corinthians 4:7**
  But we have this treasure in earthen vessels, **that the excellency of the power may be of God, and not of us**.

We are clay pots. If there is any excellency or "*power*" at all in any of us, it is not because of us. It is because of God's power working through us.

- **2 Corinthians 12:9**
  And he said unto me, My grace is sufficient for thee: for my strength is made perfect in weakness. Most gladly **therefore will I rather glory in my infirmities, that the power of Christ may rest upon me**.

- **Ephesians 3:7**
  Whereof I was made a minister, according to the gift of the grace of God given unto me **by the effectual working of his power.**
- **Ephesians 3:20**
  Now unto him that is able to do exceeding abundantly above all that we ask or think, **according to the power that worketh in us,**
- **Colossians 1:11**
  Strengthened with all might, **according to his glorious power,** unto all patience and longsuffering with joyfulness;

There is nothing wrong with having a powerful physique. *"Bodily exercise profiteth little"* (1 Timothy 4:8). But we are to be *"strong in the Lord."* There are three words in this verse which are synonymous with strength. The first one is *"strong."* The second one is *"power."* The third one is *"might."* Have strength in the Lord. Do not forget that we have the great power of His force. The Lord wants us strong in Him and not in our own abilities or our own strength. We are strong in the power of God only. When we witness or when we preach for the Lord, we are to do it in His power and in His strength.

Ephesians 6:11

"Put on the whole armour of God, that ye may be able to stand against the wiles of the devil"

"Put on the whole armour of God" We are to put on every single piece of the *"armour of God."* We are to put the armor on like a garment.

This reminds me of the account of David trying on Saul's armor in 1 Samuel 17:38-40. He tried the armor on, but decided to wear his shepherd's clothes and fight Goliath with only a sling and five smooth stones. Here was King Saul who stood head and shoulders over any other man (1 Samuel 9:2). He was a powerful king of Israel. This giant, Goliath, was even taller than king Saul. He was about nine feet nine inches tall (1 Samuel 17:4).

This giant came out twice a day to defy Israel and challenge them to have a man come fight with him. He would say that if the Israelites would win the battle, then the Philistines would be Israel's servants. But if Goliath won, then the Israelites would be servants to the Philistines (1 Samuel 17:9). Goliath taunted and cursed David and Saul's God every morning and evening for forty days (1 Samuel 17:16). When David came to camp to bring some food to his brothers, he saw Goliath, this Philistine giant. David wondered who this man was, and he wondered who gave Goliath the power to defy the armies of the living God (1 Samuel 17:36). David said that he would fight Goliath (1 Samuel 17:32). David said that God delivered him out of the paw of the bear and the lion, and he would deliver him from the giant, too (1 Samuel 17:37).

Saul told David that he would give his armor to David. So David put on Saul's armor, but it was so heavy that David could hardly stand up. He took all of Saul's armor off, and then he took five smooth stones and his sling (1 Samuel 17:38-40). You might ask why did he take five stones. Did he think that he was going to miss? Goliath had four brothers, and you know how families are. When you kill one of them, the rest of them rise up against you. Some have speculated about that.

The other thing that David had was "faith." He believed in the delivering power of his God. When that giant came out and looked at that little young fellow, he made fun of him and then cursed David (1 Samuel 17:43). David put his stone in his sling and spun it around. The stone hit that giant right in the temple where the helmet was not protecting. Goliath fell to his feet. Then David took the giant's own sword and cut off that giant's head (1 Samuel 17:51). The power of David's armor was not the armor of this world. It was the armor of God and the faith and the practice and the assurance that God was with him.

- **Luke 11:21**
   When a strong man armed keepeth his palace, his goods are in peace:

The Devil is the one who is our enemy. He wants to take away our armor. It is not the physical armor. That is why the verse says to *"be strong in the Lord and in the power of His might."*

" that ye may be able to stand against the wiles of the devil" Why is it that we have to put on the *"armour of God"*? Why do we need to put on the armor of God, not the armor of man or the armor of flesh. Why? We put it on that we *"may be able to stand against the wiles of the devil."* The armor of an ancient soldier included *"the shield, the sword, the lance, the helmet, the greaves and the breast plate."* The purpose is to have the ability *"to stand against the wiles of the devil."*

We have people who do not know how *"to stand"* these days. The church leaders do not stand. They just waver and quake and waffle and every other word you might use to describe it. I do not know who they are trying to please? Certainly they are not trying to please the Lord. The Lord has given us something to stand for and to stand upon. We are not to move or to be carried about by every wind of doctrine. God says to put on all the armor of God and all that He provides for us.

The Devil is our enemy, and we are to stand against His wiles. The word for *"wiles"* is METHODEIA. It means *"cunning arts, deceit, craft, trickery."* The Devil is so clever that he can come up on the right side of us, on the left side of us, in front of us, or in back of us. He will trick us. He will even use

some Christians who will delude us into believing that he is right even when those things are wrong. Someone has summed up who Satan is as follows:
"Satan, the prince of the demons, the author of evil, persecuting good men, estranging mankind from God, and enticing them to sin, afflicting them with diseases by means of demons who take possession of their bodies at his bidding."

Ephesians 6:12
"For we wrestle not against flesh and blood, but against principalities, against powers, against the rulers of the darkness of this world, against spiritual wickedness in high *places*" We who are saved are *"wrestling"* demonic forces not only in people but also in Satan and his demons. It is not flesh and blood that we are wrestling . We are wrestling with the *"principalities"* and the *"powers,"* the evil angels, and demons. *"Spiritual wickedness in high places"* are the wicked people in high places. These are the ones who we are fighting against. That is why we must have the *"armour of God."* It is very important that we put on every single piece of armor with "prayer." We must put it on daily so that we may be able to have success in this battle.

Ephesians 6:13
"Wherefore take unto you the whole armour of God, that ye may be able to withstand in the evil day, and having done all, to stand" Armor was defensive as well as offensive to the knights of old. This *"take unto you"* is a command. Paul is in a prison in Rome writing to the Christians at Ephesus. He says, *"take unto you."* Some Christians do not want to take, and that is a strange thing. You have to take *"the whole armour of God,"* not just part of it. If you leave a piece off, you are vulnerable in that section. You must put all the armor on. You must put every piece of armor on so that you can *"withstand"* and then *"stand in the evil day."*

To *"withstand"* means *"to resist and to fight it off."* There are a number of verses which have to do with standing and withstanding.
- **Romans 5:2**
  By whom also we have access by faith into **this grace wherein we stand**, and rejoice in hope of the glory of God.
Believers have *"standing"* with the Lord.
- **1 Corinthians 16:13**
  Watch ye, **stand fast in the faith**, quit you like men, be strong.
God doesn't want us to be moving around in our faith. He wants us to *"stand"* in place. We have the Bible. We have to *"stand"* firm.

- **Galatians 5:1**
  Stand fast therefore in the liberty wherewith Christ hath made us free, and be not entangled again with the yoke of bondage.
- **Ephesians 6:11**
  Put on the whole armour of God, that ye may be able to **stand against the wiles of the devil.**
- **Philippians 4:1**
  Therefore, my brethren dearly beloved and longed for, my joy and crown, so **stand fast in the Lord,** *my* dearly beloved.
- **1 Thessalonians 3:8**
  For now we live, if ye **stand fast in the Lord.**

Paul said, in effect, that if you Thessalonian Christians do not *"stand fast,"* I am not going to live and have a happy life because I want you to *"stand"* the way I taught you. This applied to the Ephesians as well.

- **2 Thessalonians 2:15**
  Therefore, brethren, **stand fast, and hold the traditions which ye have been taught,** whether by word, or our epistle.
- **Revelation 6:17**
  For the great day of his wrath is come; and **who shall be able to stand?**

Only those who are in Christ and saved will be *"able to stand."* Those who are saved now will be in Heaven. Those who are on this earth during this great tribulation time will not be *"able to stand."*

We are to *"put on the whole armour of God."* That *"includes the shield and the sword and the lance and the helmet and the greaves* [armor for the leg] *and the breastplate."* We have seven pieces of armor (if we include *"praying always"*) that we must use to *"withstand"* or resist the evil one.

Has there ever been a more evil day than when we live today? California was recently taking a vote to allow two same-sex people to marry. If it passes in California, then every other state in the union will probably follow its lead. This is wicked. In the military they have the "don't ask don't tell" policy. When I was a Naval Chaplain on active duty from 1960 to 1965, homosexuals were not allowed to be in the military. That was a good way. We live today in an evil day. We have smut all around us. The Internet is a pollution master.

There are some negatives in the Christian faith, and this is one of them. To withstand means to oppose. We are to oppose everything that is evil. We must stand in this evil day, too. That word *"stand,"* HISTEMI, means *"to make firm, to fix, to establish."* Concrete is something that is fixed once it drys. You can put salt on it to melt the ice, but the concrete is still standing. To stand also means *"to cause a person or thing to keep his or its place."* When you get in line in the supermarket, people will try to push ahead of you, but you need to just stand firm and keep your place. God wants us to continue standing.

Ephesians 6:14
"Stand therefore, having your loins girt about with truth, and having on the breastplate of righteousness"

"Stand therefore, having your loins girt about with truth" Here again we see the command to *"stand."* The *"loins"* are the lower parts of our waist and our legs. We are supposed to gird our loins with *"truth."* What is *"truth"*? The Bible is *"truth."* We must have the right Bible. That is why we stand for the Greek Textus Receptus text which underlies our King James Bible and the Hebrew Masoretic text which underlies our King James Bible. The King James Bible is the right Bible in the English language.

I have answered a book entitled *From the Mind of God to the Mind of Man* which was written by men connected in some way with Bob Jones University. I call my book *Fundamentalist Misinformation on Bible Versions*. One of the contentions in the *Mind of Man* book is that we should not contend over things which are not important. What they are referring to is the Bible. The Bible is the most important thing for which we should contend. The Bible is the basis of our Biblical faith. If we use the wrong Bible, then we will have the wrong faith. I have found 5,604 places of difference between the Textus Receptus Greek text on which our King James Bible is built, and the Westcott and Hort kind of text. This is a serious problem regarding *"truth."* According to an ongoing study by Dr. Jack Moorman of London, England, those 5,604 places involve over 8,000 Greek words that are different to a greater or lesser degree. Dr. Moorman has also found 356 passages in the Westcott and Hort kind of text which involve important doctrines. We have a battle on our hands in our day to stand for *"truth."*

According to their own testimony, the four "major" fundamentalist schools that stand for the wrong New Testament Greek text in our day are these: (1) Bob Jones University; (2) Detroit Baptist Seminary; (3) Central Baptist Seminary; and (4) Calvary Baptist Seminary. We have a battle on our hands with many of our fellow-fundamentalists about our Bible.

It is not pleasant to battle with your friends. They have other doctrines that I agree with completely such as Biblical separation and other fundamental doctrines. But if these schools are off on their Bible, I must contend with them. The Lord Jesus Christ has given me, as a preacher of the gospel, the duty to stand up for Him and for His Words. He said to all of us, *"Whosoever shall be ashamed of me and of my words in this adulterous and sinful generation; of him also shall the Son of man be ashamed when he cometh"* (Mark 8:38). That is the situation. If we are going to be effective soldiers for the Lord Jesus Christ, we must have our *"loins girt about with truth"*--not with *"truth"* mixed with error.

"and having on the breastplate of righteousness" The *"breastplate"* covers the very vital parts of our heart and our lungs. The Greek word for *"breastplate"* is THOROX. The *"breastplate"* covers the body *"from the neck to the navel where the ribs end, . . . protecting the body on both sides."* There is no way to get righteousness except by faith in the Lord Jesus Christ. He is our righteousness.

- Romans 5:1
  Therefore **being justified by faith**, we have peace with God through our Lord Jesus Christ:

"Being justified" is being declared righteous by faith. We have to be prepared in this battle with Satan. An unsaved person is not able to stand against the wiles of the Devil. Only believers who will take upon themselves the whole armor of God can stand against this infernal foe.

Ephesians 6:15

"And your feet shod with the preparation of the gospel of peace" Here is the third element of the warrior's armor. The feet are to be shod with the *"preparation of the gospel of peace."* The feet are important because with them we can move around. What will *"prepare"* us for this gospel? Prayer and knowing the Bible are important parts of this. Are you prepared? *"Preparation"* implies that a person is ready. Being ready is necessary. Do you know what the gospel is? Do you know how to use it? That is *"preparation of the gospel of peace."* We have to memorize some Scripture. We have to know the Scriptures that give us the gospel.

- John 3:16
  For God so loved the world, that he gave his only begotten Son, that **believeth** in him should not perish, but have everlasting life.
- Romans 3:23
  For **all have sinned**, and come short of the glory of God;
- Romans 6:23
  For the **wages of sin *is* death**; but the **gift of God *is* eternal life through Jesus Christ** our Lord.
- Romans 5:1
  Therefore **being justified by faith**, we have peace with God through our Lord Jesus Christ:

We have to be prepared. We must memorize verses so that we can talk to people about Christ. I realize that when we go to bed we do not have our shoes on unless we are camping. Normally our feet are not *"shod"* while we sleep, but once we get up in the morning we put our shoes on. God wants us to have readiness so we can walk here or walk there and be prepared to tell forth His *"gospel of peace."*

Ephesians 6:16

"Above all, taking the shield of faith, wherewith ye shall be able to quench all the fiery darts of the wicked"

"Above all, taking the shield of faith" The shield of faith is the fourth item of our armament. There are many verses which speak about the *"shield"* in the Scriptures.

- **Genesis 15:1**
After these things the word of the LORD came unto Abram in a vision, saying, Fear not, Abram: **I *am* thy shield**, *and* thy exceeding great reward.
- **2 Samuel 22:3**
The God of my rock; in him will I trust: ***he is* my shield**, and the horn of my salvation, my high tower, and my refuge, my saviour; thou savest me from violence.

God is our protector if we are saved.

- **2 Samuel 22:36**
Thou hast also **given me the shield of thy salvation**: and thy gentleness hath made me great.
- **Psalm 3:3**
But **thou, O LORD, *art* a shield for me**; my glory, and the lifter up of mine head.

God protects those whom He has redeemed.

We knew of someone in the south who had a pre-leukemia disease. She took care of a disable person. Some believe she foolishly might have developed this leukemia because of having to hold down this disabled person during various times of radiation without being protected by a *"shield."* We don't know if this contributed to this illness or not. It is true, however, that if you don't stay behind the protective *"shield"* while administering radiation, you can develop some serious problems. The *"shield"* is necessary for protection. The Lord is our *"Shield"* against all wickedness and sin.

- **Psalm 28:7**
The LORD *is* my strength and my shield; my heart trusted in him, and I am helped: therefore my heart greatly rejoiceth; and with my song will I praise him.
- **Psalm 33:20**
Our soul waiteth for the LORD: **he *is* our help and our shield**.

We need a shield from the wickedness and deceitfulness of sin.

- **Psalm 84:11**
  For **the LORD God** *is* **a sun and shield**: the LORD will give grace and glory: no good *thing* will he withhold from them that walk uprightly.
- **Psalm 115:9**
  O Israel, trust thou in the LORD: **he** *is* **their help and their shield.**
- **Psalm 144:2**
  My goodness, and my fortress; my high tower, and **my deliverer; my shield**, and *he* in whom I trust; who subdueth my people under me.
- **Proverbs 30:5**
  Every word of God *is* pure: **he** *is* **a shield** unto them that put their trust in him.

Moses needed a shield when he went before the Lord. Moses was placed in a "*clift of the rock*" and shielded by the hand of God while He passed by (Exodus 33:22) lest, seeing God, Moses would die. Our God is a flaming fire. No man can see Him. Moses saw only the "back parts" of God while he was hidden in the "*clift of the rock*" (Exodus 33:23). The Lord Jesus is our "*shield*." We must take "*the shield of faith*" if we are to be successful warriors for the Lord.

"wherewith ye shall be able to quench all the fiery darts of the wicked" This is what that "*shield of faith*" will do for us. The "*wicked*" who are throwing these fiery darts could be wicked people, or it could be the wicked one, Satan, or it could include both ideas.

During the second World War, our men tell stories about "*white phosphorous*," called "*W.P.*" or "*Willy Peter*." These were white phosphorous bombs that would travel into fox holes and burn the soldier's feet. Even though the soldiers were not hit directly, these "*fiery darts*" from the white phosphorous bombs could still do damage in the trenches. They were frightening.

God has a way of protecting us from the "*fiery darts of the wicked*" ones. That way is by the proper use of "*the shield of faith*." That "*Shield*" is the Lord Jesus Christ Himself. The wicked one is out to harm us who are saved, and the "*shield*" protects our heart, our breathing, and our lungs. Satan would kill us or wound us in battle if we did not have our "*faith*." That "faith" includes both personal and saving faith in the Lord Jesus Christ as well as faith in the Words of God. That is the kind of faith trust that David had when he went out to slay the giant. The "*shield of faith*" is a very important part of our armament.

Ephesians 6:17
"And take the helmet of salvation, and the sword of the Spirit, which is the word of God"

"And take the helmet of salvation" The *"helmet"* protects the head, the brain, and the ears. Unless you have a visor, it does not protect the eyes because you have to see. The head area of the body, as we know, is the most vital part of the body. It houses the mind which needs to be sound.

- **Genesis 3:15**
 And I will put enmity between thee and the woman, and between thy seed and her seed; it shall **bruise thy head**, and thou shalt bruise his heel.

God predicted that Satan's *"head"* would be *"bruised."* It is the seed of the serpent that will bruise the heel of the Seed of the woman, the Lord Jesus Christ. That bruise to Christ was in the heel. It hurt, but it was not fatal. That bruise took place at Calvary. The Seed of the woman, the Lord Jesus Christ, was going to crush the head of the serpent, and that is vital. On the Cross of Calvary, the head of the serpent was bruised. Satan is still around here during this age of grace, and he will be active during the tribulation period. But during the Millennial reign of Christ, he will be bound for one thousand years (Revelation 20:2). Then he will be loosed for a little while (Revelation 20:3). Finally, he will be cast into the lake of fire with the beast and the false prophet to suffer in these flames for ever and ever (Revelation 20:10).

The head is important, and we need the *"helmet of salvation"* to protect it. We have to be sure we are saved. If we are not saved, our head is absolutely open for trash, for the infusion of pornography and filth, for swearing and bad talking, for hearing and seeing wicked things. We need a *"helmet of salvation"* that will protect our head at all times from these things that would defile us.

"and the sword of the Spirit, which is the word of God" The Greek word for *"word"* here is RHEMA. This means *"that which is or has been uttered by the living voice, thing spoken, word."* It is the spoken word. That is a powerful weapon. When the Lord Jesus Christ went forty days and forty nights without food or drink, Satan came to tempt Him. Jesus responded to each of the three temptations by saying, *"It is written"* (Matthew 4:4, 7, 10). The spoken Words of God were used during the attack of Satan in the wilderness.

That phrase *"it is written"* is in the perfect tense. This shows the Bible's preservation, the preservation of the very Hebrew and, by extension, Greek Words of God. The Lord Jesus said this almost two thousand years ago. But when He said *"it is written,"* using the Greek perfect tense, He referred to Words that were written down in the past, that were preserved up to the time of the Lord Jesus Christ, and will continue to be preserved into the future. This is the proper understanding of Bible preservation. It consists of both the Hebrew and Greek Words of the original Scriptures.

The Words of God will not do us any good on the dining room table. They must be read. They must be memorized. They must be used.

The Bible–Hand, Head, and Heart

The Bible in the hand is **good.**

The Bible in the head is **bett**er.

But the Bible in the heart is **best.**

Yes, the Bible is good in the hand, better in the head, but best in the heart. We have to hold the Words of God dear to us. When people are running for their lives and must leave everything behind, I would hope they would take their Bibles with them. We need the "*sword of the Spirit.*" Do not forget to memorize the Words of God in your hearts for the emergency times when the Bible is not available.

Ephesians 6:18

"Praying always with all prayer and supplication in the Spirit, and watching thereunto with all perseverance and supplication for all saints"

"Praying always with all prayer and supplication in the Spirit" "*Praying always*" is the seventh and final part of our weapons of warfare. We must continuously pray. There is no cessation in that. Prayer is ordinary communication and fellowship with the Lord. If we have sin in our hearts and our lives, the Lord will not hear us. We must confess and forsake our sins. "*If we confess our sins, He is faithful and just to forgive us our sins, and to cleanse us from all unrighteousness*" (1 John 1:9). God wants us to continue to pray.

"*Supplication*" is asking for things from the Lord out of a sense of need. It is requesting because we need things from the Lord. Notice, we are giving supplication "*in the Spirit.*" We are not just praying with our lips but from our hearts in the Spirit if we are saved.

"and watching thereunto with all perseverance and supplication" That word for "*watching*" is AGRUPNEO means "*to be sleepless, keep awake, watch.*" Jesus asked his disciples to watch with him in the Garden of Gethsemane while he went to pray. Jesus asked, *"What, could ye not watch with me one hour?"* (Matthew 26:40) That is the same word for *"watch"* that is used here. It means to be alert. We must watch with *"all perseverance and supplication."* We must be everlastingly at it.

"for all saints" *"Saints"* is a word used in the Bible for all born-again Christians. All believers need prayer. Saved Christians in modernistic churches need our prayers for them to get out of such churches. The Christians in the Roman Catholic Churches need our prayers that they would get out of that church. Those who go to the neo-evangelical compromising churches need our prayers so that they can get out of those churches. The Christians in Fundamental churches that are asleep at the switch need our prayers for them to get in the right Fundamental church. We have to pray *"for all saints."* All believers need prayer, including pastors and their families.

Ephesians 6:19

"And for me, that utterance may be given unto me, that I may open my mouth boldly, to make known the mystery of the gospel"

"And for me, that utterance may be given unto me" Paul said, *"Please, don't leave me out in your prayers."* People might be surprised that Paul asked for prayer. After all, he was an apostle who had seen the Lord. He was commissioned directly by the Lord Jesus Christ on the road to Damascus (Acts 9:1-6). You might think that he did not need prayer because he was strong and great. We used to say this in football. *"The bigger they are the harder they fall."* It is the same way with the saints of God. The bigger the man of God, the harder he or she falls. We have to pray *"for all saints."* Paul wanted to be prayed for, too.

Why did Paul want to be prayed for? He wanted them to pray *"that utterance may be given"* unto him. Paul was a preacher. Some say that he had trouble talking, but he was a preacher, regardless. Have you ever heard a preacher who used bad grammar and did not have clear speech yet the Spirit of God was mightily upon him? The Lord blessed their ministry. I remember my pastor in my early days at the Grayton Road Baptist Church in Berea, Ohio. Being from a foreign background, he would sometimes say *"duh"* instead of *"the."* But he was and is a great man of God that the Lord has used mightily. He is in his nineties now, and just retired. Through the years his pronunciation improved. He went on to get his Master's degree. He was a dedicated and deep student of the Scriptures. We must always remember that it is the Spirit of God that allows a preacher to open up the hearts of people. It is not a preacher's education that does this. It is not a preacher's background. It is the Spirit of God getting hold of him. Paul needed prayer for *"utterance."*

"that I may open my mouth boldly, to make known the mystery of the gospel" If there were ever a man who was bold, it was Paul. Why does he say to pray for boldness? Paul prayed for boldness because he was in prison. In prison, if you cross the guards, you may get into trouble. Paul wanted to continue to preach Christ boldly even in jail. Most people would think that if they were in jail, they would take a vacation from their preaching. No, he was in jail because of his preaching, and he continued to preach while he was there. The Lord Jesus was his Saviour, and he was going to make known the "sacred secret" (the "*mystery*") which is the gospel.

- John 7:26
  But, lo, **he speaketh boldly,** and they say nothing unto him. Do the rulers know indeed that this is the very Christ?

The Lord Jesus spoke boldly, and it got Him in trouble. It often gets us in trouble when we speak boldly, but if it is the Word of God, so be it. Let us be bold as we proclaim the Word of God. If it gets us in trouble, so be it.

- Acts 4:13
  Now when **they saw the boldness of Peter and John,** and perceived that they were unlearned and ignorant men, they marvelled; and they took knowledge of them, that they had been with Jesus.

- Acts 9:27
  But Barnabas took him, and brought *him* to the apostles, and declared unto them how he had seen the Lord in the way, and that he had spoken to him, and how **he had preached boldly** at Damascus in the name of Jesus.

- Acts 9:29
  And **he spake boldly** in the name of the Lord Jesus, and disputed against the Grecians: but they went about to slay him.

Paul was a man who spoke boldly.

- Acts 14:3
  Long time therefore abode **they speaking boldly** in the Lord, which gave testimony unto the word of his grace, and granted signs and wonders to be done by their hands.

- Acts 19:8
  And he went into the synagogue, and **spake boldly** for the space of three months, disputing and persuading the things concerning the kingdom of God.

- Ephesians 6:20
  For which I am an ambassador in bonds: that therein **I may speak boldly,** as I ought to speak.

Paul wanted utterance to be given so he might speak boldly. We have preachers all over the world who are speaking timidly. You have heard of the people in those polar bear clubs who go out and swim in the freezing weather. Those people are not timid people. Then, there are people who go to a pool and stick their big toe in to test the water. They are timid.

Preachers today want to please the people instead of the Lord. That is why there is a timidity in their preaching. Paul said he did not want to be that kind of preacher. He said that the Lord called him to preach the gospel. That is why he is asking the saints at Ephesus to pray for him. We should all pray for our preachers to preach "*boldly*" the things of the Lord.

If you do not believe me, just be a chaplain in the U.S. Navy working with the Marines. When you preach "*boldly*" the Word of God there, you can get bad "*fitness reports*" by the unsaved people who are your superiors. If you preach too boldly, they do not like it. When I was a Naval Chaplain (1956-1961), I didn't know the difference. The Lord called me to preach, and I just preached the Word of God as it was written. I got some bad "*fitness reports*" written up, but that was all right. I was still going to preach boldly even though the world did not like it.

I had a senior chaplain at the Naval Air Station in Corpus Christi, Texas named Chaplain James Carter. He was a Commander, a three striper in the Navy. He gave me one of those bad reports. I preached about the Lord Jesus Christ's healing of the maniac of the Gadarenes (Mark 5:1-20). I entitled the message, "*Taming the Untamed.*" I talked about how the Lord Jesus Christ had cast out the demons who had possessed this man. After the sermon, this modernist Presbyterian Chaplain was infuriated. He said, "*Chaplain Waite, that message was intellectually barren and spiritually sterile.*" He cut me off from preaching in the morning service from then on. He wrote to Washington and told them what a bad Chaplain I was. Well, I wrote Washington myself, and answered in great detail that bad fitness report. I still have a copy in my files. The Navy Chief of Chaplains saw to it that I was put back preaching in the morning service. The only trouble was that I had started an evening service, after I had been cut off from the morning service, and there were many people coming to that service. Then, when he put me back in, he offered me a compromise for this evening service. He had these other modernistic chaplains come into the evening service. I said, "*All right, Chaplain Carter, I'm out. You take the evening service. I don't want any part of it.*" I didn't want to mix Bible truth with modernism in that service. People stopped coming to hear the modernists and the evening service soon ceased. From that point on, however, I made it a point to tape-record all of my sermons so that anyone could hear what I actually said and not what others accused me of saying.

Boldness, many times, gets us in trouble. Make sure the boldness is in line with the Word of God. If we are sure the boldness is in line with the Word of God, then speak up boldly. Those who are Christians rejoice when we are stepped upon by the Scriptures. We rejoice if our sins are exposed by the

Scriptures. We rejoice that we grow in grace and more boldness and more Christlikeness. Make sure that you are bold in accordance with the Word of God. Paul asked them to pray for him that he may have boldness in preaching. We all need such boldness.

Ephesians 6:20

"For which I am an ambassador in bonds: that therein I may speak boldly, as I ought to speak" Paul was an *"ambassador in bonds."* He was one who went out and told people about the *"gospel."* But now he was in prison, *"in bonds,"* because he was a preacher of the gospel. Paul was appointed an *"ambassador"* by the King of Kings and Lord of Lords. It was Christ who gave him his marching papers.

I looked up in the dictionary the various English expressions using the word, *"ambassador."*

Different Kinds of Ambassadors

Ambassador--*"the highest-ranking diplomatic representative appointed by one country or government to represent it in another."*

Ambassador-at-large--*"one accredited to no particular country."* He goes to any country he is sent to.

Ambassador extraordinary--*"one on a special diplomatic mission."*

Ambassador plenipotentiary--*"one having the power to make treaties."*

Paul was an ambassador, and so are we who are saved.
- 2 Corinthians 5:20
  Now then **we are ambassadors for Christ**, as though God did beseech *you* by us: we pray *you* in Christ's stead, be ye reconciled to God.

We represent the Lord Jesus Christ. Paul's being in *"bonds"* did not stop him, and it should not stop us if it ever comes to that.
- Acts 20:23
  Save that the Holy Ghost witnesseth **in every city, saying that bonds and afflictions** abide me.

Paul did not just fall into an ambush accidentally. He was warned that he would be put into bonds.

- **Acts 23:29**
  Whom I perceived to be accused of questions of their law, but to have **nothing laid to his charge worthy of death or of bonds.**

  If Paul had not appealed to Caesar, it is possible that he would have been released because he had done nothing *"worthy of death or of bonds."*

- **Acts 26:31**
  And when they were gone aside, they talked between themselves, saying, **This man doeth nothing worthy of death or of bonds.**

- **Philippians 1:13**
  So that **my bonds in Christ are manifest in all the palace,** and in all other *places*;

- **Colossians 4:3**
  Withal praying also for us, that God would open unto us a door of utterance, to speak the mystery of Christ, **for which I am also in bonds:**

The prison epistles were called "prison epistles" because they were written while Paul was in prison. These "prison epistles" are Ephesians, Philippians, Colossians, and Philemon. 2 Timothy shows that Paul was bound in jail a second time. The books he wrote while in prison the second time are 1 Timothy, 2 Timothy, and Titus.

- **Philemon 10**
  I beseech thee for my son Onesimus, **whom I have begotten in my bonds:**

The Lord wants us to be bold, no matter if we are bond or free, so that the Lord Jesus Christ may be glorified in all that we do or say.

Ephesians 6:21

"But that ye also may know my affairs, *and* how I do, Tychicus, a beloved brother and faithful minister in the Lord, shall make known to you all things" Notice Tychicus's qualifications. He was a *"beloved brother."* He was loved and a Christian brother. He was also a *"faithful minister in the Lord."* May we be faithful. *"Moreover it is required of stewards, that a man be found faithful"* (1 Corinthians 4:2). Tychicus was a faithful man. (Tychicus is referred to six times in Scripture.)

- **Acts 20:4**
  And there accompanied him into Asia Sopater of Berea; and of the Thessalonians, Aristarchus and Secundus; and Gaius of Derbe, and Timotheus; and of Asia, **Tychicus** and Trophimus.

  He accompanied Paul into Asia Minor.

- **Ephesians 6:24**
  Grace *be* with all them that love our Lord Jesus Christ in sincerity. Amen. *To the Ephesians written from Rome, by* ***Tychicus****.*

  Tychicus delivered the letter to the Ephesians.

- **Colossians 4:7**
  All my state shall **Tychicus** declare unto you, *who is* a beloved brother, and a faithful minister and fellowservant in the Lord:

- **Colossians 4:18**
  The salutation by the hand of me Paul. Remember my bonds. Grace *be* with you. Amen. *[Written from Rome to Colossians by* ***Tychicus*** *and Onesimus.]*

  The letter to the Colossians was also delivered by Tychicus.

- **2 Timothy 4:12**
  And **Tychicus** have I sent to Ephesus.

- **Titus 3:12**
  When I shall send Artemas unto thee, or **Tychicus**, be diligent to come unto me to Nicopolis: for I have determined there to winter.

Tychicus was a faithful brother and a friend. When you are in jail, you cannot do very much. In this case, it is good to have friends who will help you. It is nice for me as your Pastor to have help. The preacher cannot do everything. Paul was glad for Tychicus and I am glad for everyone who is a help in our ministry at the Bible For Today Baptist Church, whether that help is in prayer, in giving, in attendance, in some other form of service, or all of these helps.

Ephesians 6:22

"Whom I have sent unto you for the same purpose, that ye might know our affairs, and *that* he might comfort your hearts" Tychicus was sent to the Ephesians to tell them what was going on in Paul's life. They were concerned about Paul's welfare and Tychicus was to bring comfort and encouragement to the home church. If your friend were in jail, you would wonder about him, would you not? If you would not hear from him, you would wonder what was happening.

We have a number of friends who are in jail who write to us. They are pen pals, you might say. We just received a letter the other day from a man who is on death row. He said that the conditions are even worse than they ever were before. He has been saved since he has been in prison, and he loves the Lord and has been reading the Scriptures. He has had a lot of privileges taken away. They can only exercise three hours instead of four hours. They have taken away his papers, and he is in solitary confinement. He asked for prayer. He is a man who knows Greek and Latin. I do not know what is going to happen to him, but he keeps going. When you are in bonds, it is good to have a friend on the outside to help and encourage you.

Ephesians 6:23

"Peace *be* to the brethren, and love with faith, from God the Father and the Lord Jesus Christ"

"Peace *be* to the brethren" Notice the three qualities: *"peace," "love,"* and *"faith."* *"Therefore being justified by faith, we have peace with God through our Lord Jesus Christ"* (Romans 5:1). God's peace has been beautifully defined.

God's Peace

"The tranquil state of a soul, assured of its salvation through Christ, and so fearing nothing from God, and content with its earthly lot, of whatsoever sort it is."

It is the peace that *"passeth all understanding"* and guards our minds and our hearts by faith through Christ Jesus (Philippians 4:7).

"and love with faith" Christians that hate one another do not stay together. Families that hate one another do not stay together too long. *"Love"* is the glue that keeps things together and the oil that keeps the machinery running. *"Perfect love casteth out fear"* (1 John 4:18). *"Charity shall cover the multitude of sins"* (1 Peter 4:8). Love covers over. This is not that we agree with the sin, but it makes it possible for redeemed sinners to work with one another despite their failings.

Paul says *"and love with faith."* Love that is a sappy, gooey love without a proper Biblical *"faith"* is a strange kind of love. Love for sin is wrong, but *"love with faith"* for the things of Scripture is what God wants us to have. Paul asked the Ephesians to have that kind of *"love."*

"from God the Father and the Lord Jesus Christ" Notice the source of the *"peace, love, and faith."* It is *"from God the Father and the*

Lord Jesus Christ." Notice that they are co-equal. The liberals and modernists do not believe that. They think that God is one. They are unitarians. They believe and teach that Jesus was just a man. They say that Jesus was an ordinary human being. This is false. The Lord Jesus Christ is co-equal with God the Father. He is as omniscient as God the Father and God the Holy Spirit. He is as omnipotent as God the Father and God the Holy Spirit. He is as omnipresent as God the Father and God the Holy Spirit.

Ephesians 6:24

"Grace *be* with all them that love our Lord Jesus Christ in sincerity. Amen. *[To the Ephesians written from Rome, by Tychicus]"* Tychicus delivered this letter to the Ephesians. Paul wished for them *"peace, love, and faith"* in verse twenty-three. Now, he wishes for them *"grace."* *"Grace"* is getting something you don't deserve.

It is important to *"love our Lord Jesus Christ in sincerity."* *"Sincerity"* is that which is genuine, complete, and whole. There are various Scriptures which talk about that.

- **Joshua 24:14**
  Now therefore fear the LORD, and **serve him in sincerity and in truth**: and put away the gods which your fathers served on the other side of the flood, and in Egypt; and serve ye the LORD.

Sincerity is a Latin word with two parts. *"Sin"* means *"without"* and *"cerus"* means *"wax."* It means *"without wax."* In ancient times when a person broke a pot, he would mend it with wax so that no one could easily see the break. A pot that is not mended with wax is *"sincere--without wax."* Something that is *"sincere"* is wholesome. Something that is *"sincere"* is completely true.

- **1 Corinthians 5:8**
  Therefore let us keep the feast, not with old leaven, neither with the leaven of malice and wickedness; but with the unleavened *bread* of **sincerity and truth**.

Our Lord's supper should be taken with *"sincerity and truth"* by those who are genuinely saved by God's grace who have *"examined"* themselves (1 Corinthians 11:28).

Paul wishes *"grace"* to all those who love the Lord Jesus Christ *"in sincerity."* Does that mean that some Christians do not love the Lord in sincerity? Yes, it does. Paul defines it very clearly. Who would those be who do not love the Lord Jesus Christ *"in sincerity"*? I think it would be those who name His name but want to walk according to the flesh and not according to the Spirit. It would be those Christians who would not be willing to die for Him.

Someone has challenged professing Christians with this situation. What would you do if machine gun-toting, Christian-killing Communists or other murdering terrorists broke into your church meeting and asked all the Christians to line up at the side wall. How many would, at that time, line up against the wall and proclaim that they are sincerely Christians knowing that they would be shortly be machine-gunned down? Sincerity is believing in something by doing it.

- **2 Corinthians 1:12**
  For our rejoicing is this, the testimony of our conscience, that **in simplicity and godly sincerity**, not with fleshly wisdom, but by the grace of God, we have had our conversation in the world, and more abundantly to you-ward.
- **2 Corinthians 2:17**
  For we are not as many, which corrupt the word of God: but **as of sincerity**, but as of God, in the sight of God speak we in Christ.
- **Titus 2:7**
  In all things shewing thyself a pattern of good works: in doctrine *shewing* uncorruptness, gravity, **sincerity**,

Titus was a young preacher when Paul wrote him a pastoral letter.

How can I tell if a Christian is sincere? Can you ask them? You could try that. The better gauge to know if a Christian is sincere is by their actions. You can look at their life and examine it.

I trust that you can benefit from the grace that Paul has spoken about. Is He worthy of our sincere love? Yes, He is. He took our sins on His own body on the cross of Calvary (1 Peter 2:24). If we're saved, there is not a single Person who sticks closer to us than the Saviour. Your friends may fail you. Your wife or your husband may fail you, but He will never fail you. *"There is a friend that sticketh closer than a brother"* (Proverbs 18:24). Brothers usually stick close, but Jesus sticks closer than a brother. Our Saviour is worthy of our sincere love.

This book of Ephesians is truly amazing in its breadth, its depth, its reproof, its instruction, its encouragement, and its love for the truth of God's Words. It is hard to believe that it was written while Paul was imprisoned in a dirty jail in Rome, Italy. God used this time, when Paul was all alone, to write the Prison Epistles of Ephesians, Philippians, Colossians, and Philemon. They may never have been written had Paul been traveling from place to place continuously. We who are saved should be thankful to God for the times He sets us aside from our busy lives. May we use such times to draw closer to Him in the reading of our Bibles, in fellowship with our Saviour, and in prayer!

Index of Words and Phrases

1 Timothy	1, 22, 44, 74, 91, 152, 153, 179, 193
1,800 places	72
160 Names for the Lord Jesus Christ	79
1611	72
1945	120
1956-1961	191
1-800-JOHN 10:9	I, 81
2 Timothy	1, 43, 67, 69, 72, 115, 119, 147, 153, 167, 193, 194
2,886 places	83
356	83, 105, 183
356 places of doctrinal changes	83
5,604 places	72, 82, 83, 105, 183
600 B.C.	170
700 B.C.	170
8,000 Greek words	83, 183
85 verses per day	150
856-854-2464	I
856-854-4452	I
9,970 Greek words	83
Abednego	145
About the Author	iv
Abraham	44, 52, 74, 76
Abraham's bosom	108, 109
Absalom	118
ABWE	132
accepted	10
access	14, 17, 58, 64, 65, 86-89, 181
Adam's rib	158
admonition	159, 170, 172
adoption	8, 9, 25
Adoptionists	83
adultery	88, 146, 159, 168, 169
Africa	53, 91
Ahithophel	118
alcoholic beverages	152, 153
Allen	120
always when they need it	172
ambassador	190, 192
American Standard Version	72, 82, 84, 137

androgynous	113
anger	125, 130-132, 170, 171
angry	116, 125, 133, 152, 154
anti	136
ants	157
apostle	2, 77, 79, 98, 120, 152, 189
apostles	2, 34, 66, 73-76, 79, 86, 98, 110, 120, 190
Arabia	73, 78
Aramaic	66, 71-73
Arizona	48, 90
Arminians	24, 114
armour of God	179, 181, 182
Assyrian captivity	170
Atlantic Ocean	114
August of 1948	160
Avoiding Temptation	126
Babylonian captivity	170
bad language	128
baptism	83, 106, 140
Baptist Churches	67, 152, 155
Baptists	98, 103, 113, 132, 159
Barbara Egan	ii
beasts	99, 158
Berea	19, 189, 194
Berea, Ohio	19, 189
Bethel Baptist Church	40
BFT #1997	82
BFT2973	I
Bible For Today	I-iii, 67, 77, 83, 86, 91, 99, 105, 149, 194
Bible For Today Baptist Church	iii, 67, 77, 86, 91, 99, 149, 194
Bible For Today Press	I
BibleForToday.org	I
Biblical separation	142, 183
Bill Gothard	169
Bill Gothard's father	169
Billy Graham	110
bitterness	130-132
blessed section	109
blood	4, 6, 10-16, 21, 32, 49, 54-59, 61, 64, 87, 88, 90, 114, 121, 140, 149, 175, 181
blood of Christ	10-15, 21, 54-59, 114
board of education	172

Index of Words and Phrases

Bob Jones University 72, 83, 113, 183
bold 86, 87, 91, 190, 192, 193
boldness 14, 58, 65, 86, 87, 89, 190-192
bonds 23, 190, 192-195
Book of Mormon 71
breadth of Christ's love 93
breastplate 53, 153, 182-184
Bremerhaven, Germany 114
Brooklyn, New York 114
by Jesus Christ 8, 9, 17, 61, 82
By the Waters of Galilee 121
Caesar 1, 2, 78, 193
Caesarea 2
Calvary .. 30, 42, 49, 61-63, 72, 83, 85, 88, 94, 121, 136, 162, 183, 187, 197
Calvary Baptist Seminary 83, 183
Calvary Baptist Theological Seminary 72
Calvary's Cross 7, 175
Camping 30, 39, 48, 184
cancer 148, 149
canon 66, 75
canon of Scripture 66, 75
Captain Kirk 124
Carl Elgena 40
Carl McIntire 63
cart before the horse 51
CCM 154
Central Baptist Seminary 83, 183
Central Baptist Theological Seminary 72
Chafer 16, 111, 128
Chaplain 77, 92, 114, 152, 182, 191
Chaplain James Carter 191
Charismatics 71, 89, 98, 110, 155
chemotherapy 147
Chief of Chaplains 191
children ..... iii, 3, 8-10, 17, 26, 36, 40, 42-44, 61, 67, 88, 90, 98, 111, 113,
             114, 135, 138, 140-143, 156, 159, 163, 164, 167-173, 175
chosen 2, 5, 17, 76
Christ as a male 112
Christ Our Threefold Shepherd 38
Christian Beacon 63
Christian rock 154
Christian Science 71, 75, 114

Christmas	52, 53
church covenants	152
cleansing	13, 57, 161
Cleveland	19
cockroaches	145
Collingswood	I, iii, 63, 90, 164
Colossians	1, 11, 13, 16, 21, 28, 46, 48, 53, 55-57, 61, 73, 130, 179, 193, 194
communication	127, 128, 188
computer	ii, 19, 73, 122
concepts	12, 97
confession	162
confidence	65, 86
conformed to the image of His Son	8
conning tower	157
contemporary Christian music	154, 155
corporate	5
Corpus Christi, Texas	191
corrupt communication	127, 128
covetousness	88, 138-140
cross	7, 13, 24, 33, 41, 42, 49, 50, 56, 57, 60-63, 108, 109, 120, 125, 135, 136, 162, 175, 178, 187, 190, 197
cults	114
Dallas	2, 16, 48, 67, 111, 128, 174
Dallas Theological Seminary	2, 16, 48, 67, 111, 128, 174
Damascus	77, 85, 104, 189, 190
Daniel S. Waite	ii
Daniel's seventieth week	19
darkness	16, 17, 21, 60, 75, 118, 130, 136, 142, 143, 145-148, 181
David	34, 44, 118, 179, 180, 186
deacons	67, 87, 98, 113, 152-154
dead	4, 13-15, 20, 24, 34-36, 39, 44-46, 54, 57, 58, 81, 98, 104, 109, 141, 147, 148
death	1, 7, 10, 12, 15, 22, 29, 35, 49, 54-56, 58-61, 63-65, 87, 106, 108, 117, 124, 148, 149, 158, 160, 164, 170, 177, 184, 193, 195
Deity	4, 31, 82, 99, 144, 164
departed spirits	108, 109
depraved	44, 122
depth of Christ's love	94
descended into hell	109
desert of Arabia	73, 78
despair	53, 131

Index of Words and Phrases

Detroit Baptist Seminary 83, 183
Detroit Baptist Theological Seminary 72
devil . 15, 20, 35, 40, 41, 43, 51, 59, 103, 106, 115, 116, 125, 126, 143, 146, 149, 180, 182, 184
Dianne W. Cosby ii
Different Kinds of Ambassadors 192
discipline 172
dispensation 20, 70, 74, 76
dispensation of conscience 70, 74
dispensation of grace 70, 74
dispensation of human government 70, 74
dispensation of innocence 70, 74
dispensation of promise 70, 74
dispensation of the kingdom 70, 74
dispensation of the law 70
dispensationalism 70
dispensations 70, 74
dissonance 155
Docetism 83
doctrinal position 103
Dr. Carl McIntire 63
Dr. H. A. Ironside iii
Dr. Jack Moorman 73, 83, 183
Dr. Jung 77, 78
Dr. Lewis Sperry Chafer 16, 111, 128
Dr. McIntire 63
Dr. Moorman 183
Dr. Peter Ruckman 71, 75, 128
Dr. Thomas Strouse 82
drivers 48
drugs 124, 148, 162
eating daily for eighteen hours 123
eighteen hours to eat 123
election 5
elephants 123
Elgena 40
Elijah 32, 34
English versions 19
Ephesians 2:1-10 48
Ephesians Chapter Five iv
Ephesians Chapter Four .... iv, 107
Ephesians Chapter One iv

Ephesians Chapter Six iv
Ephesians Chapter Three iv
Ephesians Chapter Two iv
Ephesus 1-3, 21, 23, 28, 31, 40, 88, 107, 126, 138, 150, 152, 181, 191,
                194
Episcopalians 98, 113
eternal life 24, 42, 49, 50, 52, 54, 184
evangelists 66, 76, 98, 110
everlasting life 6, 24, 94, 105, 140, 161, 184
e-mail I
faith .... iii, 3, 7, 10, 12, 16, 19, 21, 23, 24, 26-28, 33, 39, 40, 43-46, 48-53,
           56, 61, 62, 65, 68, 70, 78, 80, 81, 86-88, 90-92, 101, 102, 104-
           106, 110-112, 129, 133, 135, 143, 148, 153, 161, 180-186, 195
faithfulness 3, 122
Family Radio 30, 39, 48
fanatic 120
fax I
fellowship .. 3, 12, 14, 17, 25, 29, 35, 38, 54, 56, 57, 65, 67, 75, 82, 88, 92,
                117, 142, 143, 145, 188
fiery darts 185, 186
five levels 97
Five Tasks of a Shepherd 111
five-point Calvinists 39
Florida 145
follow me 25, 135, 148
Foreword .... iii, iv
forgiveness 10, 11, 13, 16, 21, 27, 55-57, 132, 133
fornication 137, 138, 146, 159
foundation of the world 5-7
fourteen effects 11, 54
fourteen years 109
from the heart 175
From the Mind of God to the Mind of Man 72, 124, 183
fruit 51, 83, 124, 126, 129, 139, 143, 144, 151
fruit of the Spirit 143
fundamental churches 156, 189
fundamentalist 72, 73, 75, 83, 183
fundamentalist institutions 72, 83
Fundamentalist Misinformation on Bible Versions 183
GARBC 152, 153
gender-neutral 113
Germany 114

Index of Words and Phrases

Gertrude G. Sanborn ... 19
Gnostic ... 82, 83, 105
Gnostic Heresies Invaded the Critical Text ... 82
Gnostics ... 82, 105
God .... iii, 1-13, 15-21, 23-38, 41-79, 81-99, 101, 103, 104, 106-119, 122-130, 132, 133, 135-152, 154, 155, 157-159, 161-165, 167-171, 173-193, 195-197
God the Father . 4, 17, 24, 34, 35, 37, 46, 47, 64, 65, 68, 82, 88, 96, 97, 155, 195, 196
God the Son ... 4, 24, 90, 96, 99, 155
God-Man ... 95
God's Peace ... 60, 195
God's power ... 32-34, 36, 91, 98, 143, 178
God's will ... 14, 19, 58, 78, 121, 150
God's Word ... 66, 119, 124, 147, 150, 157, 168
Golden Rule of Interpretation ... 10
Goliath ... 34, 179, 180
good fruit ... 139
Good Shepherd ... 37, 38, 81
good tree ... 139
gospel . 1, 7, 20, 23, 24, 28, 31, 32, 39, 40, 42, 50, 53, 61, 66, 69, 74-77, 85, 87, 111, 118, 120, 178, 183, 184, 190-192
Gothard ... 169
grace 3-5, 7, 10, 11, 13, 15-19, 21, 28, 33, 39, 44-52, 54, 55, 57, 59, 65, 70, 71, 74, 77, 79, 86-88, 91, 99, 102, 107-111, 116, 127, 128, 130, 131, 150, 153, 163, 178, 179, 181, 186, 187, 190, 192, 194, 196, 197
Grace and Mercy Contrasted ... 45
Graham ... 110
Grayton Road Baptist Church ... 189
Great Tribulation ... 14, 58, 177, 182
greatest need ... 27
Greek . iii, 8, 10, 16, 18, 19, 23, 24, 39, 43, 47-49, 54, 59, 62, 66, 67, 71-73, 75, 76, 78, 82-85, 88, 92, 101-105, 109, 113, 116-118, 124, 127, 128, 132, 135, 136, 138, 142, 144, 145, 148, 150, 153, 154, 156, 162, 163, 172, 178, 183, 184, 187, 188, 195
Greek New Testament ... 19, 72, 83, 84
haima ... 54
Hamilton ... 65
Harold Camping ... 30, 39, 48
Harvard College ... 29
hate ... 27, 60, 62, 63, 73, 195

head 37, 38, 81, 106, 115, 157, 158, 165, 175, 179, 180, 185, 187, 188
heart .. 26, 31, 43, 51, 52, 61, 63, 79, 91, 92, 108, 118, 119, 124, 125, 131, 146, 151, 154, 155, 173, 175, 184-186, 188
Heaven ... 4, 8, 13, 20-24, 26, 31, 32, 35, 36, 39, 41, 42, 45, 47, 49-51, 53, 56, 57, 61, 64, 68, 79, 84, 86, 88, 89, 95, 96, 99, 104, 107-110, 140, 141, 161, 176, 177, 182
Heaven of Heavens 35
heavenly places 4, 34, 35, 46, 47, 84
Hebrew 10, 18, 19, 23, 24, 66, 71-73, 75, 76, 78, 105, 183, 187, 188
Hebrew Old Testament 18, 72
height of Christ's love 95
hell 24, 27, 37, 42, 45, 49, 51, 84, 96, 109, 117, 140, 141
helmet 53, 153, 180, 182, 187
help ... iii, 38, 45, 68, 87, 122, 131, 142, 160, 162, 176, 185, 186, 194, 195
high school class 120
high school janitor 120
Hiroshima 32
Hodgkin's 148, 149
Hodgkin's Disease 148, 149
holiness 7-9, 112, 123, 128, 140, 152
holy .. 3-5, 7, 8, 11, 17, 23-26, 31, 33, 44, 46-48, 53, 55, 64, 67, 68, 74, 75, 80, 81, 83, 87-89, 91-93, 96-98, 101, 103, 106, 107, 110, 115, 116, 122, 124, 128-130, 132, 135, 140, 141, 143, 144, 151, 154, 155, 161, 162, 178, 192, 196
holy rollers 7
Holy Spirit .. 3, 4, 7, 17, 23-26, 31, 44, 47, 64, 68, 75, 83, 89, 91, 92, 96-98, 101, 103, 106, 107, 115, 116, 122, 124, 128-130, 132, 135, 143, 144, 151, 154, 155, 178, 196
homosexuals 182
honor 156, 169
Hort 82-84, 105, 183
huper 136
husbands 94, 156-160, 162-165, 175
Hushai 118
hymns 37, 89, 154, 155
hyper-Calvinists 24, 39, 48, 93
ideas 73, 186
idolater 139
Inchon 78
independent Baptists 103
Index of Words and Phrases iv
Internet 146, 150, 182

Index of Words and Phrases

Ironside iii
ISBN #1-56848-031-8 I
Israel 4, 5, 16, 34, 52, 54, 61, 62, 76, 142, 169-171, 179, 186
janitor 120
Jesus ... 1-4, 7-10, 12-15, 17, 19-21, 23-32, 34-40, 42-52, 54, 56-71, 73, 74,
    77-93, 95, 97-99, 101, 103-113, 115-125, 127, 129, 130, 132, 133,
    135, 136, 139, 141-144, 148-150, 153, 155, 157, 159-164, 170,
    173-177, 183, 184, 186-197
Joah 53, 91
Job 79, 112, 162, 174
John E. Mitchell 174
John MacArthur 10, 15, 54, 56, 59, 85, 114, 132
Judaism 76
Judas 2, 110
judgment seat of Christ 176
Jung 77, 78
justification 12, 56
justified 3, 8, 11, 12, 17, 54-56, 61, 65, 88, 133, 140, 184, 195
King James ... 18, 19, 23, 24, 66, 71-73, 75, 78, 82, 84, 103, 105, 114, 137,
    150, 155, 161, 183
King James Bible .. 18, 19, 23, 24, 66, 71, 72, 75, 78, 82, 84, 103, 105, 114,
    137, 150, 155, 161, 183
Korea 77, 78
labor 116, 127
Lamb 7, 11, 12, 14, 15, 19, 54-56, 58, 59, 74, 99, 141
Lamb of God 7
Lamb slain 7, 19, 74
land of Palestine 170
Lazarus 44, 90, 108
length of Christ's love 94
level 96, 97
levels 97
liars 124, 126
liberation 159
Liberia 22, 53, 91, 152
Liberians 53, 91
light .. 10, 14, 16, 17, 21, 31, 57, 60, 77, 105, 108, 118, 130, 142, 143, 145-148
literal blood 10-15, 54, 56-59
literal blood of Christ 10-15, 54, 56-59
lock, stock, and barrel 118, 130
Logos 30, 161

London 73, 83, 183
London, England 73, 83, 183
Lord ... iii, 1-5, 7, 8, 10, 15, 17, 19-21, 23-52, 54, 58-71, 73, 74, 77-82, 84-86, 88-95, 97-99, 101-125, 127, 129-133, 135-137, 139, 141-145, 147-151, 155, 157-165, 167-196
Lord Jesus .. 1-4, 7, 8, 10, 15, 19-21, 23-26, 28-31, 34-40, 42-52, 58-68, 70, 71, 73, 74, 77-79, 81, 82, 85, 86, 88-90, 92, 93, 95, 97-99, 101, 103-113, 115-125, 127, 129, 130, 132, 133, 136, 141-144, 149, 150, 155, 159-164, 170, 173-177, 183, 184, 186-196
Lord Jesus Christ .. 1-4, 7, 8, 10, 19, 21, 23-26, 28-31, 34-37, 39, 40, 42-52, 59-68, 70, 71, 73, 74, 77-79, 81, 82, 85, 86, 88-90, 92, 93, 95, 97-99, 101, 103-112, 115-117, 119, 120, 123, 125, 129, 130, 132, 133, 136, 141-144, 150, 155, 159-161, 163, 164, 170, 173-176, 183, 184, 186-189, 191-194, 196
love . 8, 26-28, 35, 37, 42, 44, 48, 53, 63, 65, 92-96, 98, 102, 107, 108, 111, 115, 116, 129, 135, 136, 140, 143, 145, 147, 153, 155, 156, 158-160, 162, 163, 165, 172, 175, 194-197
Lutherans 98, 113
lying 89, 119, 124, 126
lymph glands 148, 149
Lystra 109, 120
MacArthur 10, 15, 54, 56, 59, 85, 114, 132
make-overs 123
male 62, 112, 113, 139
male/female 113
man ... 1, 4, 10, 16, 17, 24, 28, 32, 34-36, 39, 44-46, 48-51, 62, 65, 66, 69, 72, 77, 79-81, 83, 86, 88, 90-92, 94-97, 99, 106-109, 112, 113, 119, 122-124, 137, 139, 140, 144, 148, 156, 158, 161, 163, 165, 167, 168, 175-177, 179, 180, 183, 186, 189-191, 193, 195, 196
maniac of the Gadarenes 191
Marine Corps 105
marriage 156-158, 160, 163-165
Mars 35
Masoretic 18, 71, 78, 105, 183
Masoretic Text 18, 105, 183
Master 48, 66, 104, 105, 155, 156, 164, 174-177, 182
Master of Theology 48
masters 104, 156, 173, 175, 176
Master's degree 189
Matthias 2
maturity 14, 58, 115, 163
mechanical engineering 77

Index of Words and Phrases

meet	1, 20, 21, 67, 79, 142, 177
melody	154, 155
mercy	44, 45, 48, 86, 87, 148
Meshach	145
message	iii, 38, 78, 113, 120, 159, 191
metonym	10, 54
Michigan	19, 72
might	2, 6, 8, 9, 13, 16, 19, 20, 22, 28, 29, 34-36, 41, 46, 47, 50, 53, 56, 57, 61, 62, 64, 70, 72, 73, 83, 84, 90-93, 95, 99, 102, 103, 107, 109, 110, 119, 128, 132, 145-147, 151-153, 160, 161, 168, 171, 175, 177-180, 185, 189, 190, 194, 195
millennial reign	177, 187
millennium	37, 71, 74
Mitchell	174
modernistic Chaplains	191
Molenkott	113
Monopoly	109
Moorman	73, 83, 183
Mormon	66, 71
Mormon Church	66, 71
Moses	12, 29, 32, 55, 79, 141, 142, 186
Mother-Father God	113
Mrs. Waite	120, 123, 160
music	154, 155
mystery	19, 20, 53, 71, 73, 76, 82, 85, 87, 164, 189, 190, 193
Names for Christ	80
NASV	72, 82, 83
Naval Air Station	191
Naval Chaplain Corps	152
navy	77, 114, 191
Navy Chaplain	77, 114
neo-evangelical	189
NEPHALEOS	153, 154
NEPHO	153, 154
New American Standard Version	72, 82, 84, 137
New Century Version	137
New International Version	18, 72, 82, 84, 105, 137
New Jersey	I, iii, 40, 63, 113, 146, 160, 164
New King James Version	72, 137
New Revised Standard Version	82
NIV	72, 82-84, 105
no fellowship	145

nurture 170, 172
obedience 156, 168, 169, 174, 175
obey 43, 156, 165, 167-169, 173-175
Okinawa 152
one flesh 158, 164
Order Blank Pages iv
orders .... I, 174, 176
our greatest need 27
Palestine 161, 170
Palestinians 170
parents 156, 163, 167-170, 172, 175
passover 12, 54, 55
Pastor D. A. Waite, Th.D., Ph.D. .... I, iii
Pastor Joah 53, 91
Pastor Richard N. Waite ii
pastors 1, 37, 66, 76, 87, 96, 110, 112, 115, 153
patience 53, 78, 102, 153, 179
Patterson College 113
Paul .... iii, 1, 2, 21-23, 26-29, 31, 32, 35, 40, 48, 50, 52, 53, 62, 64, 69-71,
73, 74, 77-79, 82, 85, 87-89, 92, 93, 95, 98, 99, 101, 103-105,
108-110, 114-118, 120, 126, 127, 129, 133, 137, 138, 140, 142,
148, 150-152, 159, 164, 170, 173, 181, 182, 189-197
Pensacola 78
Pensacola Christian College 78
Pentecostals 89, 98
periscope 114, 148, 149
perseverance 5, 188, 189
Pharisees 43, 94, 106, 125, 140
Philadelphia 51, 167, 174
Philemon 1, 69, 193
Philippians 1, 28, 29, 35, 36, 41, 61, 73, 87, 177, 182, 193, 195
Philistines 179
phone I
Pilgrim's Progress 44
Plymouth Brethren 52
polite drivers 48
pollution 182
power .. 16, 17, 21, 28, 29, 32-36, 40, 41, 44, 53, 60, 68, 69, 78, 85, 90, 91,
96-99, 104, 106, 107, 118, 120, 143, 167, 177-180, 192
preacher 2, 6, 67, 74, 81, 82, 92, 98, 113, 154, 155, 183, 189, 191, 192,
194, 197
predestinate 8

Index of Words and Phrases

predestinated 8, 9, 21
preparation 184
preservation 72, 73, 187, 188
preservation of God's Words 72
Princeton 29
prison epistles 1, 193
prisoner 21, 23, 69, 70, 88, 89, 101
promise 22, 26, 32, 52, 70, 73, 74, 76, 169, 170
promised 4, 25, 71, 73, 76, 162, 169, 170
promised to preserve 71, 73
prophets 6, 29, 66, 74, 75, 110
propitiation 12, 17, 56
provoke 170, 171
Psalm 22 38
Psalm 23 .... 38, 148
Psalm 24 38
psalms 91, 154, 155
punishment 15, 58, 59
rapture 19, 104, 177
reconciliation 13, 57, 63
redemption ... 4, 10, 11, 13, 16, 21, 22, 24-26, 54, 55, 57, 84, 109, 116, 129
Reformation Building 63
Regular Baptist Press 153
remembrance 14, 58
repent 24, 31, 52, 93, 111
repentance 16, 23
reprove 145, 147
revelation .. 2, 7, 12, 14, 15, 19, 20, 28-30, 55, 58, 59, 66, 71, 73-76, 85, 90, 99, 110, 114, 141, 150, 153, 182, 187
Revelator 30
Revised Standard Version 82
Revised Text 84
rich man 108, 109
Riches of Divine Grace 17
right hand 4, 6, 16, 34-36, 47, 68, 110, 167, 177
righteousness 12, 36, 43, 48, 56, 86, 111, 123, 132, 140, 143, 144, 147, 184
rightly dividing 119
rock 17, 142, 154, 155, 185
Roman Catholic Church 3, 26
Roman Catholics 36, 65, 113
Ron Hamilton 65

Ruckman	71, 75, 128
saint	112
saints	2, 3, 5, 17, 20, 21, 26, 27, 65, 76, 79, 86, 93, 109, 112, 189, 191
salutatorian address	120
salvation	3, 7, 11, 23-25, 36, 38, 40, 45-51, 53, 54, 60, 62, 82, 85, 86, 93, 95, 103, 105, 111, 114, 117, 141, 153, 163, 178, 185, 187, 195
Sanborn	ii, 19, 130, 131, 150
Satan	15, 16, 21, 40-42, 52, 59, 90, 98, 106, 125, 126, 144, 181, 184, 186, 187
Saul	179, 180
scars	30
School District of Philadelphia	167
Science and Health	71
sealed	23-26, 116, 128, 129
seat of learning	172
sections	108, 164
Seed	51, 187
seminary	2, 16, 18, 48, 67, 72, 75, 78, 83, 111, 128, 174, 183
Senate	157
separation	142, 183
Serenity Prayer	18
servants	22, 86, 102, 156, 173, 174, 176, 179
Seven Stop Signs	116
Shadrach	145
Shatner	124
shepherd	15, 37, 38, 58, 66, 80, 81, 111, 112
shield	67, 148, 180, 182, 185, 186
sincere	23, 197
sober	53, 153
Solomon Joah	91
Some Names For Christ	80
South Korea	77, 78
Southampton, England	114
spank	171-173
spanking	172
spiritual blessings	4
spiritual songs	154, 155
St. Solomon Joah	91
stand	23, 33, 65, 88, 102, 110, 145, 147, 153, 159, 165, 174, 179-184
Startrek	124
stealing	116, 127
Stephen	177

Index of Words and Phrases

```
stoned .................................................. 109, 177
stop sign .............. 116, 125, 127, 128, 137, 140, 142, 145, 150, 151
strong in the Lord ............................. 34, 91, 102, 177, 180
Strouse ...................................................... 82
submission ......................................... 156, 157, 173
suicide .................................................. 52, 148
sword ............................... 60, 141, 148, 180, 182, 187
sword of the Spirit ........................................... 187
systematic theology ........................................ 16, 18
Table of Contents ............................................. iv
tape-record ................................................. 191
teacher .......... 16, 19, 75, 77, 111, 120, 121, 128, 154, 167, 173, 174
teachers .................... 1, 39, 66, 76, 79, 121, 124, 132, 152, 167
Temple University ............................................ 29
Texas .................................................. 145, 191
Textus Receptus .................... 19, 72, 73, 78, 82, 84, 105, 183
thanatos ..................................................... 54
thanks ........................................ 21, 28, 138, 155
thanksgiving ............................................... 5, 28
theology ............................... 16, 18, 19, 24, 48, 106
thesis ....................................................... 48
third Heaven ......................................... 35, 42, 109
Third Marine Division ...................................... 152
thoughts ......................................... 92, 97, 147
Titus .............. 1, 43, 48, 54, 74, 78, 104, 152, 153, 193, 194, 197
tormented section ...................................... 108, 109
tract ........................................................ 52
traitor ................................................ 110, 120
tree ................................................... 126, 139
tribulation period ...................................... 75, 141, 187
truth . iii, 23, 24, 29, 30, 40, 43, 53, 73, 83, 86, 87, 105, 106, 115, 117, 119,
             121, 124, 125, 129, 136, 140, 143, 144, 183, 191, 196
TULIP ....................................................... 5
twelve foundations ........................................ 2, 76
two sections .............................................. 108
Tychicus ........................................ 193, 194, 196
Uncle Charles Allen ........................................ 120
Unitarians .............................................. 4, 196
United States Senate ....................................... 157
University of Michigan ...................................... 19
veil ........................................ 32, 60, 64, 65, 88, 142
Vermilion ................................................... 22
```

Vermilion Yacht Club	22
victory	15, 34, 44, 59, 78, 129
Victory Baptist Church	78
Victory Baptist Church of Inchon, South Korea	78
Virginia Molenkott	113
vows	156
Waite	I-iii, 102, 120, 123, 152, 160, 191
washing	13, 29, 48, 57, 160, 161
watch	28, 89, 111, 117, 138, 153, 181, 188, 189
waves	98, 114
website	I, iii
wedding vows	156
West Africa	53, 91
Westcott	82-84, 105, 183
Westcott and Hort	82-84, 105, 183
Wheaton College	152
white phosphorous	186
whole armour	179, 181, 182
whosoever will	135
wife	ii, 22, 45, 66, 77, 107, 124, 137, 139, 148, 153, 154, 157-163, 165, 197
wiggle-room	160
wiles of the devil	180, 182, 184
will of God	2, 50, 129, 137, 144, 150, 154, 174, 175
William Pettingill	150
William Shatner	124
wine	41, 141, 151, 152, 154
withstand	181, 182
wives	153, 156-160, 162-165, 175
women deacons	113
women preachers	74, 113
women's liberation	159
works	6, 13, 22-24, 26, 39, 40, 46-51, 57, 85, 98, 124, 127, 145, 146, 150, 171, 172, 197
world	iii, 2, 5-8, 10, 15, 19, 20, 31, 33, 34, 36, 38-41, 43, 44, 48, 50-54, 59, 61, 63, 64, 67, 68, 72, 75-77, 82, 90, 91, 93, 94, 96, 98, 99, 102, 107, 109, 112, 118-122, 132, 136, 139, 142, 143, 145-150, 158, 160, 162, 167, 173, 177, 178, 180, 181, 184, 186, 191, 197
World War II	112
wrath	6, 11, 12, 42, 55, 56, 116, 125, 130-132, 140, 141, 167, 170-172, 182
Yvonne Sanborn Waite	ii

About the Author

The author of this book, Dr. D. A. Waite, received a B.A. (Bachelor of Arts) in classical Greek and Latin from the University of Michigan in 1948, a Th.M. (Master of Theology), with high honors, in New Testament Greek Literature and Exegesis from Dallas Theological Seminary in 1952, an M.A. (Master of Arts) in Speech from Southern Methodist University in 1953, a Th.D. (Doctor of Theology), with honors, in Bible Exposition from Dallas Theological Seminary in 1955, and a Ph.D. in Speech from Purdue University in 1961. He holds both New Jersey and Pennsylvania teacher certificates in Greek and Language Arts.

He has been a teacher in the areas of Greek, Hebrew, Bible, Speech, and English for over fifty-two years in ten schools, including one junior high, one senior high, three Bible institutes, two colleges, two universities, and one seminary. He served his country as a Navy Chaplain for five years on active duty; pastored three churches; was Chairman and Director of the Radio and Audio-Film Commission of the American Council of Christian Churches; since 1971, has been Founder, President, and Director of THE BIBLE FOR TODAY; since 1978, has been President of the DEAN BURGON SOCIETY; has produced over 700 other studies, books, cassettes, or VCR's on various topics; and is heard on both a five-minute daily and thirty-minute weekly radio program IN DEFENSE OF TRADITIONAL BIBLE TEXTS, presently on 25 stations. Dr. and Mrs. Waite have been married since 1948; they have four sons, one daughter, and, at present, eight grandchildren. Since October 4, 1998, he founded and has been the Pastor of the 𝕭𝖎𝖇𝖑𝖊 𝕱𝖔𝖗 𝕿𝖔𝖉𝖆𝖞 𝕭𝖆𝖕𝖙𝖎𝖘𝖙 𝕮𝖍𝖚𝖗𝖈𝖍 in Collingswood, New Jersey. His sermons are heard both on radio and the Internet over "www.BibleForToday.org/audio_sermons.htm"

Order Blank (p. 1)

Name:_____

Address:_____

City & State:_____Zip:_____

Credit Card #:_____Expires:_____
[ ] Send *Ephesians--Preaching Verse by Verse* by Pastor D. A. Waite ($12+$5 S&H) hardback, 224 pages.
[ ] Send *Galatians--Preaching Verse By Verse* by Pastor D. A. Waite ($12+$5 S&H) hardback, 216 pages.
[ ] Send *First Peter--Preaching Verse By Verse* by Pastor D. A. Waite ($10+$5 S&H) hardback, 176 pages.
[ ] Send *Fundamentalist MIS-INFORMATION on Bible Versions* by Dr. Waite ($7+$3 S&H) perfect bound, 136 pages
[ ] Send *Holes in the Holman Christian Standard Bible* by Dr. Waite ($3+$2 S&H) A printed booklet, 40 pages
[ ] Send *Central Seminary Refuted on Bible Versions* by Dr. Waite ($10+$3 S&H) A perfect bound book, 184 pages
[ ] Send *Fundamentalist Distortions on Bible Versions* by Dr. Waite ($6+$3 S&H) A perfect bound book, 80 pages
[ ] Send *Burgon's Warnings on Revision* by DAW ($7+$3 S&H) A perfect bound book, 120 pages in length.
[ ] Send *The Case for the King James Bible* by DAW ($7 +$3 S&H) A perfect bound book, 112 pages in length.
[ ] Send *Foes of the King James Bible Refuted* by DAW ($10 +$4 S&H) A perfect bound book, 164 pages in length.
[ ] Send *The Revision Revised* by Dean Burgon ($25 + $4 S&H) A hardback book, 640 pages in length.
[ ] Send *The Last 12 Verses of Mark* by Dean Burgon ($15+$4 S&H) A hardback book 400 pages.
[ ] Send *The Traditional Text* hardback by Burgon ($16 + $4 S&H) A hardback book, 384 pages in length.
[ ] Send *Summary of Traditional Text* by Dr. Waite ($3 +$2)
[ ] Send *Summary of Causes of Corruption*, DAW ($3+$2)

Send or Call Orders to:
THE BIBLE FOR TODAY
900 Park Ave., Collingswood, NJ 08108
Phone: 856-854-4452; FAX:--2464; Orders: 1-800 JOHN 10:9

Order Blank (p. 2)

Name:_____

Address:_____

City & State:_____Zip:_____

Credit Card #:_____Expires:_____

Other Materials on the KJB & T.R.
[ ] Send *Causes of Corruption* by Burgon ($15 + $4 S&H) A hardback book, 360 pages in length.
[ ] Send *Inspiration and Interpretation*, Dean Burgon ($25+$4 S&H) A hardback book, 610 pages in length.
[ ] Send *Summary of Inspiration* by Dr. Waite ($3 + $2 S&H)
[ ] Send *Contemporary Eng. Version Exposed*, DAW ($3+$2)
[ ] Send *Westcott & Hort's Greek Text & Theory Refuted by Burgon's Revision Revised--Summarized* by Dr. D. A. Waite ($7.00 + $3 S&H), 120 pages, perfect bound.
[ ] Send *Defending the King James Bible* by Dr. Waite $13+$4 S&H) A hardback book, indexed with study questions.
[ ] Send *Guide to Textual Criticism* by Edward Miller ($7 +$4)
[ ] Send *Westcott's Denial of Resurrection*, Dr. Waite ($4+$3)
[ ] Send *Four Reasons for Defending KJB* by DAW ($3+$3)
[ ] Send *Vindicating Mark 16:9-20* by Dr. Waite ($3+$3 S&H)
[ ] Send *Dean Burgon's Confidence in KJB* by DAW ($3+$3)
[ ] Send *Readability of A.V. (KJB)* by D. A. Waite, Jr. ($6 +$3)
[ ] Send *NIV Inclusive Language Exposed* by DAW ($5+$3)
[ ] Send *26 Hours of KJB Seminar* (4 videos) by DAW ($50.00)
[ ] Send *Defined King James Bible* lg.prt. leather ($40+$6)
[ ] Send *Defined King James Bible* med.prt. leather ($35+$5)
[ ] Send the "DBS Articles of Faith & Organization" (N.C.)
[ ] Send Brochure #1: "1000 Titles Defending KJB/TR"(N.C.)

Send or Call Orders to:
THE BIBLE FOR TODAY
900 Park Ave., Collingswood, NJ 08108
Phone: 856-854-4452; FAX:--2464; Orders: 1-800 JOHN 10:9
E-Mail Orders: BFT@BibleForToday.org; Credit Cards OK

Order Blank (p. 3)

Name:_____

Address:_____

City & State:_____Zip:_____

Credit Card#:_____Expires:_____

More Materials on the KJB &T.R.

[ ] Send *Heresies of Westcott & Hort* by Dr. Waite ($7+$3)

[ ] Send *Scrivener's Greek New Testament Underlying the King James Bible*, hardback, $14+$4 S&H

[ ] Send *Scrivener's Annotated Greek New Testament*, by Dr. Frederick Scrivener: Hardback--$35+$5 S&H; Genuine Leather--$45+$5 S&H

[ ] Send *Why Not the King James Bible?--An Answer to James White's KJVO Book* by Dr. K. D. DiVietro, $10+$4 S&H

[ ] Send *Forever Settled--Bible Documents & History Survey* by Dr. Jack Moorman, $20+$4 S&H. Hardback book.

[ ] Send *Early Church Fathers & the A.V.--A Demonstration* by Dr. Jack Moorman, $6 + $4 S&H.

[ ] Send *When the KJB Departs from the So-Called "Majority Text"* by Dr. Jack Moorman, $16 + $4 S&H

[ ] Send *Missing in Modern Bibles--Nestle-Aland & NIV Errors* by Dr. Jack Moorman, $8 + $4 S&H

[ ] Send *The Doctrinal Heart of the Bible--Removed from Modern Versions* by Dr. Jack Moorman, VCR, $15 +$4 S&H

[ ] Send *Modern Bibles--The Dark Secret* by Dr. Jack Moorman, $5 + $2 S&H

[ ] Send *Early Manuscripts and the A.V.--A Closer* Look, by Dr. Jack Moorman, $15 + $4 S&H

Send or Call Orders to:
THE BIBLE FOR TODAY
900 Park Ave., Collingswood, NJ 08108
Phone: 856-854-4452; FAX:--2464; Orders: 1-800 JOHN 10:9

The Defined King James Bible

UNCOMMON WORDS DEFINED ACCURATELY

I. Deluxe Genuine Leather

✦Large Print--Black or Burgundy✦
1 for $40.00+$6 S&H
✦Case of 12 for✦
$30.00 each+$30 S&H

✦Medium Print--Black or Burgundy✦
1 for $35.00+$5 S&H
✦Case of 12 for✦
$25.00 each+$24 S&H

II. Deluxe Hardback Edition

1 for $20.00+$6 S&H (Large Print)
✦Case of 12 for✦
$15.00 each+$30 S&H (Large Print)

1 for $15.00+$5 S&H (Medium Print)
✦Case of 12 for✦
$10.00 each+$24 S&H (Medium Print)

Order Phone: 1-800-JOHN 10:9

CREDIT CARDS WELCOMED

www.ingramcontent.com/pod-product-compliance
Lightning Source LLC
Chambersburg PA
CBHW062206080426
42734CB00010B/1810